Words for the Wise

Sixty-Two Insights on Hebrew, Holidays, History and Liturgy

Mitchell First

KODESH PRESS

WORDS FOR THE WISE
Sixty-Two Insights on Hebrew, Holidays, History and Liturgy

© Mitchell First 2022

Hardcover ISBN: 978-1-947857-96-4
Paperback ISBN: 978-1-947857-97-1

The publisher extends it gratitude to Rabbi Eliezer Barany for assistance editing this volume.

All rights reserved. Except for brief quotations in printed reviews, no part of this publication may be reproduced, stored in a retrieval system, or transmitted in any form or by any means (printed, written, photocopied, visual electronic, audio, or otherwise) without the prior permission of the publisher.

PUBLISHED AND DISTRIBUTED EXCLUSIVELY BY
Kodesh Press LLC
New York, NY
www.kodeshpress.com
kodeshpress@gmail.com

Set in Minion Pro by Raphaël Freeman MISTD, Renana Typesetting
Printed in the United States of America

Sponsors

The author would like to express his appreciation to the following individuals for their generous donations which helped fund the publication of this book:

Arielle and Chanan Cohen, in honor of the marriage of their daughter Chavi to Michael Fagin

Michele and Dr. Ben Cooper

Dean Rachel and Allen Friedman

Roz and Ira Friedman, in loving memory of their parents, David J. & Rose Anne Friedman, z"l, and Abraham & Charlotte Remer, z"l

Ellen and Dr. Richard Gertler

Seryl and Dr. Elliot Goldofsky and Family

Amy and Ziggy Hirsch

Altie Karper

Rabbi Avrohom Lieberman

Aliza and Kal Staiman

Rabbi Simcha Weinberg, in gratitude to the author

Barbara and Neal Yaros, in honor of their grandchildren: Gavi, Tzvi, Tamar, Liana, Shani, Caleb, Aiden, Rikki and Tobias

The Zell Family

Contents

Guide to Reading this Book by Parashah ... ix
Preface ... xi

Holidays

1. *Le-David Hashem Ori*: The Origin of Our Elul–Tishrei Recital Custom ... 1
2. The Fast of Gedaliah: The Overshadowed Fast Day ... 4
3. Yom Kippur: The Day We Afflict Our נפש ... 9
4. Interesting Words in the Book of Jonah ... 14
5. The Etymology of the Word *Lulav* ... 17
6. The Meaning of *Atzeret* ... 20
7. חנך: The Connection Between the Meanings "Dedicate" and "Educate" ... 24
8. The Meaning of the Verb פסח ... 27
9. Interesting Words in the Book of Ruth ... 31

Liturgy

1. The Prayer for Rain in *Birkat Ha-Shanim* in the Diaspora: The Issue of Different Climates ... 37
2. The Origin of the Recital of the *Kedushah* Prayer in *U-Va Le-Tziyon* ... 43
3. The *Shalom Aleikhem* Prayer: Origin and Insights ... 47
4. *Anim Zemirot*: Origin and Insights ... 52
5. God as *Boḥen Kelayot* (= Examiner of the Kidneys) ... 58
6. *Maoz Tzur Yeshuati*: Authorship and Insights ... 64

7. *Ve-Heishiv Lev Avot al Banim:* What did Malachi Mean?   71
8. *Ha Laḥma Anya:* Which *Matzah* is it Referring to?   75

History

1. The History of the City of Acco   79
2. Moses' Raised Hands at Exodus 17:9–12   83
3. The *Urim* and the *Tumim*   86
4. Archaeology and the Assyrian Kings   91
5. The Unusual Interpretive Approach of Rashbam   94
6. Rashbam: Life and Works   98
7. An Important Manuscript of Rambam's *Mishneh Torah*: Huntington 80   102
8. The Mashhadi Jews of Northeastern Iran   106
9. Bukharan Jewry and the Dynamics of Global Judaism   109
10. The Fascinating Life of Judah Touro (1775–1854)   112
11. 1827: Russia Begins to Draft its Jews   116
12. On July 3, 1861, the Pasha Gave the Keys of Jerusalem to the Chief Rabbi   120
13. The *Navemar*: The "Ship from Hell" That Sailed to the U.S. in 1941   123
14. Golda Meir: The Early Years   126
15. Yigael Yadin: Archaeologist, Military Man, Politician   132
16. The Heroism of Kibbutz *Yad-Mordechai*   135
17. James McDonald: The First U.S. Ambassador to Israel (1948–1951)   139
18. Insights into Jewish Names and Modern Israel   142

Hebrew Roots

1. בער: The Multiple Meanings of the Root בער   147
2. גדד: The Root גדד and the Prohibition of *Lo Titgodedu*   151
3. הביט: Various Words for "Seeing" in *Tanakh*   154
4. זהר: Is There A Connection between "Light" and "Warn"?   157
5. זמר: The Three Meanings of the Root זמר in *Tanakh*   160

6. חול: The Meaning of חול When Contrasted with קדש 164
7. חרף: The Season חורף and the Marital Word נחרפת 167
8. ישן: The Two Meanings of ישן: Sleep and Old 174
9. כברת: The Meaning of *Kivrat Ha-Aretz* (Genesis 35:16) 177
10. כשף: What is the Meaning of מכשפה? 180
11. לעט: *Hal'iteni Na Min Ha-Adom Ha-Adom Ha-Zeh* (Genesis 25:30) 184
12. מופת: What is the Root of *Mofet* (= Wonder, Sign)? 188
13. מות: The Meaning of Death 192
14. מטה: מטה and Other Words for "Stick" in *Tanakh* 195
15. ממזר: The Etymology of the Word *Mamzer* 198
16. עבר הנהר: The Meanings of *Ever Ha-Nahar* and *Ever Ha-Yarden* 201
17. ערב: The Meaning of *Erev Rav* at Exodus 12:38 205
18. פלא: Insights into This Wondrous and Marvelous Root 208
19. פסים: What is the Meaning of כתנת פסים? 212
20. פתה: *Pen Yifteh Levavkhem* (Deuteronomy 11:16) 215
21. רגע: The Multiple Meanings of the Root רגע 218
22. רפא and רפה: The Two Meanings of *Refaim* in *Tanakh* 222
23. שׂכל: *Sikkel et Yadav* (Genesis 48:14) 226
24. שׂער: Is There a Connection in *Tanakh* Between Hair Standing Up and Fear? 230
25. Interesting Words in *Hallel* 233
26. Hendiadys: Two Separate Words Understood as One Idea 237
27. Miscellaneous Words of Interest 241

Abbreviations of Frequently Cited Sources 249
Corrections Page 251

Guide to Reading this Book by Parashah

Since many people today focus their learning and *divrei Torah* by *parashah*, I thought it would be helpful to make a list suggesting articles that were relevant in some major or minor way to each *parashah* or its season. I did not do this for the entire yearly cycle. But I am presenting suggestions from *Bereshit* through *Mishpatim*. (Of course, the list below only includes a small portion of the articles in this book.)

Bereshit:	The *Shalom Aleikhem* Prayer: Origin and Insights
	Anim Zemirot: Origin and Insights
	Le-David Hashem Ori: The Origin of Our *Elul–Tishrei* Recital Custom[1]
Noah:	חרף: The Season חורף and the Marital Word נחרפת
Lekh Lekha:	רפא and רפה: The Two Meanings of *Refaim* in *Tanakh*
Va-Yera:	פלא: Insights into This Wondrous and Marvelous Root
	הבים: Various Words for "Seeing" in *Tanakh*
Chayey Sarah:	מות: The Meaning of Death
Toledot:	לעט: Hal'iteni Na Min Ha-Adom Ha-Adom Ha-Zeh (Genesis 25:30)
	Ve-Heishiv Lev Avot al Banim: What did Malachi Mean?

---

1. OK, *Bereshit* is late for this topic, but it is still pretty close!

Va-Yetze:	ישן: The Two Meanings of ישן: Sleep and Old
Va-Yishlaḥ:	כברת: The Meaning of *Kivrat Ha-Aretz* (Genesis 35:16)
Va-Yeshev:	פסים: What is the Meaning of כתנת פסים?
Miketz:	זמר: The Three Meanings of the Root זמר in *Tanakh*
Va-Yigash:	בער: The Multiple Meanings of the Root בער
Va-Yeḥi:	שׂכל: *Sikkel et Yadav* (Genesis 48:14)
	עבר הנהר: The Meanings of *Ever Ha-Nahar* and *Ever Ha-Yarden*
Shemot:	מטה: מטה and Other Words for "Stick" in *Tanakh*
Va-Era:	מופת: What is the Root of *Mofet* (= Wonder, Sign)?
Bo:	The Meaning of the Verb פסח
	Ha Laḥma Anya: Which *Matzah* is it Referring to?
	ערב: The Meaning of *Erev Rav* at Exodus 12:38
Be-Shalaḥ:	Moses' Raised Hands at Exodus 17:9–12
Yitro:	זהר: Is There a Connection between "Light" and "Warn"?
Mishpatim:	כשף: What is the Meaning of מכשפה?

* * *

Also, in the *Hebrew Roots* section:

- "Interesting Words in *Hallel*" is relevant many times throughout the year.
- "Hendiadys: Two Separate Words Understood as One Idea" is relevant to many *parshiyyot*.
- "Miscellaneous Words of Interest" is relevant to many *parshiyyot*.

Preface

I started writing columns for the *Jewish Link* newspaper in 2014. This is my third book based on these columns. When I prepare the books, I typically improve the original weekly column with additional material, and add more Hebrew and some footnotes.

As I did in the introductions to *Roots and Rituals*, and *Links to Our Legacy*, I would again like to thank Moshe Kinderlehrer, co-founder and co-publisher of the *Jewish Link*, for giving me the opportunity to write regularly for this paper. When I started, I had no idea that I would learn so much from writing these columns and that they would enable even one book, let alone three!

Writing for the *Jewish Link* was the third time that I was fortunate enough to find a regular place for my writings. My first two opportunities came with the founding of the print journal Ḥakirah and the online site seforimblog.com. With each of these, I had the opportunity to publish relatively long scholarly articles, and these articles ended up forming the basis for my second book, *Esther Unmasked: Solving Eleven Mysteries of the Jewish Holidays and Liturgy* (Kodesh Press, 2015).[1] Then, just when I needed it, along came the *Jewish Link* newspaper, giving me the opportunity to write shorter articles on a wider variety of topics.

* *

---

1. My first book, *Jewish History in Conflict: A Study of the Major Discrepancy Between Rabbinic and Conventional Chronology*, published in 1997, was based on my M.A. paper at the Bernard Revel Graduate School of Yeshiva University.

I would like to thank the following individuals who read portions of this book and improved it with their criticisms and suggestions: Sam Borodach, Michoel Chalk, Ira Friedman and Rabbi Avrohom Lieberman.

I would again like to thank Sam Borodach, Rabbi Ezra Frazer, Allen Friedman, Rabbi Avrohom Lieberman, Meylekh Viswanath and Rabbi Moshe Yasgur for many years of extensive discussions and sharing of sources with me.

Also very important is my *chavruta* for the last two decades, Josh Teplow. He has provided many ideas and much encouragement.

I would also like to acknowledge some of the many others who contributed over the years towards my efforts, either by sharing and discussing particular ideas and sources, or by encouraging me in my research: Joey Adler, Michael Alweis, Ze'ev Atlas, David Barach, Leonard Berkowitz, Lazer Borgen, Menachem Butler, Avi-Gil Chaitovsky, Myron Chaitovsky, Joel Chudow, Chanan Cohen, Craig Cohen, Fred Cohen, Ben Cooper, Mollie Fisch, David Fisher, Howard Friedman, Ira Friedman, Rabbi Mordy Friedman, Rachel Friedman, Aharon Gal, David Gertler, Richard Gertler, Jeff Glazer, Rabbi Jay Goldmintz, Elliot Goldofsky, Binyamin Goldstein, Azriel Haimowitz, David and Shulamis Hes, Dick Harris (of blessed memory), Ziggy Hirsch, Rabbi Aryeh Kaplan, Daniel Klein, Heshie Klein, Rabbi Reuven Chaim Klein, Rabbi Stephen Knapp, Rabbi Ariel Kopitnikoff, Steve and Abby Leichman, Ari Leifer, Arvin Levine, Yehiel Levy, Moshe Markovitz, Yaakov Metzger, Yehuda Miller, Jeff Neugroschl, Efraim Palvanov, Rabbi Michael Pariser, Lenny Presby, Rabbi Baruch Price, Michael Rapoport, Moshe Rosenberg, Chanani Sandler, Eli Schaap, David Schachter, Steve Schaffer, Richie Schiffmiller, Fred Schulman, Menachem Shapiro, Mark Siletski, Rob Sperber, Kal Staiman, Zalman Suldan, Nati Sulimanoff, Rabbi Chaim Sunitsky, Kovie Wagner, Josh Waxman, Rabbi Simcha Weinberg, Zvi Weissler, Barry Weissman, Rabbi Richard Wolpoe, Rabbi Benjamin Yablok, Neal Yaros, Joshua Zakheim, Heshey Zelcer, Rabbi Alan Zelenetz, Rabbi Shawn Zell, and Ariel Zell.

I have learned much over the past thirty-four years from the *shiurim* of the Rabbis of Congregation Beth Aaron: Rabbi Ephraim Kanarfogel and Rabbi Laurence Rothwachs.

I would like to thank Rabbi Reuven Chaim Klein of Beitar Illit for his continuing "What's in a Word?" posts, and David Curwin of Efrat for his continuing posts at his site balashon.com. Both of them continually provide me with ideas and material for columns.

I would particularly like to thank Rabbi Simcha Weinberg and Michael Rapoport for their exceptional feedback and encouragement to me on my weekly columns. Also, Leonard Berkowitz, Mollie Fisch, Aharon Gal, Abby Leichman, Jesse Schwartzman, and Kal Staiman provide regular encouragement and feedback.

Over the past several years, Rabbi Moshe Schapiro, Rachel Berliner, Rebekah Shoemake, and Mary Ann Linahan have saved me hundreds of trips to the Yeshiva University library by graciously responding to my requests for sources. I could not have written my weekly columns and these several books without their assistance.

I would also like to again thank Daniel A. Klein, whose 1998 edition of S.D. Luzzatto's commentary on Genesis introduced me to the world of close analysis of the meanings and subtleties of Hebrew roots. (Prior to this, my special area of interest in Judaic studies was chronology, not etymology.)

Special thanks to Rabbi Alec Goldstein of Kodesh Press for his fourth tremendous job of publishing for me. Alec has always been a pleasure to work with. Moreover, he knows ancient languages (better than I do) and has contributed many insights.

I would again like to thank my beloved wife Sharon for allowing me to live this additional life as a scholar, outside my legal career, and pursue my research and writing interests.

Please feel free to contact me with comments on any of the topics that I have addressed. I can be reached at MFirstAtty@aol.com. (I still use AOL as it helps me relate to the ancient world!)

Mitchell First
Teaneck, N.J.
July 2022

P.S. I wanted to share the following:

People have always made fun of my last name with comments like "second," "last," etc. Recently, I had a new experience. Someone moved to my community and had a question on some Jewish scholarly matter and was told to ask "Mitch First." Since he had not been in the community that long, he thought they were telling him to ask "Mitch first," i.e., before he asked others. My last name is now more and more becoming a path to respect!

Holidays

1. *Le-David Hashem Ori*: The Origin of Our Elul–Tishrei Recital Custom

The *Mishnah Berurah* (R. Yisrael Meir Kagan, d. 1933) records its recital at the end of every morning and evening prayer in the High Holiday season. First he writes that "in our countries" we recite it from Rosh Hodesh Elul to Yom Kippur. Then he adds that *anu nohagin* to recite it through Shemini Atzeret.[1] I.e., his specific locale recited it for longer than "our countries" did.

But where does the practice of reciting *Le-David* (Psalm 27) during this period come from? It is not in the Talmud or the Rishonim. It is not in the *Shulhan Arukh* (sixteenth cent.). Scholars have spent much time tracking down the origin of this custom.

There is a work called *Hemdat Yamim*, published in 1731, that is an early source for many of our customs. The recital of *Le-David* is mentioned in this work. (The precise practice mentioned here is to recite it *be-ashmoret ha-boker be-selihot*.)

But scholars have tracked down earlier sources. The earliest source is a work called *Shem Tov Katan*, from 1706. The author writes: "I would like to tell you a great secret. Whoever recites this Psalm from Rosh Hodesh Elul through Simhat Torah, even if an evil decree has been inscribed from heaven against a person, he can annul it. He will annul from himself all evil and harsh decrees, and go free, and be meritorious in his judgment. One must be very, very careful to say this Psalm evening and morning, every day, from Rosh Hodesh Elul

---

1. See his comments on *OH* 581.

through Simhat Torah. Then one will be assured that one will live his years and days in goodness and it will be pleasant for him, and through this, he will subdue all kinds of accusers."

The author even gives the reason for the recital. *Le-David* has the four-letter Divine Name 13 times (including Divine Names with prefixes) and this corresponds to the 13 *Middot*. As we know, the 13 *Middot* are much recited in our prayers during the High Holiday period.

But *Le-David* also includes the words *be-sukkoh* and *teruah*. More importantly, the chapter's themes, which include requests for salvation, are fitting for the High Holiday season. Thus, even though the author mentioned only the reason of correspondence to the 13 *Middot*, the psalm's content was surely also a factor in leading him to promote its recital.

It is of course interesting that the author does not cite *Midrash Tehillim* (also known as *Midrash Shocher Tov*) which had stated that אורי represents Rosh Hashanah and ישעי represents Yom Kippur and finds allusions in the psalm to Sukkot and Hoshanah Rabbah as well. This is suggested by many later sources as the reason for the recital of Psalm 27 during the Elul-Tishrei season.[2]

The author of *Shem Tov Katan* was a kabbalist: Rabbi Binyamin Beinisch ha-Kohen. He was from Krotoszyn (Poland).

In the *Shem Tov Katan*, R. Binyamin did not provide the specific time in the evening and morning prayers that *Le-David* should be recited. But he published a different work ten years later, *Amtahat Binyamin*. There he specified that the time for its recital was after the *Amidah* of *shaharit*. (Presumably he meant that it should be recited after the *Amidah* of *maariv* as well.)

The remaining issue is whether R. Binyamin was the one who first introduced the Elul-Tishrei recital custom or whether he was just reporting an earlier custom. He does not clearly state that he was introducing a new custom. But there is a work *Shirei Ha-Leviim*, published in Lublin around thirty years before *Keter Shem Tov*, which attempted to record all of the yearly daily *Tehillim* recital customs. Extensive research went into this work. Here there is no mention of any Elul-Tishrei *Le-David* recital custom. This is evidence that R. Binyamin was the one who introduced the custom.

---

2. See, e.g., *Mateh Ephraim* (d. 1828), *OH* 581 (6).

R. Binyamin's *Shem Tov Katan* was very popular, and came out in many editions. Also, the practice he mentioned was cited by many others after him. This explains how the custom spread after its first mention by R. Binyamin.[3]

* * *

A few other observations:

1. There are other chapters in the book of Psalms with 13 mentions of the Divine Name (including Divine Names with prefixes). For example, chapter 33: *Rannenu Tzaddikim*.[4] *Hemdat Yamim* had also suggested its recital together with chapter 27. (This is further evidence that the content of chapter 27 was a factor in motivating R. Binyamin to propose its recital, as he did not suggest chapter 33.)
2. Until recent decades, it was believed by many that *Hemdat Yamim* was the earliest source for the *Le-David* custom. This work was viewed by many as having been authored by a follower of Shabbetai Tzevi. The belief that this work had a Sabbatean origin discouraged many communities from reciting *Le-David*.[5]
3. One major figure who did not endorse the recital of *Le-David* was Vilna Gaon (d. 1797). See *Maaseh Rav*, sec. 53, which rejects the practice of reciting it between Elul and Yom Kippur.
4. Shnayer Leiman, in a lecture in 2009, mentions a story in a certain Hasidic work, *Nezer Ha-Kodesh* (2000), which claims an earlier origin of the recital custom.[6] The story claims the recital was introduced in perhaps the sixteenth century by a certain R.

---

3. The post at strangeside.com (see below) wrote that R. Binyamin is mentioned by R. Yonatan Eybeschuetz as the greatest of his teachers. I do not know what his source is for this statement.
4. I have not checked whether there are other psalms with 13 mentions of the Divine Name.
5. The identity of the author of this work has always been a mystery. But the most recent scholarship argues strongly that the author was the person who first printed the book: Israel Jacob b. Yom Tov Algazi (d. 1756). See the article by R. Yechiel Goldhaber in *Sefer Zikhron le-Professor Meir Benayahu* (2019). Algazi was not a Sabbatean. But the *Hemdat Yamim* is problematic in a different way. It borrows and adapts material from many earlier sources without acknowledgement.
6. See pp. 147–48.

Eliyahu Baal Shem.⁷ But the story found in this source includes details that are hard to believe (including someone making a pact with the Satan). Separate from that, the lack of reference to any Elul-Tishrei *Le-David* recital custom in *Shirei Ha-Leviim* is a difficulty for anyone who would follow this alternative approach to the recital's origin.⁸

* * *

Mitchell First has not made any pacts with the Satan (so far).

2. The Fast of Gedaliah: The Overshadowed Fast Day

The background to the Fast of Gedaliah is inevitably overlooked as the day is overshadowed by Rosh Hashanah. This is my attempt to rectify this.

The story of Gedaliah and his assassination is told in the book of Jeremiah, chapters 40 and 41.⁹

Gedaliah was appointed by Nebuchadnezzar to be in charge of the small Jewish community that remained in various cities of Judea after the destruction of the Temple in 586 BCE and the forced exile of the overwhelming majority of the population. Only the poorest were allowed by the Babylonians to remain in the land.

Gedaliah set up his headquarters in Mizpah, in the tribe of Benja-

---

7. The precise R. Eliyahu intended in the story is unclear. There are at least two candidates. See strangeside.com for a summary of the story (cited below).

As to the meaning of *Baal Shem*, I had always thought it referred to someone who had a "good name." But actually it refers to "one who possessed the secret knowledge of the Tetragrammaton and the other 'Holy Names,' and who knew how to work miracles by the power of these names." See *EJ* 8:5–7. (There is evidence that this term already existed with this meaning in the Geonic period.) Even with the addition *Tov*, the term seems to have the same meaning.

8. My main sources for this article were: 1) E. Brodt, "The Source for the Recitation of LeDovid," seforim.blogspot.com, Sept. 21. 2009, 2) Brodt, *Likkutei Eliezer* (2020), pp. 1–25, and 3) S. Leiman's lecture from Aug. 27, 2009, at YUTorah.com. Also useful was the post at strangeside.com, July 1 2016: "Le-Dovid Prayer."

9. A brief version is at 2 Kings, chapter 25.

min. Upon his appointment, he advised the Jews to stay loyal to the Babylonians and that all would be well with them.

Archaeology has unearthed a clay seal from Lachish from around the time of Gedaliah with the inscription: "(Belonging) to Gedalyahu who is in charge of the house." A widespread view is that this belonged to our Gedaliah.[10]

At some point after Gedaliah's appointment, Baalis king of Ammon made an alliance with Ishmael son of Netanyah (who was from the Davidic line) and instructed Ishmael to kill Gedaliah.[11] Gedaliah was warned that Ishmael was planning to kill him, but he discounted the rumor.[12]

Shortly thereafter Ishmael had his opportunity. During a meal, Ishmael and the ten men that were with him suddenly got up and struck Gedaliah with a sword, killing him. They also killed the other Jews that were with Gedaliah and killed the Babylonian officers present. Ishmael managed to escape to Ammon with eight of his men. The end of the story is that the Jewish community in all the cities of Judea decided to flee to Egypt out of fear that the Babylonians might take revenge against them for the actions of Yishmael and his men.[13] They fled to Egypt even though Jeremiah, in the name of God, warned them not to go there and that God would destroy them in Egypt.

Jeremiah and his scribe Baruch went with them to Egypt.[14] Perhaps they were forced to go or they eventually agreed since they would have been of little use in Judea without an organized Jewish community.[15]

---

10. See the article by T. Ganzel in *Shnaton* 20 (2010), pp. 51–69 (53). Seals belong to people of importance.
11. The Soncino commentary suggests that Baalis was trying to hinder the rehabilitation of Judea so that it might fall to his own expansionist plans. It also mentions Ishmael's possible resentment at being passed over as leader of Judea.
12. One adviser even offered to preemptively kill Ishmael, but Gedaliah refused to allow this.
13. 2 Kings 25:26 tells us: *va-yakumu kol ha-am, mi-katon ve-ad gadol*.
14. See Jer. 43:6.
15. Although we usually assume that Judea was empty of Jews after the time of Gedaliah and for the decades thereafter, this is an oversimplification. It was probably just the organized Jewish community that ended with Gedaliah.

The *Tanakh* does not clearly state how long after his appointment Gedaliah was killed. *Seder Olam* (chap. 26) takes the position that Gedaliah was killed "fifty-two days after the destruction of the Temple." But many scholars believe that he could not have been killed that fast and that it was at least the next Tishrei that he was killed, or perhaps a subsequent one.[16]

* * *

After all that background, why do we fast on the third of Tishrei?[17] There is a statement in the sixth chapter of the Tosefta that the fast was enacted to teach us that the death of righteous individuals is as hard for God as the destruction of the Temple.[18] But this seems like a homiletical explanation.[19] Moreover, the three other fast days were established to commemorate national traumas. We would expect this fast day to also commemorate such a trauma.

I mentioned above that the flight to Egypt of the Jewish community that had been ruled by Gedaliah marked the end of the organized Jewish community in Judea. This trauma is likely the reason for the fast. Rambam takes this position. In his *Hilkhot Taaniyot* 5:2 he writes that upon Gedaliah's death, "the remaining embers of Israel were extinguished and the completion of the exile was brought about." Perhaps Rambam was just expressing what all understood intuitively for hundreds of years before him.

In the many centuries between the Talmud and Rambam, there

See Ganzel, p. 53, n. 15. Jeremiah 52:30 mentions 745 *Yehudim* as exiled by the Babylonians a few years after the destruction of the Temple. The verse does not say exiled from where. On the simplest level, the reference is to an exile from Judea. (But *Seder Olam*, chap. 26, interprets the verse as a reference to an exile of *Yehudim* from neighboring countries. See also Josephus, *Antiquities* X, 182.)

16. See Ganzel, pp. 56–58, and see in particular Jer. 40:11–12. The longer that Gedaliah ruled before his assassination, the more traumatic his killing and the sudden change in their fate would have been for the community.

17. The earliest mentions of our fast in the seventh month are at Zech. 7:5 and 8:19.

18. This passage is also found at *Sifrei*, Deut. 31, with almost identical wording. The passage is also found at *Rosh Hashanah* 18b with slightly different wording.

19. Moreover, at *Niddah* 61a Gedaliah is blamed for discounting the assassination warning and held accountable for the death of the others killed with him.

is at least one other authority who has written enough for us to determine how he understood the reason for the establishment of the fast. That authority is R. Saadiah Gaon (d. 942). He wrote at least three *selihot* for the Fast of Gedaliah (two of which are included in his *siddur*).[20] In an article on thetorah.com, Tzvi Novick focused on one of these *selihot: Avlah Nafshi*.[21] Novick concluded that R. Saadiah took an approach similar to Rambam. The *selihah* only mentioned Gedaliah one time, and several times pointed out that the fast marks the destruction of the remnant that survived the Babylonian assault on Jerusalem.[22]

* * *

Precisely when in Tishrei did the assassination of Gedaliah take place? The *Tanakh* merely records: *ba-hodesh ha-shevii*.[23] At first glance it looks like the *Tanakh* did not specify the date. But sometimes in *Tanakh* the word *hodesh* means "the first of the month." This is seen, for example, at Exodus 19:1: *ba-hodesh ha-shelishi…ba-yom ha-zeh….*"[24] This reasonable interpretation of *hodesh* in our story is found in the time of the Rishonim.[25] In this view, the observance of the fast was postponed to the third day of Tishrei because of Rosh Hashanah.[26] The earlier view in our sources is that Gedaliah

---

20. Probably, between the time of the Talmud and the Rambam, others also wrote *piyyutim* for the Fast of Gedaliah. From their *piyyutim*, we can see how they understood the reason for the establishment of the fast. This is an area that needs further research.
21. This one is included and translated in *The Complete ArtScroll Selichos*, pp. 472–474.
22. Tzvi Novick, "Tzom Gedaliah: Why Commemorate His Assassination?," thetorah.com, Sept. 3 2021.
23. 2 Kings 25:25 and Jer. 41:1.
24. S.D. Luzzatto writes here that the first of the month was the principal meaning of *hodesh* and that the meaning later expanded to denote the entire length of the month. Another example of *hodesh* meaning the first of the month is at Ps. 81:4: *tiku va-hodesh shofar*. See, e.g., Radak, Rashi and *Daat Mikra* there. There are many other examples of this usage of *hodesh* in *Tanakh*.
25. The earliest sources that I am aware of who interpret our *ba-hodesh* this way are Ibn Ezra (comm. to Zech. 8:19) and Radak (comm. to Jer. 41:1 and Zech. 7:5).
26. This leads to the issue of when the Jews started observing two days of Rosh Hashanah.

was assassinated on the third of the month. This view is found in *Seder Olam* (chap. 26), Tosefta *Sotah* chap. 6, and *Sifrei* Deut. 31. It is impossible to derive this date from the verses. If this date is correct, it must have been an ancient tradition.

* * *

An interesting issue is whether this fast and the three others fasts enacted in connection with the first ḥurban were observed during the period of the Second Temple. There is no clear answer to this question and the topic is too broad for me to address here. But here are a few thoughts:

- Perhaps there was distinction between the fast in Av[27] and the other fast days.
- We should not assume that the practice in Babylonia was the same as the practice in *Eretz Yisrael*.
- We should not assume that the practice in *Eretz Yisrael* was uniform.
- Finally, the practice in any individual community could have varied over the many centuries as well.

I have also found one scholar's observation to be noteworthy: "It is difficult to imagine... that for a period of close to 600 years... these fast days had fallen into oblivion and then were suddenly reinstituted.... Especially puzzling is the supposed reinstitution of the fast days of Tebet 10 and the Fast of Gedaliah, since these have nothing to do with the Second Temple.... We are therefore led to accept the assumption that these fast days continued to be observed by the people during the Second Commonwealth."[28] I would just modify this conclusion by changing it to "some of the people."

There is one source on this topic that relates specifically to the third of Tishrei and that one I will discuss here. The passage is in *Megillat Taanit*. This is a list of about thirty-five dates on which one

---

27. I am purposely not referring to it as the ninth of Av, as the Biblical verses refer only to the seventh and tenth.
28. See J. Rosenthal, "The Four Commemorative Fast Days," *Jewish Quarterly Review* 57 (1967), pp. 446–459 (458). There are traditional sources that agree with Rosenthal. See his n. 64.

was **not allowed** to fast.²⁹ The earliest layer of *Megillat Taanit* is the Aramaic layer which dates to around 50 CE and is a collection of earlier traditions. Here there is a listing for the third of Tishrei as a date where one is not allowed to fast. The reason given is: *itnetilat adkarta min shetaraya* (= removal of God's name from documents). The later layer of *Megillat Taanit* offers the following explanation.³⁰ The holiday was established some time in the Hasmonean period after it was agreed that God's name would no longer be written in *shetarot*. The practice had been problematic because a *shetar* might end up in the garbage once the obligation was satisfied.

The fact that the third of Tishrei could suddenly be declared a holiday suggests that there was no practice of fasting on this day before its enactment, at least in those areas where the custom was to observe the *Megillat Taanit* holidays.³¹

* * *

Mitchell First makes sure not to use God's name in the *Jewish Link* articles that he writes each week, so as to avoid halakhic issues with their disposal.

3. Yom Kippur: The Day We Afflict Our נפש

The noun נפש occurs over seven hundred times in *Tanakh*. The word has a range of meanings including: person, life, life-force, breath,³²

---

29. For an excellent discussion of this work, see V. Noam, "Megillat Taanit – The Scroll of Fasting," in *The Literature of the Sages* (Second Part), eds. S. Safrai et al (2006), pp. 339–62. *Megillat Taanit* was not the original title of this work, as it does not fit the work. The work is referred to in Mishnah *Taanit* 2:8. Based on the earliest manuscripts, the work is referred to here as the *"Megillah"* (= Scroll). This was probably its original title. See Noam, p. 340.
30. The later layer is in Hebrew. Scholars today very often do not accept the explanations offered in this later layer.
31. We do not have to assume that these holidays were observed in all of *Eretz Yisrael*.
32. I have even seen the suggestion that perhaps every time the *Tanakh* uses *nefesh* to mean "person," it literally means "breather"!

desire, and appetite.[33] נפש is also often translated as "soul," something separate from the body.

נפש also has the meaning: "throat." See, e.g., Isa. 5:14: "*She'ol* has opened wide its throat" and Ps. 69:2: "Water reached to the throat." Most probably, "throat" was its original meaning[34] and נפש then expanded to the other meanings, as the throat is the organ for breathing and eating.

The root only appears three times as a verb.[35] One of the three times the word appears as a verb is in the Shabbat morning *kiddush*: *shavat va-yinnafash* (Ex. 31:17).[36] Here *va-yinnafash* certainly has a meaning related to "breathing." One suggestion is "caught His breath."[37] See, e.g., Rashi: *meshiv nafsho u-neshimato*. Another suggestion is "breathed easily." See, e.g., *Theological Dictionary of the Old Testament*, vol. 9, p. 504.[38]

Let us return to the noun. The recent trend in scholarship is to avoid translating the word as "soul." According to this view, the idea of a "soul," something separate from the body, may be a post-Biblical idea. In the ancient Israelite world view, this approach asserts, the נפש was always connected to life in the flesh. Consistent with this approach, the scholar Robert Alter, in his recent translation of the Bible, decided to avoid the word "soul" altogether.[39]

But many believe that "soul" is still a proper translation in many verses. Richard Steiner, who taught at Yeshiva University for decades, wrote a monograph on this for the Society of Biblical Literature, disagreeing with the view that the "soul" meaning is a post-Biblical one. He admits that נפש has so many meanings that it is easy to claim that the meaning is not "soul" in almost any verse. But he finds one verse, Ezekiel 13:18, in which he argues that נפש can only have the

---

33. For the last, see, e.g., Isa. 56:11: "dogs have a strong appetite."
34. See Tawil, p. 244.
35. Scholars suspect that the word started out as a noun.
36. I wrote about this word in *Links to Our Legacy* (2021), pp. 67–68.
37. Even though God's creations were with words and not through physical effort, the Torah speaks *bi-leshon bnei adam*.
38. See similarly, Kaddari, p. 723: נשם לרווחה. See also *BDB*, first suggestion: "take [a] breath."
39. See Alter, *The Hebrew Bible: A Translation with Commentary* (2018).

meaning "soul." This legitimizes the possible interpretation "soul" in other verses.

Another scholar who agrees with Steiner's approach has written: "Emphasizing the Hebrew Bible's concrete approach to life should not obstruct its occasional reach toward otherworldliness. Nefesh deserves to have its soul restored."[40] One example this scholar points to is 1 Kings 15:21–22, where Elijah miraculously brings back the נפש of a child. The alternative view would translate it with something like: "life force." But it does seem that the נפש here is something that existed, at least temporarily, outside of the body.

Bearing all this in mind, let us see how נפש is translated in the context of fasting on Yom Kippur. In the context of Yom Kippur, the Torah uses the idiom "ענה [=afflict] + נפש" (with ענה preceding) five times: two times in Lev. chapter 16, two times in Lev. chapter 23, and one time at Num. 29:7.[41] Let us focus on the first occasion: Lev: 16:29: *te'anu et nafshoteikhem*.

All can agree that ענה + נפש is an idiom for fasting. According to the Even-Shoshan concordance, outside the Yom Kippur context it appears four times. Admittedly the context at Num. 30:14 is vague. But at Isa. 58:3, it is parallel to צמנו, at Isa. 58:5 it is parallel to צום, and at Psa. 35:13, we have the phrase *ineiti va-tzom nafshi* (= I afflicted my נפש with a fast). See also Isa. 58:10.[42]

Given that ענה + נפש is an idiom for fasting, how should we translate נפש in the Yom Kippur context? The King James Bible (1611) and the Jewish Publication Society of America translation of 1917 (included at the top in the *Pentateuch* of Rabbi Dr. Hertz) translate: "ye shall afflict your souls." Rabbi Dr. Hertz is very happy with this

---

40. B. French, "Putting 'Soul' Back in the Hebrew Bible," *Wall Street Journal*, April 5, 2019.
41. One might interpret this phrase as requiring an affirmative act of discomfort. A *baraita* at Yoma 74b considers this interpretation, e.g., the possibility that one is obligated to sit in the heat or the cold and cause oneself discomfort. But the *baraita* rejects this approach and decides that no such obligation is implied in the verse.
42. This verse is not cited for the idiom in this concordance because here נפש precedes the affliction word. There may be other occurrences of the two words in this order.

translation. He writes: "This Heb. phrase well indicated the spiritual aim of fasting.... The abstention from all food and from gratification of other bodily desires, however, must be accompanied by deep remorse at having fallen short of what it was in our power to be and to do as members of the House of Israel. Without such contrite confession, accompanied by the solemn resolve to abandon the way of evil, fasting in itself is not the fulfillment of the Divine command...."

The above statement of Rabbi Dr. Hertz is quoted approvingly in the Soncino comm. to Ps. 35:13. Moreover, their commentary here begins: "To *afflict the soul* is the Hebrew term for a fast."

On the other hand, afflicting the **physical** self seems to be the simpler meaning of the deprivation. For example:

ArtScroll's *Chumash* (Stone edition) translates: "You shall afflict **yourselves**."

S.D. Luzzatto uses an Italian phrase that means "**your persons**."[43]

Etz Hayim (the Conservative movement's flagship *Ḥumash*) offers: "you shall practice **self-denial**."

I have also seen the translation: "afflict your appetite."

Moreover, since our idiom ענה + נפש also appears outside the Yom Kippur context, we can argue that there is no reason to read the "soul" meaning into the word נפש in the Yom Kippur context. (But R. Hertz might respond that all fasting in Judaism is ultimately for a spiritual aim!)

Finally, I note that Rav S.R. Hirsch translates: "you shall starve your **vital spirits**." He seems to be straddling the line between the spiritual interpretation and the physical.[44]

* * *

What about the four other activities prohibited on Yom Kippur? All five are listed together at Mishnah *Yoma* 8:1. But all authorities agree that it is only the violation of eating or drinking that warrants the *karet* penalty. Many authorities believe that nevertheless all five are considered Torah-level prohibitions. But there is an alternative view

---

43. See D. Klein, *Shadal on Leviticus* (2021), p. 149. The phrase he used was *le vostre persone*.
44. See also the note in *The Living Torah* which mentions both possibilities.

that the three other prohibited activities are rabbinic in origin, and the verses cited in the Talmud are merely *asmakhtot*.

* * *

The above ArtScroll *Chumash* makes an inspiring observation about the language of Rambam at *Shevitat Asor* 1:5. Based on the phrase *Shabbat Shabbaton* in the context of *Yom Kippur* (Lev. 16:31), Rambam here describes the goal of the day as לשבות from those five activities. The ArtScroll commentary writes that this "indicates that [according to Rambam] the purpose of fasting is not that one should suffer, but that he should transcend the normal human limitations that prevent him from functioning properly unless he eats. On *Yom Kippur*, a Jew is like an angel who serves God without need for food."[45]

* * *

Naḥmanides on Lev. 16:29 mentions that there are Karaites who disagree with the view that the idiom נפש + ענה means "fast." I could not find such a view. In recorded Karaite sources, they do fast on Yom Kippur.[46] I then consulted with a professor who is very knowledgeable about Karaites. He was also not aware of such a view. He advised that this may be the only time that Naḥmanides mentions Karaites. Most likely, Naḥmanides merely inferred that there was such a Karaitic view from Ibn Ezra's brief comments on this verse.[47]

* * *

Mitchell First enjoys making *kiddush* on Shabbat morning and taking a breather.

---

45. P. 644 (comm. to Lev. 16:29).
46. But Karaites have always had different ideas about *Yom Teruah* (= Rosh Hashanah). See the article by P. Miller in *Ki Baruch Hu*, eds. R. Chazan et al (1999), pp. 537–541.
47. It is of course possible that there was such a Karaitic view in an early stage. The professor I consulted with advised me that the easily accessible Karaite commentators, who wrote in Hebrew, are after Ibn Ezra and after a major Karaite rapprochement with rabbinic views. The Judeo-Arabic Karaite commentators, which are often earlier, are mostly still in manuscript.

4. Interesting Words in the Book of Jonah

נינוה (1:2 and elsewhere): It is of interest that the cuneiform sign for this city is a fish within a house. Also, *nun* means fish in Aramaic. But the entry in the *EJ* (12:1168) concludes that the name of the city is of Hurrian origin, so we do not know what it means. Hurrian is an old language, not related to any Semitic one.

As further background to the story, a prophet Jonah son of Amittai is mentioned at 2 Kings 14:25 in connection with the reign of Jeroboam son of Joash (early eighth century BCE). Presumably this is our Jonah, so we now know the time period of our story. A century later (late seventh century BCE), Assyria was attacked by its former vassals: Babylonians, Chaldeans, Medeans, Persians and others. The Assyrian city of Nineveh was destroyed in 612 BCE.

מלחים (1:5): This word for sailors only appears here and in the book of Ezekiel. I was sure its origin had to do with מלח and the saltiness of the sea. But it turns out that it is a word that Akkadian borrowed from the older language of Sumerian (a non-Semitic language). In Sumerian, *ma* means "ship" and *lah* means "to steer." Hence, the word means: one who steers a ship.

רב החבל (1:6): The root חבל has four different meanings. One of them is "bind" (e.g., with a rope). These men are all involved with the ropes of the ship. The *rav* is the chief.

The other meanings of this root are: destroy/damage, pains of the expectant mother, and pledge. (Perhaps the "pledge" meaning derives from the "bind" meaning.)

התעטף (2:8): Here we have the root עטף with the meaning "feeble, faint." The phrase here is: *be-hitattef alay nafshi*. The continuation of the verse is that at that point he remembered God and prayed.

This root appears with this meaning thirteen times in *Tanakh*. Yet this root appears a few other times in *Tanakh* with a different meaning: "cover." See, e.g., Ps. 65:14 and 73:6.

Ernest Klein writes that "most scholars" derive the "feeble, faint" meaning from the "cover" meaning. I did not find this to be true. I think most scholars do not see a relation here. Also, Klein did not even mention the suggested relation. *Daat Mikra* on our verse suggests that a feeble person's strength is being covered up. See also *Daat Mikra* to Ps. 61:3 and 107:5.⁴⁸

In *Tanakh*, the *hitpael* is used only in connection with the "feeble, faint" meaning. Yet our Sages took the *hitpael* and used it in our blessing for the *tallit*, using it instead with the "cover" meaning (= cover oneself)!

As to the meaning of "feeble, faint" in the *hitpael*, it is difficult to understand. Sometimes words that are in the *nifal* develop an added ת, and misleadingly look as if they are in the *hitpael*. I think that is what happened here.⁴⁹ *Daat Mikra* to Ps. 102:1, n. 2, subsection 3, essentially agrees. It comments, with regard to this meaning of עטף, that there is no meaningful distinction between the *kal*, *nifal* and *hitpael*.

היכל (2:5 and elsewhere): This word appears many times in *Nakh*. (But it is never in Joshua or Judges.) It means "big house, palace." It is found in Akkadian (*ekallu*) and was borrowed from Sumerian.

שק (3:5 in the plural, and elsewhere): The Hebrew word means both: 1) a sack to hold items like grain and 2) a garment worn in mourning and humiliation. The widespread view is that the origin of the English word is the Greek *sakkos* and that this Greek word was borrowed from the Semitic word.

The next step is to figure out which of the two Semitic word meanings came first: the sack of grain meaning or the garment meaning? Could one have developed from the other? Most likely, that is not what happened. Rather, the word origin is the material used for both. The word refers to something made from goat's hair or a similar animal.⁵⁰

---

48. Mandelkern cites Radak for a different suggestion and Rav S.R. Hirsch makes a suggestion as well (see, e.g., his comments on Ps. 61:3). I did not find these suggestions convincing.
49. I gave many examples in my *Roots and Rituals* (2018), p. 245. See, e.g., Ps. 92:10: *yitpardu kol poalei aven*. (Despite the use of the *hitpael*, the evildoers are not scattering themselves.) See also Prov. 31:30: *ishah yirat Hashem hi tithallal*. (Despite the use of the *hitpael*, the woman is not praising herself.)
50. See the post at balashon.com of Dec. 24, 2006, *The JPS Torah Commentary: Leviticus* (2003) on Lev. 11:32, *KB*, pp. 1349–1350, and *Daat Mikra* to Est. 4:1.

One can see this meaning by comparing Lev. 11:32 with Num. 31:20. Both verses list common categories of objects. The first verse has the word שק, while

Our book, at verse 3:8, is the one place in *Tanakh* where animals wear a שק.

קיקיון (4:6 and elsewhere): This word appears five times in our book. Surprisingly, or perhaps unsurprisingly, it appears nowhere else in *Tanakh*. Ernest Klein suggests "castor tree, ricinus."[51] (Perhaps that is helpful to some readers. Neither is helpful to me!)

שאול (2:3): The netherworld location שאול is mentioned over sixty times in *Tanakh*. On the simplest level, it is a large place, located deep underground, where the bodies and spirits of dead people dwell, perhaps spending most of their time sleeping.

But some of these times, שאול refers only to an individual grave, and other times, it is used merely as a metaphor for distress. In our verse Jonah cries out from the *beten* of *She'ol*. Perhaps "distress" is the meaning of *She'ol* here, or perhaps the depths of the belly of the large fish was analogous to *She'ol*, or perhaps Jonah already considered himself among the dead when he cried out.

The most likely explanation for the etymology of *She'ol* is that it derives from the root שאה and that the final ל is not part of the root. The root שאה has meanings like "loud noise," "crash into ruins," and "desolation." Although the first two of these meanings do not fit, "desolation" can be seen as a main aspect of שאול. It is viewed as desolate of material objects, or at least desolate of comforting material objects. At Isaiah 14:11, it is implied that when one lies down there, one lies on top of maggots and one is covered with worms. I.e., there is nothing to lie down upon there, and no blankets to cover oneself.

I mentioned many other suggestions for the etymology of the word in *Roots and Rituals* (2018), pp. 143–147. It is of course ironic that scholars have made extensive efforts **inquiring** about the meaning of the word שאול.

On a homiletical level, and in the spirit of Yom Kippur, perhaps

---

the second has "*ma'aseh izzim*" (= everything made of goat's hair). This suggests a rough equivalency with the שק of the other verse.

51. Yehuda Feliks has written much on topics like this. See, e.g., his *Olam Ha-Tzomeaḥ Ha-Mikra'i*.

שאול is called this to remind us that we are all on "borrowed time" and that we should use our time on earth wisely!

* * *

Mitchell First is a personal injury attorney and Jewish history scholar. While still on earth, he can be reached at MFirstAtty@aol.com.

5. The Etymology of the Word *Lulav*

The word לולב never appears in *Tanakh*. It is a word from rabbinic Hebrew. But what is its origin?

A widespread view is that it derives from an underlying verb לבלב. This also seems to be the view of our Sages. See *Yoma* 81b which refers to *lulavei gefanim* (grapevine shoots) and then uses the verb לבלבו.

Everyone agrees that the verb לבלב means "blossom." See, e.g., Targum Onkelos on Genesis 40:10, which uses the word לבלבין as a translation for the word נצה (blossoms).

But how do we get this "blossom" meaning from the letters לבלב?

In one view, it comes from the underlying letters לב, with its "heart" meaning.[52]

But Marcus Jastrow (p. 689) had taken a different approach. He connected the word לבלב with the root לבה, and wrote (p. 688) that the latter was a contraction of להב, a word with the meaning: "flame, brightness." Then David Curwin[53] (*HaMizrachi* magazine, Sukkot 2020) took this same position. He wrote that לולב was derived from לבלב (blossom) and then explained that "the blossoming of a plant radiates like the shine of a fire." I prefer this explanation over the "heart" explanation.[54]

In the *Yah Eli piyyut*, the word לבלב is preceded by a phrase with

---

52. Klein, p. 292.
53. Curwin is the author of the balashon.com site.
54. I have been told by my wife Sharon that there are studies that show that talking to plants makes them grow. This makes me think that there might be some merit to the "heart" etymology. But I am not convinced. I have also heard that these studies found that plants grow faster to the sound of a female voice than to the sound of a male voice!

the word לב. One can make the argument from this proximity that the author of this *piyyut* related לבלב to the word "heart." But this can easily be mere wordplay by the *paytan*.

* * *

Now I would like to quote a very important passage from Rambam's *Guide to the Perplexed*. It gives his view of midrash in general and also provides his interesting explanation of the mitzvah of the four species. The Torah tells us to use these items on Sukkot but never explains why.

This is what he writes in Book III, chapter 43:

> As regards the four species... our Sages gave a reason for their use by way of Agadic interpretation, the method of which is well known to those who are acquainted with the style of our Sages. They use the text of the Bible only as a kind of poetical language [for their own ideas], and do not intend thereby to give an interpretation of the text. As to the value of these Midrashic interpretations, we meet with two different opinions. For some think that the Midrash contains the real explanation of the text, whilst others, finding that it cannot be reconciled with the words quoted, reject and ridicule it. The former struggle and fight to prove and to confirm such interpretations according to their opinion, and to keep them as the real meaning of the text; they consider them in the same light as traditional laws. Neither of the two classes understood it, that **our Sages employ biblical texts merely as poetical expressions**, the meaning of which is clear to every reasonable reader. This style was general in ancient days; all adopted it in the same way as poets [adopt a certain style]. Our Sages say, in reference to the words "and a paddle (*yated*) thou shalt have upon thy weapon" [*azeneka*, Deut. xxiii,14]: Do not read *azeneka*, "thy weapon," but *ozneka*, "thy ear." You are thus told, that if you hear a person uttering something disgraceful, put your fingers into your ears. Now, I wonder whether those ignorant persons [who take the Midrashic interpretations literally] believe that the author of this saying gave it as the true interpretation of the text quoted, and as the meaning of this precept: that in truth

yated, "the paddle," is used for "the finger," and *azeneka* denotes "thy ear." I cannot think that any person whose intellect is sound can admit this. The author employed the text as a beautiful poetical phrase, in teaching an excellent moral lesson, namely this: It is as bad to listen to bad language as it is to use it. This lesson is poetically connected with the above text. In the same sense you must understand the phrase, "Do not read so, but so," wherever it occurs in the Midrash.

I have departed from my subject, but it was for the purpose of making a remark useful to every intellectual member of the Rabbanites. I now return to our theme. I believe that the four species are a symbolical expression of our rejoicing that the Israelites changed the wilderness, "no place of seed, or of figs, or of vines, or of pomegranates, or of water to drink" (Num. xx. 5), with a country full of fruit-trees and rivers. In order to remember this **we take the fruit which is the most pleasant of the fruit of the land, branches which smell best, most beautiful leaves, and also the best of herbs**, i.e., the willows of the brook. These four kinds have also these three purposes: First, they were plentiful in those days in Palestine, so that every one could easily get them. Secondly, they have a good appearance, they are green; some of them, viz., the citron and the myrtle, are also excellent as regards their smell, the branches of the palm-tree and the willow having neither good nor bad smell. Thirdly, they keep fresh and green for seven days, which is not the case with peaches, pomegranates, asparagus, nuts, and the like.

* * *

- The above translation from the Arabic is from the edition of M. Friedländer. (The bolding is my own.)
- One of the phrases above (second paragraph, third sentence) is an awkward and misleading translation. A better translation is: "I believe that the four species of the *lulav* symbolize our rejoicing of leaving the wilderness ... to a country full of fruit-trees and rivers."[55] He seems to mean that every year we would be celebrating

---

55. See the many other translations of this passage.

this transition from the barren wilderness to the beautiful land of Israel.
- When Rambam wrote at the outset: "As regards the four species, our Sages gave a reason for their use by way of Agadic interpretation," he does not state what Aggadic interpretation he is referring to. But surely he is referring to the midrash at *Leviticus Rabbah* 30:12 where the *etrog* is viewed as symbolizing those with Torah knowledge and good deeds, the *lulav* as those with Torah knowledge but without good deeds, the *hadas* as those who have good deeds but lack Torah knowledge, and the *aravah* as those who lack both Torah knowledge and good deeds. (The midrash continues that they are all joined together in this commandment, so that each can atone for the other.) Rambam must reject a literal understanding of this midrash because he is viewing all the four species in a positive light.
- Certainly, a factor in motivating Rambam's interpretation of the commandment is that the Torah mentions an obligation of ושמחתם in connection with it. See Lev. 23:40.

* * *

Rambam's remark that "they keep fresh and green for seven days" does not square with the reality of Mitchell First's experience with *hadassim* and *aravot*, for reasons unknown to him.

6. The Meaning of *Atzeret*

The word עצרת is used in *Tanakh* to refer to the last day of Sukkot (Lev. 23:36 and elsewhere) and to the last day of Pesaḥ (Deut. 16:8). What precisely does it mean?[56]

---

56. The Sages use the word עצרת as the name of the holiday of Shavuot, even though this term is not used for it in *Tanakh*. One possible explanation is that the Sages viewed Shavuot as an appendage to Pesaḥ, just like the eighth day of Sukkot and the seventh day of Pesaḥ are appendages to their first days. Pesaḥ and Shavuot are of course connected by the counting of the *Omer* throughout the period.

Josephus, writing around 100 CE, uses the Aramaic form of the name:

The word appears six times in *Tanakh*, along with an *atzroteikhem* at Amos 5:21. Also, an alternative form of this word, עצרה (*atzarah*), appears four times.

As further background, three out of the six times that the word *atzeret* appears, it is followed by a prohibition on doing any *melekhet avodah* (Lev. 23:36 and Num. 29:35) or any *melakhah* (Deut. 16:8). When used as a verb, עצר usually means "**restrain**."

Let us look at Lev. 23:36 regarding the eighth day of Sukkot. The relevant part of the verse reads: "The eighth day will be a *mikra kodesh* to you, and you shall bring an offering made by fire to God; it is an *atzeret*, you shall do no *melekhet avodah*."

Here are various approaches to *atzeret*:

1. Rashi on this verse understands the meaning as: "**restrain yourselves from leaving**." I.e., God wants the people to stay another day.[57]
2. Rashbam and Ibn Ezra understand the meaning as: "**restrain yourself from doing work**."[58]
3. Targum Onkelos and many others understand the meaning as: "**gathering**."[59] Targum Onkelos uses the term כנישין.
4. Another view is that עצר means "close up" here. This is its meaning in the phrase from *Shema* at Deut. 11:17: *ve-atzar et ha-shamayim*. The meaning in our context would be **a day that "closes up" the holiday**.[60]

Which view is to be preferred?

With regard to approach #2, three times the phrase with *atzeret* is followed by a prohibition on doing *melekhet avodah* or *melakhah*. On

---

asartha (in Greek characters). See *Antiquities* III, 252. (He then states that it means "fifty"!)
57. Rashi's explanation here is based on *Sifrei* Deut. 151 and *Sukkah* 55b.
58. This interpretation is found at *Hagigah* 18a and earlier at *Sifrei* Deut. 135. It is also the first interpretation that Rashi offers at Num. 29:35 and Deut. 16:8.
59. See, e.g., *Sifrei* Num. 151: *kenisah*.
60. This suggestion is one of several mentioned in *Daat Mikra*. Also, Rabbi Dr. Hertz suggests the term "closing festival" in his commentary, seeming to prefer it over the term "solemn assembly."

the simplest level, this suggests that *atzeret* is teaching us something different.

Most significantly, *atzeret* means "gathering" at Jer. 9:1. See similarly Amos 5:21 (*atzroteikhem*). Also, the alternative form of the same word, *atzarah*,[61] appears four times and probably means "gathering" each time. (*Atzarah* probably refers to gatherings that are not related to the appointed holidays.) For these reasons, approach #3 is most likely and *atzeret* probably means "gathering" in our holiday context.[62]

But what type of gathering? The King James Bible (1611) used the term "solemn assembly."[63] But why "solemn"? Would not "assembly" be a better translation, to allow for the possibility of a "festive" assembly?[64]

One possibility is that the "gathering" is a merely a reference to all those assembled for the holiday.

But another possibility is that *atzeret* was a reference to a concluding ceremony, such as a concluding prayer ceremony. I have seen the suggestion that at Pesaḥ it was a prayer for a successful harvest and at Sukkot a prayer for rain. Another possibility is a concluding feast.[65]

Note that regarding the eighth day of Sukkot, the people would still have been in Jerusalem. But regarding the seventh day of Pesaḥ,

---

61. Initially, we might think *atzeret* is the construct form of *atzarah*. But scholars today do not treat *atzeret* as a construct form. Rather, it is treated as an alternative form of the same word. (But some treat the *atzeret* of Jer. 9:1 as the construct form.) There are many other examples of word pairs like *atzarah/atzeret*, where the latter is not treated as a construct form. One example is *tifarah/tiferet*.

62. See, e.g., D. Henshke, *Simḥat Ha-Regel Be-Talmudam Shel Tannaim* (2007), p. 209.

But we can speculate that there was a double meaning intended in the *Yamim Tovim* context. The "gathering" meaning was the primary meaning but a "close up the holiday" meaning was also intended.

63. Perhaps they followed an earlier English translation in their choice of words here. I have not researched this issue. Also, perhaps "solemn" did not have the same connotation then as it does now.

64. "Festive assembly" is one of the possibilities suggested in *KB*.

65. Something like this is stated by Philo of Alexandria (first century CE), *Laws* 2:211–213, writing about the eighth day of Sukkot.

it would seem from Deut. 16:7 that they already returned home. So the gathering would have been in their home cities.⁶⁶

Rashi at Deut. 16:8, in his second opinion, suggests that *atzeret* is a reference to a gathering for food and drink. But that verse began with a reference to eating. Rashi did not make this suggestion on the other *atzeret* holiday verses.

What about that similar word *atzarah*? At Joel 1:14 and 2:15, the context of the *atzarah* gathering was a drought and locust invasion, suggesting a solemn prayer gathering. But at 2 Kings 10:20, the context was a joyful feast for Baal. See similarly the meaning at Isa. 1:13.

So, after all that, we cannot determine the nature of the "gathering" and have only offered suggestions.

* * *

One final detail needs to be addressed: How does a verb that means "restrain" turn into a noun that means "gathering"? The explanation is that when people are gathered together it is because they have confined themselves to one location. See, e.g., Radak, *Sefer Ha-Shorashim*, and *Brown-Driver-Briggs*, p. 783 (bottom).

* * *

Finally, I would also like to quote from the inspiring words of Rav S.R. Hirsch on Lev. 23:36:

"If we examine the places where the root עצר is used in Tanach, we find, in the far predominating number of cases, that it has the meaning of retaining, keeping back persons, things, or forces to guard against their being withdrawn or lost.... We accordingly think we are not wrong if we take עצרת to designate a day which is not fixed to bring new lessons and new truths... but which has the mission to keep us still before the Presence of God... to strengthen and solidify the impressions and knowledge we have already gained, so that they remain with us permanently, and do not become lost in the hurly-burly of life.... [It] is a gathering up of all the spiritual 'treasures' that we have collected during the days of the Festival before the Presence of God, so that we can, at the end of this seventh

---

66. I have seen the suggestion that, if the reference is to a prayer gathering, the verse might reflect the origin of synagogues!

day, step over into the course of our ordinary life which then begins, truly enriched by them.... Therein lies the dual conception of עצר: persistence, remaining with God, and holding fast to all the spiritual acquisitions obtained...."⁶⁷

* * *

Mitchell First is an attorney and Jewish history scholar. His mission is to **stop work** early and **gather** up his sources and write articles that all can enjoy in this book that has been **assembled** for you.

7. חנך: The Connection Between the Meanings "Dedicate" and "Educate"

We are all used to this root having the meanings of "dedicate" and "educate." Are these meanings related? How did this root come to have both these meanings?

The clue is found at Deuteronomy 20:5: "The officers shall speak to the people saying: Who is the man that has built a new house and did not חנכו? Let him go and return to his house, lest he die in battle and another man יחנכנו."

There is no evidence for dedication ceremonies of individual houses in ancient Israel. (And we are certainly not talking about "educating" the houses!) It is clear in this verse that our root means: "**use for the first time.**" This is how Rashi understands the verb here and elsewhere (see, e.g., Rashi to Gen. 14:14). See also Radak, *Sefer Ha-Shorashim*. In modern times, many scholars agree that "use for the first time" is the basic meaning of the verb.⁶⁸

The verb is used in *Tanakh* in various contexts: 1) the founding of the *mishkan*, Numbers chap. 7 (four times); 2) the founding of Solomon's Temple, 1 Kings 8:63 (and its parallel at 2 Chron.); 3) the rebuilding of the Second Temple, Ezra 6:16–17; 4) the completion of the wall around Jerusalem, Neh. 12:27; 5) Psalms 30:1; and 6) an image built by Nebuchadnezzar, Dan. chap. 3.

---

67. The above statements are made by R. Hirsch regarding the seventh day of Pesaḥ. But he gives a similar explanation regarding the eighth day of Sukkot.
68. See Reif (next note), p. 495.

In English, "dedicate" typically has the implication of consecrate for sacred use. It is possible that the "use for the first time/initiate" meaning expanded to "dedicate/consecrate" in some of the above passages. But there is also an alternative view: the root never had such a meaning in *Tanakh*, and always meant something like "use for the first time/initiate."

This view is advocated by Stefan Reif.[69] Reif points out that קדש and משח are the verbs in *Tanakh* that meant "dedicate/consecrate for a sacred use." This suggests that חנך must have had a different meaning. He maintains that in *Tanakh* it always meant to "initiate." He writes that "such initiations would naturally represent ideal opportunities for celebrations and festivities but they are not to be confused with dedication or consecration ceremonies." He argues, for example, that the meaning in Numbers is "an initiation gift for the altar." Another similar word that Reif proposes for his translation is "inauguration," which is something less than a dedication/consecration for sacred use.

Even if Reif is not correct, we can understand how a verb that started off meaning "use for the first time/initiate" expanded in *Tanakh* to the meaning "dedicate/consecrate for sacred use."

But what about the "educate" meaning? Where does that come from? The answer is that when you "initiate" someone into an activity, you are "training" him. From these, the verb expanded to "educate."

Perhaps the "educate" meaning is found in *Tanakh*. At Prov. 22:6, we have: ḥanoch la-naar al pi darko; gam ki yazkin lo yasur mi-menah. Most see a "train" or "educate" meaning here. This would be the only time in *Tanakh* that the verb has such a meaning. But Reif argues that our root means "initiate" here: "Start a boy..."

As to the "train" meaning, at Gen. 14:14, Abraham is going off to rescue Lot and calls his three hundred eighteen חניכיו to assist him. Reif first suggests "initiates" or "trainees" here, but then points out that this word may be of Egyptian origin.[70]

* * *

---

69. See *Vetus Testamentum*, vol. 22 (1972), pp. 495–501. The article is humorously titled: "Dedicated to חנך." For several decades, Reif was the Director of the Taylor-Schechter Genizah Research Unit in Cambridge.

70. He is likely correct in allowing for an Egyptian origin for this word. This

In Arabic, *chanaka* has the primary meaning of rubbing the gums of a newborn child with the juice of dates or oil. In this way, the parent "initiates" the newborn into eating. Since the noun חך in *Tanakh* means "palate, roof of mouth, gums," many scholars see a relation between the noun חך and the "initiate" verb חנך and postulate that perhaps the original meaning of the verb was "to rub the palate of a newborn child" with such items. But this custom of rubbing the gums of a newborn child is only attested to from Islamic times. It is only conjecture that it existed in early Biblical or pre-Biblical times.

Nevertheless, the suggestion that חך = "palate, roof of mouth, gums," was originally חנך has much evidence to support it.[71] For example, the Syriac and Arabic cognates have that middle *nun*.[72]

* * *

Now let us address the name of the holiday Chanukah. The name certainly does not mean "educate." (Although on a homiletical level, I would suggest that people need to educate themselves more about the holiday and read I and II Maccabees! If you do not own them, you can read them online.) Reif does not like the "Dedication" meaning even here, post-Biblically. But I can accept that the meaning of חנך expanded to "dedicate/consecrate" even in Biblical times, and certainly in the latter portion of the Second Temple period when the holiday received this name.

Is there a possible alternative translation? The fourth chapter of I Macc. tells us that Judah and his men tore down the defiled altar and built a new one and made new holy vessels. Then it continues (4:54–59):[73] "At the very time of year and on the very day on which the gentiles had profaned the altar, it was **dedicated** to the sound

---

is one of the Egyptian words listed by T. Lambdin in his important article on this subject. See his "Egyptian Loan Words in the Old Testament," *Journal of the American Oriental Society* 73 (1953), pp. 145–55.

71. See, e.g., *BDB*, p. 335.

72. Another instance of a *nun* dropping from the name of a body part is the case of אף = nose, face. Here the original noun was אנף. See, e.g., Klein, p. 45. These three letters as a verb for "anger" appear many times in *Tanakh*. See, e.g., Deut. 1:37, *hitanaf*. The nose/face is where one's anger is revealed.

73. Translation from the edition of J. Goldstein.

of singing and harps and lyres and cymbals... They celebrated the **dedication** of the altar for eight days, joyfully bringing burnt offerings and sacrificing peace offerings and thank offerings.... The people were overjoyed as the shame inflicted by the gentiles was removed. Judas and his brothers and the entire assembly of Israel decreed that the **days of the dedication of the altar** should be observed at their time of year annually for eight days, beginning with the twenty-fifth of the month of Kislev, with joy and gladness."

I Maccabees was originally written in Hebrew. But the Hebrew was lost early on. (The last person to mention the Hebrew was the church father Jerome. He lived in *Eretz Yisrael* around 400 CE.) That English word "dedicate" is a translation of a Greek word that meant something like "renovate" or "reconsecrate." Most likely, the Hebrew words used here were from the root חנך, as suggested by A. Cahana in his Hebrew edition.[74] Based on the above passages, are we being described a "dedication/consecration" story, or a mere "inauguration" story? On the one hand, it seems that many items were consecrated at the time. On the other hand, each time that the חנך word was (presumably) being used, we could read it as meaning "inauguration."

* * *

I would like to acknowledge the article on *Chanukah* at balashon.com from Dec. 12, 2006 which pointed me to many sources and ideas.[75]

* * *

Mitchell First uses his initiative and dedicates himself to continually educating himself so he can provide his readers with new interesting material.

8. The Meaning of the Verb פסח

We are all accustomed to the idea that the verb פסח means "pass over" and that our holiday gets its English name from this meaning.

But there are many scholars who disagree. They offer two alterna-

---

74. *Ha-Sefarim Ha-Ḥitzonim* (2 vols. 1970).
75. See also A. Goldstein, *A Theology of Holiness* (2018), pp. 34–36.

tive interpretations of the verb פסח in the several times it appears in the twelfth chapter of Exodus. They cite Targum Onkelos and other early rabbinic sources for their interpretations. In fact, a leading Bible scholar has written that the "pass over" interpretation is the "least likely" of the three possibilities.[76] I write this article to refute these claims. I agree with Rashi that this "pass over" interpretation is the best one for the twelfth chapter and that it fits the underlying meaning of the root פסח throughout *Tanakh*.

Here are the key phrases in the twelfth chapter:

- 12:13: *ve-ra'iti et ha-dam* **u-fasahti** *aleikhem...*
- 12:23: *u-fasah Hashem al ha-petah...*
- 12:27: *zevah pesah hu...* [God was] *pasah al batei vnei Yisrael be-Mitzrayim be-nogpo et Mitzrayim ve-et bateinu hitzil...*

The first alternative interpretation is that פסח means חוס. Marcus Jastrow gives many meanings to חוס: e.g., protect, spare, have consideration for, have affection for, and bend over. Whatever it means, it is different from passing or skipping over.

Targum Onkelos consistently translates our four פסח words in chapter 12 with words from the root חוס. Also, there is an anonymous passage in *Mekhilta Bo* (sec. 7) that expresses the חוס interpretation at Ex. 12:13. Also, a few lines later, R. Yoshiah expresses the דלג view, while R. Yonatan expresses the חוס view.

Among our early commentators, we have some who seem to follow the חוס approach: For example, R. Saadiah uses the phrase *zevah hemlah* in his translation of Ex. 12:27.[77]

Another alternative interpretation is from the root גנן: to cover, to protect. See Tosefta *Sotah* 4:1, which uses the word הגין in its interpretation of the פסח of Ex. 12:23. There is also a similar passage using הגין in the *Mekhilta*.[78] Also, Targum Yonatan uses the word ויגין, from the גנן root, for the פסח of 12:23.[79]

---

76. See N. Sarna, *Exploring Exodus* (1986), p. 87.
77. See also Ibn Ezra.
78. See Glasson (next note), p. 80.
79. For more sources, see T.F. Glasson, "The 'Passover,' a Misnomer: The Meaning of the Verb *Pasach*," *The Journal of Theological Studies*, 10 (1959), pp. 79–84.

Let us now review the instances of the root פסח in *Tanakh* which are not references to the holiday itself. With regard to the noun, there is a noun that appears many times that refers to a person or animal that limps.⁸⁰ With regard to the verb, it has a meaning like "skip" or "jump" at 1 Kings 18:21, where we have the expression *poshim al shetei ha-se'ipim*. This is an idiom for someone who cannot decide between two opinions. *Daat Mikra* suggests that the idiom originated with a bird that **skips or jumps** from one branch to another because it cannot decide which one to land on.

Similarly it has a meaning like "skip" or "jump" at 1 Kings 18:26, where the prophets of Baal do this around the altar: *va-yefashu al ha-mizbeaḥ*. Most likely, this is their religious ritual: a dance of ecstasy, involving jumping and/or skipping.⁸¹

Of course, the "skip, jump" meaning of the verb is related to the "limp" meaning. A person or animal that limps is doing a form of skipping or jumping.

So on what basis does anyone give an interpretation of our פסח words in Exodus that is **not related** to limping? The claim is that one can get a completely different meaning of the root פסח from Isaiah 31:5. This verse reads: "As birds flying (= hovering above their children), so will the Lord of Hosts protect Jerusalem: *ganon ve-hitzil*, **pasoaḥ ve-himlit**."⁸²

This verse ends with four words, and the other three have a "protect, rescue" meaning. This suggests, at first glance, that *pasoaḥ* has this meaning here too.

But when looked at carefully, one sees that it is very easy to read in the "skip, jump" meaning here. The context is that God is being compared to a bird. A bird flies. The Jewish Publication Society of America translation of 1917 translates the last two words as: "He will rescue it as He passeth over." Even better is *Daat Mikra* which explains that the way a bird guards its nest involves moving/jumping between the surrounding branches.

---

80. The leg injury can even be more serious than a limp. This would be an expansion from the original "limp" meaning. See 2 Sam. 4:4.
81. See *Daat Mikra*.
82. When the *Mekhilta* gave the חוס interpretation, this is the verse that it cited.

Rashi on Ex. 12:13 gives an interpretation of Isa. 31:5 within the framework of skipping and jumping. But it is a bit unclear and I have seen several different translations of it. But Rashi does state clearly here: "*kol pesiḥah leshon dillug ve-kefitzah*" (= every time the verb פסח appears, it has a meaning of skipping or jumping).

If there was one verse which clearly used a "protect, rescue" meaning for פסח, then it would be legitimate to attempt to read it into the verses in Exodus. (But it still would be an unlikely interpretation, given that every other instance of the root is related to a limp/skip/jump meaning.) But we do not have even one clear example of a "protect, rescue" meaning of the root פסח in *Tanakh*. Nor do we have such a meaning in any of the other Semitic languages.

I once wrote about meaning "minimalists" and meaning "maximalists."[83] I quoted from an article by Richard Steiner, who taught at Yeshiva University for decades: "Saadia believed that words have many meanings, while Rashi held that they often have only one basic meaning. Saadia made the multiplication of meanings a cornerstone of his exegesis, while Rashi pursued a reductionist policy. In short, Saadia was a meaning-maximalist, while Rashi was a meaning-minimalist."[84]

I agree with the meaning-minimalist approach of Rashi. Our initial presumption should always be that words with the same three-letter root derive from one underlying meaning. We should not claim an entirely different meaning of a root unless there is a strong basis for doing so. There is an insufficient basis for doing so here.

* * *

Finally, I have to briefly comment on those statements of our early Sages that offer the חוס and גנן meanings. (As to Targum Onkelos, it has been suggested that this commentary was merely trying to avoid a meaning that implied a bodily movement of God.)

Anyone familiar with the statements of our Sages realizes that they sometime give interpretations of a word that apply to that verse only

---

83. See *Links to Our Legacy* (2021), pp. 107–110.
84. See his "Saadia vs. Rashi: On the Shift from Meaning-Maximalism to Meaning-Minimalism in Medieval Biblical Lexicology," *Jewish Quarterly Review* 88 (1988), pp. 213–58 (214–15).

or to only a limited number of verses. They offer these interpretations homiletically, or even non-homiletically, to emphasize a certain point. They obviously do not have a concordance in their hand when they make their statements and are often not concerned about the "global root impact" of their interpretations.[85]

* * *

As many have noted, it is interesting that the different root פסע has the meaning: "to step." (ה and ע sometimes substitute for one another.)

* * *

Mitchell First usually tries not to skip any instances of a word in *Tanakh* when discussing a root.

9. Interesting Words in the Book of Ruth

1. תעגנה (1:13): The root עגן only appears here. Here is the full passage: "Would you wait for them until they were grown? *Ha-lahen te'ageinah* so as not to belong to a man…?"

   Daat Mikra suggests that the meaning of our word is *kashar, asar* (= tie, bind). It has this meaning in Aramaic.[86] Taking a slightly different approach, the *Brown-Driver-Briggs* lexicon had suggested: "shut oneself in or off." This meaning also exists in Aramaic.[87] The Koehler-Baumgartner lexicon is similar: "locked in." Another source I saw suggested "wait," parallel to the earlier part of the verse.

   Most likely, our word in Ruth is the origin of the rabbinic word עגונה, a woman who is not able to remarry.

   In his commentary on Ruth, Rashi wrote that the נ is not a root

---

85. In contrast, medieval lexicographers, if they are meaning-minimalists, are conscious of all the instances of a root in *Tanakh* and are trying to give interpretations that work globally to the extent that they can. (Rashi is usually trying to do the same thing, even though his *Tanakh* commentary is not a dictionary.)
86. See Jastrow, p. 1042.
87. Ibid.

letter in the word. If it were, the word would have two *nuns* or there would be a *dagesh* in the one *nun*. Accordingly, he connects the word with the phrase: *ag ugah ve-amad be-tokhah* (= he made a circle and stood in its midst). Accordingly, Rashi believes that the word means something like "imprisoned." (Scholars who believe that the root is עגן take the position that the lack of a *dagesh* and lack of a second *nun* are not fatal problems with their approach.)

But Rashi on the Talmud takes a different approach to our word. At *Bava Kamma* 80a, he writes that the Rabbinic word עגונה means "delayed" and he cites our verse in Ruth.

2. יבמתך (1:15 and 1:18): Words reflecting the male form are found two times in *Tanakh* and words reflecting the female form are found five times. Perhaps the basic word for the male was *yavam* and the basic word for the female was *yevamah*, although those precise forms are not found in *Tanakh*.

The verb for the procedure appears at Gen. 38:8, and Deut. 25:5, 7. Most likely, the verb יבם arose after the nouns. We do not know the underlying meaning of the original nouns.

3. להכרני and נכריה (2:10): "Why have I found favor in your eyes to notice me (להכרני), [as] I am a stranger (נכריה)?"

The root נכר means both "strange" and "recognize."[88] Our verse is a word play, using both meanings. A similar word play is at Gen. 42:7. There Joseph recognizes his brothers (ויכרם) and then makes himself a stranger to them (ויתנכר).

How can this one root נכר have both the meanings "recognize" and "strange"? Here is the suggestion of Rav S.R. Hirsch (commenting on this verse). When you recognize something what you are doing initially is understanding its strangeness and uniqueness. "The more signs of difference we see in an object, the more specially do we recognize it. With every such sign, we 'estrange' it from all other spheres..."

It is possible that the reason הכיר is in the *hifil* is that when you

---

88. Please trust me that נכר is the root of הכיר = recognize, and its variants. The word should be understood as if it was written הנכיר.

are recognizing something you are causing the object to stand out in your mind.

4. וילפת (3:8): The verse reads: "It was midnight, the man was startled, *va-yillafet*, and behold there was a woman lying at his feet."

   This root לפת only appears two other times in *Tanakh*. It means to "grasp" or "twist" at Judges 16:29. At Job 6:18, it refers to a path that twists. (It may be related to the root פתל via a metathesis.) In our verse, it may mean that Boaz twisted himself from one side to the other (see, e.g., Ibn Ezra), perhaps in an attempt to get up and see who it was.

   Rashi believes it refers to Ruth grasping Boaz in an effort to calm him. But from the context, it does not seem to be referring to an action by Ruth. For an interesting alternative approach to our word, see *Sanhedrin* 19b.

5. פלני אלמני (4:1): This phrase appears two other times: at 1 Sam. 21:3 and 2 Kings 6:8. Also, at Dan. 8:13, we have פלמני, which is probably a contraction of the two words.

   There is a Hebrew root פלה which means "separate, distinct." That is likely the root of the first word. The second word derives from אלם with its meaning "silent." Therefore, the phrase means something like "the separate/distinct person who is not mentioned." See the *Brown-Driver-Briggs* lexicon, and the *Daat Mikra* to the above verses. (I had always thought it was essentially jibberish, like "Joe Shmoe"!)

6. אמנת (*omenet*) (4:16): We all know this root אמן. It usually has meanings like "trust, believe, verify, confirm." But one time in *Tanakh*, at Song of Songs 7:2, it means "craftsman." The "trust/believe" meaning and the "craftsman" meaning are not related,[89] as the latter comes from Akkadian (borrowed from Sumerian, a non-Semitic language).

   Ok, so what did Naomi do for Ruth's baby? And what did Mordechai do for Esther (2:7)? Were they teaching them crafts?

---

89. See Tawil, p. 24 and Klein, p. 35. But I did see one source that did not realize this (or did not accept it) and translated the אמן of Song of Songs 7:2 as a "dependable worker"!

Many translate the word here and elsewhere (e.g., Num. 11:12) as "nurse." But the application of this word to Mordechai (and other men, see, e.g., 2 Kings 10:1) is difficult! *Daat Mikra*, in the cases of Mordechai and Naomi, offers מגדל and מחנך (raise and educate). But we would prefer not to invent new meanings for the root.

Here is the better approach. A fundamental meaning of the root אמן is "trust." The *omein* and *omenet* were individuals who were entrusted with the child and trusted with its care.[90] In this explanation, there is no reason to postulate a "nurse" meaning.[91]

* * *

When the book of Ruth refers to marriage at 1:4, it uses a form of the verb נשא: וישאו. This is the verb for marriage used in the **later** books of *Tanakh*: Chronicles, Ezra, and Nechemiah. (Another וישאו is found at Judges 21:23.) In the Torah and the earlier books of *Nakh*, the verb לקח is almost always the one used.[92] (The book of Ruth does use לקח in the context of marriage at 4:13.)

The use of the late form for marriage at Ruth 1:4 and Judges 21:23 has some relevance to the date of authorship of, or at least the date of final editing of, these books. But a response is that many styles that we ordinarily think of as late are really early styles from the different dialect of Hebrew in northern Israel.[93]

More interesting is what the import of נשא is in the context of marriage. Could it mean that the man is raising the spiritual level of his wife, or of the lives of the two of them? Or is it that he is raising her status? Or was there some kind of physical raising involved in the ancient marriage ceremony? I wondered about this for years and finally decided to look into it. I realize now that the explanation is probably a very mundane one. נשא does not only mean "raise." It

---

90. See *TDOT*, vol. 1, p. 294.
91. Because *omein* has been commonly thought to mean "nurse," the 1917 Jewish Publication Society of America translation (included in the *Pentateuch* of Rabbi Dr. Hertz) was forced into the following translation at Num. 11:12: "as a **nursing-father** carries the suckling child"! The word *omein* is, of course, male, unlike *omenet*.
92. For many citations, see the Even-Shoshan concordance, p. 607.
93. See *EJ* 14:522.

also has the meaning "carry away." (Raising something is the first step in carrying it away.) Most likely, "carry away" is the meaning of נשא that is being used in the marriage context, very close to the meaning of לקח.[94]

* * *

Mitchell First "carried away" his wife Sharon in 1987.

---

94. See, e.g. *BDB*, p. 671 (column on the right), and Radak, *Sefer Ha-Shorashim*.

Liturgy

1. The Prayer for Rain in *Birkat Ha-Shanim* in the Diaspora: The Issue of Different Climates

Mishnah *Taanit* 1:3 discusses when the Jewish community in *Eretz Yisrael* should begin to pray for rain in *Birkat Ha-Shanim*. There are two views stated, the third and the seventh of Marḥeshvan.[1]

But what about the diaspora? What is their starting date for this prayer? The Mishnah (a work from *Eretz Yisrael*) does not record one. The Talmud records a *baraita* that a *tanna* stated that the Jews in the *Golah* (= Babylonia)[2] begin to pray for rain on the sixtieth day after the *tekufah* (= the autumnal equinox in September),[3] and the *halakhah* is recorded as following this opinion.[4] The different date is obviously due to different conditions in Babylonia. (How this date in November evolved into what we do in this century, December 4, is a separate topic.[5])

---

1. R. Gamliel is the one who gives the latter date, giving time for those returning from their pilgrimage to the Temple to reach the Euphrates River. At *Taanit* 10a, the *halakhah* for the land of Israel is stated to be according to R. Gamliel.
   R. Gamliel's view would seem to apply only when the Temple was standing. (See Lasker, p. 142, n. 3.) Nevertheless, it is widely treated as being applicable today as well.
2. Although *Golah* literally means "diaspora," the usual interpretation of this passage is that it is being used with the more narrow meaning of "Babylonia."
3. *Taanit* 10a and J. Talmud *Taanit* 1:1. The *tanna* quoted here is Hananiah (nephew of R. Joshua b. Hananiah). He lived for many years in Babylonia and was a leading authority there. See *EJ* 7:1253.
4. *Taanit* 10a.
5. It is partially explained by the dropping of 10 days from the calendar in 1582.

In the Mishnaic and Talmudic periods, the overwhelming majority of world Jewry lived in *Eretz Yisrael* or Babylonia. But what happened when major sections of Jewry began to live elsewhere, with conditions that were different from *Eretz Yisrael* and Babylonia? Should each region's own condition determine when the community should pray for rain? But do we really want each community to recite the prayer in a season that they see fit? Perhaps the *halakhah* should take the position that Israel and Babylonia are the two paradigms and every community must pick one or the other? Or perhaps Babylonia should be the paradigm for the entire diaspora, no matter how contrary the region's own climate is?

As further background, I hope you realize that in the U.S. today we start our prayer for rain on the day that our ancestors in Babylonia would have started it, despite whatever differences in agricultural conditions exist between the two regions.

An article by Arnold and Daniel Lasker discusses all these issues and my discussion for the rest of this essay is based on their article: "The Jewish Prayer for Rain in the Post-Talmudic Diaspora," *AJS Review* (Fall 1984), pp. 141–168.[6]

Already in the Talmud (*Taan.* 14b), there is a story about *Bnei Ninveh* (in Assyria, north of Babylonia) who asked R. Yehudah Ha-Nasi (200 CE) what to do, as they needed rain in the summer. He responded that they were not considered a רבים and in the summer they should only recite their prayer for rain in the blessing *Shome'a Tefillah*. The Talmud then records views of the *tanna* R. Yehudah and of the *amora* R. Naḥman who would have allowed *Bnei Ninveh* to recite their prayer for rain in *Birkat Ha-Shanim* in the summer. But the Talmud concludes that the *halakhah* follows R. Sheshet who disagreed with R. Naḥman.[7]

At the time of the Talmud, there were Jewish communities in places

---

The day after Thursday, Oct. 4, was declared to be Friday Oct. 15. I discussed this in *Roots and Rituals* (2018), pp. 211–13.

6. More recently an article in Hebrew by D. Sabato on our topic came out in the online journal *Oqimta*: vol. 8 (2022), pp. 117–40.

7. The Jerusalem Talmud has a slightly different version of this story. See *Taan.* 1:1 and *Ber.* 5:2. It has also been argued that the locale involved was not Nineveh, but Nawe, in Jordan.

such as Rome and Alexandria, but the Talmud does not record their rain prayer practices.

In the post-Talmudic period, the question arose in late Geonic times among the Jews in Tunisia. Tunisia is in Africa, bordered on its west by Algeria and on its east by Libya. It seems that they followed the custom of the land of Israel: the seventh of Marḥeshvan.[8]

Beginning in the eleventh century, accurate records of rabbinic decisions have been preserved. Numerous sources from the eleventh through the fourteenth centuries record that the Jews in Europe (i.e., France, Germany, Italy, and Spain) followed the Babylonian paradigm. The only exception was Provence (southern France). Most of the sources from Provence state that they followed the *Eretz Yisrael* paradigm: the seventh of Marḥeshvan. For example, Meiri writes that while it is true that in general Babylonian customs are followed in his region, an exception has to be made if the nature of the land is different and needs rain earlier.[9]

The Laskers point out that we do not know the origin of these European practices. Were the practices justified by halakhic thinking? Or do these practices merely reflect the origins of the earliest Jewish settlers in each region?

In Rambam, however, we have clear (but contradictory!) discussions. In his commentary on Mishnah *Taanit* 1:3, he writes that any place with a climate similar to *Eretz Yisrael* should follow what is in the Mishnah. Everywhere else, they should make the request in *Birkat Ha-Shanim* "at the time that is fit for rain in that locale." He calls any other approach *sheker* and concludes that his approach is *nakhon u-barur*.[10]

But a few years later in his *Mishneh Torah* (*Tefillah* 2:16–17), he writes differently. First he sets up two categories: 1) *Eretz Yisrael* and 2) Babylonia, Syria, Egypt and places that are near them and similar to them.[11] He instructs all the latter to follow the Babylonian date. Then

---

8. But the Laskers admit that their evidence here is based on unreliable readings.
9. See, e.g., Meiri, *Beit Ha-Beḥirah*, Taan., p. 34.
10. I am here following R. Kafaḥ's translation from the Arabic.
11. I believe he means "or similar to them." Otherwise he has not given any guidance for Europe.

he adds: "Places that need rain in the summer, such as the faraway sea islands, should ask for rain in *Shome'a Tefillah* when they need it." Thus, he has not permitted each region to use *Birkat Ha-Shanim* to ask for rain in the time it needs it.

Aside from Rambam's view in his commentary on the Mishnah, another authority who strongly argued for the regional approach was Rosh (= R. Asher b. Yeḥiel). He wrote about this at length in a responsum written due to a drought in Spain in 1313.[12]

In this responsum, Rosh described his lifetime of efforts on this issue. Rosh lived approximately the first fifty years of his life in Germany. There he felt that rain was necessary from the middle of Tishrei to Shavuot and he urged his fellow Jews in this area to pray for rain in *Birkat Ha-Shanim* between the seventh of Marḥeshvan and Shavuot. He took the position that the Nineveh precedent described in the Talmud did not apply because Nineveh was only a city, while Germany was an entire region/country. Since the entire region/country needed rain at a time other than the traditional diaspora period, he took the position that the Jews there were within their rights to incorporate the prayer for rain into *Birkat Ha-Shanim* at the time they needed it. But the Jews of Germany refused to change their custom.

Rosh wrote further that in 1303 he passed through the region of Provence (on his way to his new community in Spain). There he was pleased to learn that the Jews in Montpellier began their *Birkat HaShanim* rain prayer on the seventh of Marḥeshvan. When he was told that this region needed rain even after Passover, he urged them to extend their recital period. Their response was the same as that of the Jews of Germany. His logic was sound, but they felt obligated to follow their traditional custom.

Then Rosh reached Spain. He saw that the need for rain there was even greater than in Germany and Provence. He mentioned to his colleagues in Spain that they ought to ask for rain through Shavuot, but he did not make a public issue of it in his early years there. But then the drought of 1313 came. Rosh saw that the Jews in Spain were even fasting for rain. He thought this would be a good time to bring about the change he wanted. If he could convince Spanish Jewry to

---

12. *Teshuvot Ha-Rosh*, section 4, no. 10.

extend the rain prayer request deadline this year, they would hopefully repeat their extension in the following years.

But the Jews of Spain refused to change their custom. The Rosh lost his battle in three separate regions! Logic was not enough to change practices which were deeply rooted. Rosh also finally agreed that the need for uniformity is as important a principle on which to base *halakhah* as are logic and a correct interpretation of texts. Therefore Rosh yielded. Even his son the *Tur* (early fourteenth cent.) ruled that the diaspora prayer for rain in *Birkat Ha-Shanim* should span only the traditional period: starting sixty days from the equinox and continuing up to Passover.[13]

In the sixteenth century, R. Yosef Caro codified his position. He wrote that the period for the request for rain in the diaspora begins on the sixtieth day after the autumnal equinox and continues only until just before Pesaḥ. Then he added: Individuals who need rain in the summer can ask for rain but only in *Shome'a Tefillah*; even large cities like Nineveh, or an entire country like *Sepharad* or Germany are only considered like individuals.[14]

This resolved matters for a while, but the issue arose again when Jews started to move to the southern hemisphere. There the seasons are opposite from what they are in the northern hemisphere.

Jewish immigrants from the Netherlands established a synagogue in Brazil in 1637, the first one in the Americas. Determining when to recite the prayer for rain was one of their first ritual problems. They sent their inquiry to R. Ḥayyim Shabbetai of Salonika. (This seems to have been the first halakhic question to come from the New World!) In their question, they advised that they needed rain from Nissan to Tishrei, and that in the other months rain would be harmful to them. R. Shabbetai decided that he did not want them to pray for

---

13. *OH* 117. In the fourteenth century, R. Nissim ben Reuben of Gerona (= Ran) wrote that there were some diaspora communities that followed the seventh of Marḥeshvan date. He also wrote that R. Gamliel's statement only applied during Temple times, and that in post-Temple times, the prayer for rain in *Eretz Yisrael* should begin immediately after Shemini Atzeret. I believe some communities in *Eretz Yisrael* in the time of the Rishonim did follow this practice.
14. See also his comments in his *Beit Yosef* and *Kesef Mishneh*.

rain when it would be harmful to them. Therefore, he concluded that they should not pray for rain in *Birkat Ha-Shanim* at any time of the year. In the months they needed rain, they should pray for it in *Shome'a Tefillah*.[15]

In the early twentieth century, the southern hemisphere question was posed again by the Jews of Argentina. A number of inquiries were addressed by various groups to different authorities. Some endorsed R. Shabbetai's view. Others maintained that the standard diaspora practice should be followed, despite the different climactic conditions. The question has also been relevant in Australia and the Laskers discuss what happened there as well.

* * *

For most Ashkenazim today, the difference between whether one is praying for rain or not praying for it is only two additional words. But it is not that simple. For example, our earliest siddur is the *Siddur Rav Saadiah Gaon*. The difference between the two prayers is significant there.[16] In Rambam, too, there is a significant difference between the two prayers.[17] Similarly, for Sepharadim today, if one looks at ArtScroll's *Siddur Chaim Yehoshua Hashalem* (Nusach Sefard, 1999), p. 48, one sees two different paragraphs depending on the season.[18]

To view several versions of both prayers over the centuries, see B.S. Jacobson, *The Weekday Siddur* (1978), pp. 191–193.[19]

* * *

If someone erroneously inserted the prayer for rain in the summer in

---

15. See also *Eshel Avraham*, OH 117.
16. Compare p. 18 with p. 21.
17. See his *Seder Tefillot Kol Ha-Shanah* in his *Mishneh Torah*.
18. There is a note on this page that the separate summer paragraph reflects the version of only *ketzat kehillot*. But in B.S. Jacobson, *The Weekday Siddur* (1978), pp. 192–93, different paragraphs for summer and winter are presented under the title "current Sefardi wording," and there is no statement that only a small number of Sephardic communities follow this custom.

I would be remiss if I did not mention that there is a community (not a Sephardic one) whose custom is the addition in the rainy season of only one word: *u-matar*. (In the summer, their text is: *ve-tein tal li-verakhah*.) See I. Elbogen, *Jewish Liturgy* (1993, Eng. edition), p. 39.

19. For further discussion see Elbogen, p. 39.

a region which does not need rain (and has concluded his *Amidah*), the *halakhah* is that he must repeat his *Amidah* without the insertion. This is because if the original prayer would be answered, God will send rain and it will be in the wrong time. We see from here the seriousness with which our Sages treated the effectiveness of our prayers.

* * *

Mitchell First recalls the famous joke among modern Ashkenazim (two words versus four words): On the evening of Dec. 4, the *Yekke* said to his wife on his way to the evening prayer: "I will be home late tonight!"

2. The Origin of the Recital of the *Kedushah* Prayer in *U-Va Le-Tziyon*

When I refer to the *Kedushah* prayer, I am referring to the juxtaposition of the *kadosh, kadosh, kadosh* phrase from Isaiah 6:3 with the *barukh kevod Hashem mi-mekomo* phrase from Ezekiel 3:12. On a regular weekday, we recite such a prayer three times at *shaharit*: once before the morning *Shema*, once in the repetition of the *Amidah*, and once in *U-Va Le-Tziyon*. The last recital differs from the first two in that in the last we recite each verse followed by a translation in Aramaic.

What is the origin of our third daily *Kedushah* recital in *shaharit*? Of course, one theory is that it originated for the benefit of latecomers.[20] Another theory is that it arose as a replacement during a period of persecution when one or both of the earlier *Kedushot* were prohibited, and the guards left after the *Amidah*. After the persecution ended, it was decided to leave the new post-*Amidah Kedushah* in place.[21] Of course, both of these theories are entirely conjectural and are difficult for a variety of reasons.[22]

---

20. See, e.g., *Abudarham* (fourteenth cent.). He also suggests that the latecomers, i.e., the uneducated, would have needed the recital to be in Aramaic, as they were not fluent in Hebrew.
21. See *Likkutei Pardes*, 9a, quoting a Geonic responsum, and *Or Zarua* (thirteenth cent.), quoting *Sefer Ha-Miktzaot*.
22. For example, why would the endurance of the world be dependent on

Our post-*Amidah Kedushah* is mentioned in the Talmud at *Sotah* 49a.[23] It is referred to as *Kedushah De-Sidra*. The Talmud here states that the endurance of the world is dependent on the recital of *Kedushah De-Sidra* and on the recital the *Yehei Shemei Rabbah* of the *Aggadeta*.[24]

There is a source from the ninth century that suggests a detailed scenario for how *Kedushah De-Sidra* arose. The source is a responsum of R. Natronai Gaon.[25] R. Natronai writes that at the end of the daily prayer service the practice was to read and translate ten verses from the Prophets to fulfill the Talmudic statement (*Kidd.* 30a) that one should spend one-third of one's time learning *Mikra*, one-third learning Mishnah, and one-third learning Talmud. The verse from Isaiah and the verse from Ezekiel and their translations were added as a fitting ending to these ten.[26] In a later period, there was no longer

---

it (see the next paragraph), if it only came about as a result of latecomers or persecution?

23. This is an anonymous statement, and is commenting on a statement by Rava (fourth cent.).

24. In those times, the reference was probably to a public lecture on aggadic material, and the lecture was followed by *Kaddish*. Today, we substitute brief aggadic material such as the statement by R. Ḥananya ben Akashya (*ratzah Ha-Kadosh Barukh Hu...*) or the *amar R. Elazar* passage with its homiletical interpretation of *banayikh*.

Regarding the *Yehei Shemei Rabbah* of the *Aggadeta*, it is reasonable to assume that the Talmud considered it as a *seder*. The *seder* was either: 1) the set of all the *Kaddish* statements together or 2) the combination of aggadic lecture followed by *Kaddish*. Otherwise the homiletic interpretation of *ve-lo sedarim* (see below) would not be relevant to the *Yehei Shemei Rabbah* of the *Aggadeta*.

The Talmud makes this statement about the world being dependent on these two recitals based on a homiletic interpretation of Job 10:22. (But see the *Arukh* who rejects this interpretation as an *asmakhta* and gives a different interpretation.) This verse describes a land of gloom and uses the phrase *ve-lo sedarim* (= without *sedarim*). The Talmud deduces that when there are *sedarim*, light will emerge out of the gloom.

Based on this passage in the Talmud, codified in *OH* 132 are the laws that one is not allowed to leave synagogue before the recital of *Kedushah De-Sidra* and that it is important to recite it with *kavanah*.

25. See *Otzar Ha-Geonim, Sotah,* pp. 274–75.

26. R. Natronai does not refer to our third verse of *Kedushah De-Sidra*.: Ex.

time to read and translate ten verses, but the custom of reciting and translating the Isaiah and Ezekiel verses remained. Why? Because the word *kadosh* is repeated three times at Isaiah 6:3, it was felt that *Kedushah* should be recited three times per day.²⁷

The title of the prayer in the standard text of the Talmud, *Kedushah De-Sidra*, seems to fit R. Natronai's explanation. I.e., the *Kedushah* that was recited at the end of the *seder* of verses. But I have also seen the suggestion that there used to be a daily rabbinic discourse (= *seder* of learning) after the morning prayers, and this *Kedushah* originated at the conclusion of this *seder*.²⁸

Rashi on *Sotah* 49a gives an explanation somewhat similar to that of R. Natronai. He does not mention the studying and translating of ten verses and that the two verses were appended to this. But he does write that the recital of the two verses and their translation was instituted as a manner of ensuring that everyone study a small amount of "Torah" each day and that reading and translating verses into Aramaic is considered a manner of such study.²⁹

One more view found in the Geonim, and citing an earlier source, is that *Kedushah De-Sidra* was instituted so that we should recite one more *Kedushah* daily than the angels, who recite two.³⁰ We recite this

---

15:18. It seems that it was not part of his *Kedushah De-Sidra* and it would not have fit his origin explanation. But the later sources, *Siddur Rav Saadiah Gaon* and *Seder Rav Amram Gaon* do include this third verse.

27. The fact that *kadosh* is repeated three times at Isa. 6:3 was apparently not enough on its own to justify the commencement of a practice to recite *Kedushah* three times daily (assuming the two other *Kedushot* were already being recited). But once the third recital already arose for a different reason, the three instances of *kadosh* at Isa. 6:3 were enough to justify the third *Kedushah*'s continuance.

28. See *EJ* 10:876. But note that Tosafot, *Ber.* 3a, *ve-onin*, has a different reading in the Talmud for the name of the prayer: *Sidra De-Kedushta*. Abudarham has something similar: *Sidra De-Kedushah*.

29. The Aramaic translation of Isa. 6:3 that we recite (from Targum Yonatan) is not a translation but an expansion. The translation of the Ezekiel verse also has a minimal expansion.

There are statements elsewhere that record that Rashi adopts the persecution explanation. See, e.g., *Mahzor Vitry*, p. 108.

30. *Shaarei Teshuvah, Teshuvot Ha-Geonim*, #55.

Kedushah in Aramaic because Aramaic is a language that the angels do not understand.

It is of interest that the third verse in *Kedushah De-Sidra* is Exodus 15:18 (*Hashem yimlokh le-olam va-ed*), while the third verse in the *Kedushah* of the *Amidah* is Psalms 146:10 (*yimlokh Hashem le-olam...*).

Kedushah De-Sidra is also recited as part of the Saturday night service. A very interesting reason for this is given in *Seder Rav Amram Gaon*: to prolong the *Shabbat*-ending prayer service for the benefit of the wicked.[31] There is a tradition that as long as we are still reciting our *seder* of *Shabbat*-ending prayers, the angel in charge of *Gehinnom* is not permitted to order the wicked ones back into *Gehinnom*. They have a respite from punishment on Shabbat. This tradition is based on Job 10:22 which includes the phrase: *tzalmavet*, ולא *sedarim*. The homiletic interpretation is: The angel in charge is entitled to say to the wicked ones: *tzeu la-mavet* (= go to that place of death), but he can only say this when the *sedarim* are no longer being recited. See *Tanḥuma Ki Tissa*, sec. 33.

The recital of *Kedushah De-Sidra* is moved from the end of *shaḥarit* to the beginning of *minḥah* on Shabbat and festivals. Various reasons have been suggested.[32] The simplest explanations are so as not to prolong the morning service,[33] or because there was a discourse before *minḥah* and that discourse was followed by the recital of verses of *geulah* and *kedushah*.[34]

* * *

An unresolved issue is the order in which the various *Kedushah* recitals arose: the one recited before *Shema*, the one recited with the *Amidah*, and the one we have addressed here. I am not going to address this issue. But I would like to address the following issue: What is the earliest source that juxtaposes the *kadosh, kadosh, kadosh* phrase of Isaiah 6:3 with the *barukh kevod* phrase of Ezekiel 3:12?

---

31. *Seder Rav Amram Gaon*, p. 81.
32. See I. Baer, *Siddur Avodat Yisrael* (1868), p. 259 and M. Nulman, *The Encyclopedia of Jewish Prayer* (1993), pp. 333–34.
33. *Rokeach* and *Kol Bo*.
34. Abudarham.

The earliest juxtaposition of these two phrases is found in a statement by R. Yehudah (second century CE) in the first chapter of Tosefta *Berakhot*.³⁵ First comes an anonymous statement about not answering with the *mevarekh*. Then comes the statement of R. Yehudah: "R. Yehudah used to answer with the *mevarekh*: *kadosh, kadosh, kadosh Hashem Tzevaot... u-barukh kevod Hashem mi-mekomo...*" The precise import of the statement is unclear. But most likely, the context is the *Kedushah* before *Shema* or the *Kedushah* of the *Amidah* or both.³⁶

* * *

Mitchell First's recent books are full of *sedarim*: sets of articles in categories and in order. Based on the interpretation of Job 10:22 found in the Talmud, the world may be dependent upon them!

3. The *Shalom Aleikhem* Prayer: Origin and Insights

We all sing this song peacefully. Could anything be controversial about it? (This is aside from the mild disagreement that might occur over whether each stanza should be recited three times!) Let us analyze the history of this prayer.

The idea for the prayer is based on a *baraita* at *Shabbat* 119b that states that two *malakhei ha-sharet* escort a person home from the synagogue on Friday night. If there is a lamp burning, a set table and a *mittah* that is prepared,³⁷ the good angel says: "May it be this

---

35. It is at 1:11 in the standard printed edition.
36. One reasonable interpretation (offered by S. Lieberman) is that the anonymous statement is pointing out that in general, where blessings and prayers require a response, the response is to be stated afterwards and not simultaneously. R. Yehudah then points out that he disagrees (or explains that the above does not apply) in the context of *kadosh, kadosh, kadosh* and *barukh kevod*, where the proper procedure is for the *mevarekh* and responders to recite the phrases at the same time.
37. *Mitah* is usually translated here as a reference to a bed. But more likely the reference is to "a dining couch" (= a couch that was reclined on during the meal). See Tosefta *Shabbat* (standard printed edition), end of chapter 13, passage in brackets, beginning with מציעין. See similarly Jastrow, p. 827 (right

way next Shabbat," and the evil angel is compelled to answer "Amen." If the three above items are not prepared, then the evil angel says: "May it be this way next Shabbat," and the good angel is compelled to answer "Amen."

The author of the prayer felt it was appropriate to write a prayer greeting these two angels and seeking their blessing. The first stanza says *shalom* to these angels; the second says: "may your coming be in peace"; the third asks "bless me for peace," and the fourth concludes: "may you depart in peace."

The prayer first appears in one of the early editions of *Seder Tikkunei Shabbat*. *Seder Tikkunei Shabbat* was a *siddur* that incorporated much kabbalistic material.[38] There were many editions of this type of *siddur* and the earliest editions usually have no date. A scholar who has studied these editions concluded that *Shalom Aleikhem* first appeared in an edition published in Prague sometime between the years 1615 and 1629.[39]

The prayer's author is unknown,[40] but perhaps it was authored by

---

side, end of first entry). I thank Michoel Chalk for pointing out the "dining couch" approach and the passage in the Tosefta to me. For each diner, next to the couch there would be a small table with the food.

Probably many Jews had dining couches in Tannaitic times. We should be able to accept that the Tannaitic *baraita* at Shab. 119b would include a dining couch situation. Also, many Jews probably used cheaper substitutes to recline on. The words *mitah* and *mitot* can also include those cheaper substitutes.

The root of מטה is נטה. The main meaning of this root in *Tanakh* is "stretch out, extend." In *Tanakh*, *mitah* could refer to a bed, or to a type of couch for reclining on while eating. For the latter meaning, see Amos 6:4, Ezek. 23:41, and Est. 1:6 and 7:8.

38. The meaning of *tikkunei* in kabbalistic thought is "spiritual rectifications." Accordingly, the title of the *siddur* indicates that it contains the proper liturgy to lead to the rectifications of one's soul associated with Shabbat.

39. See H. Leiberman, "*Sefer 'Tikkunei Shabbat'*," *Kiryat Sefer* 38 (1963), pp. 401–14, 407–408. But the new Rabbinical Council of America siddur, *Siddur Avodat Halev* (Nusaḥ Ashkenaz, 2018), p. 420, states that *Shalom Aleikhem* is found in an edition published in 1613. I am not aware of their source and fear that this may be a typographical error for 1615.

40. In contrast, we do know the author of *Lekhah Dodi*. This is R. Shelomo Halevi Alkabetz. (According to the entry for him in the *EJ*, he died around

a Kabbalist from Tzefat shortly before its first appearance in *Seder Tikkunei Shabbat*.

It is well-established that Kabbalists from Tzefat in the middle of the sixteenth century were the ones who authored the *Kabbalat Shabbat* service.[41]

Many editions of *Seder Tikkunei Shabbat* state that they are based on the teachings of the ARI (R. Isaac Luria). But R. Ḥayyim Vital kept a record of ARI's *Kabbalat Shabbat* service and there is no mention of *Shalom Aleikhem* there. ARI died in 1572.

* * *

In the third stanza, we ask for these angels to bless us. Many objected. For example, R. Ḥayyim of Volozhin (d. 1821) wrote: "One must not address petitions to angels since they do not possess any power, even to the lightest [degree]. Whatever they do is by compulsion. If man is worthy, they are forced to bless him; and if not, they are forced, God forbid, to curse him."[42] Earlier, R. Yaakov Emden (d. 1776) had also objected to asking for a blessing from angels.[43]

In the last stanza, we ask the angels to leave: *tzeitekhem le-shalom*. This is objected to by many as well. For example, R. Emden writes: "It would be better for them to tarry a while and rejoice at the meal...." R. Emden concludes that he was willing to recite the first stanza only.[44]

Of course, the angels are not really being asked to leave. The phrase

---

1584.) The acrostic *Shelomo Halevi* is built into the first letters of each stanza (until the last stanza בואי).

41. But there was already a custom among some Sepharadim to recite Psalm 92. See B.S. Jacobson, *The Sabbath Service* (1981), pp. 7–8, citing a responsum of Rambam.

42. Jacobson, p. 124.

43. See his commentary in his *siddur* (first published in 1745, under the title *Shaarei Shamayim*). Of course, there are responses to these objections. For example, *Siddur Avodat Halev* (p. 421) has the following explanation: "We know that the angels are enjoined to bless the home when they see the lit candles and the table prepared for Shabbat. Thus, ברכוני לשלום does not mean "Please bless me." It means, 'Do what you are required to do.'"

44. When R. Emden first published his *siddur*, he left the prayer out altogether, but it is included in the modern editions of his *siddur*.

can merely mean: "when you decide to leave, leave in peace."⁴⁵ This is a simple solution.

There is another possible solution. Some early editions (including the edition from 1650, see below) have a slightly different text than what we have. The second stanza starts with בבואכם, and the fourth starts with בצאתכם. With this reading, our question disappears. But the second and fourth stanzas then do not read smoothly.

A comment in a *siddur* published in 1880 (*Siddur Yeshuat Yisrael*) states that if there has been a quarrel in the home, the last stanza should be omitted. The idea is that the angels remaining in the home will cause the quarrel to end!⁴⁶

Ḥatam Sofer wrote that one should not recite *Shalom Aleikhem*, as it was presumptuous of anyone to consider himself worthy of an angelic escort.⁴⁷ But his student Maharam Shick wrote that his teacher did recite it, but recited it silently lest he give the impression that he considered himself worthy of this escort.⁴⁸

The standard Sepharadi text of *Shalom Aleikhem* has an added stanza, *be-shivtekhem le-shalom*, between the traditional third and fourth stanzas.⁴⁹

There is a prayer *Ribbon Kol Ha-Olamim* that typically follows *Shalom Aleikhem* in our *siddurim*. It followed it in many of the early editions of *Seder Tikkunei Shabbat*. The prayer has some of the same ideas as *Shalom Aleikhem*. *Siddur Avodat Halev* (Rabbinical Council of America, 2018) takes the position that this prayer and *Shalom Aleikhem* are one unit, by the same author. If this is true,⁵⁰ one can use the ideas expressed in this prayer to shed light on our (too short) *Shalom Aleikhem* prayer.

There is also language in this prayer that suggests that it was

---

45. For further explanations, see Rabbi N. Scherman, *Zemiros and Bircas Hamazon* (1990), p. 15.
46. Jacobson, p. 125.
47. Scherman, p. 14.
48. Ibid.
49. Probably what motivated this additional stanza was the hastily asking of the angels to leave in *be-tzeitekhem*. Some Sepharadim recite the first three stanzas and then omit *be-tzeitekhem*.
50. I am hesitant to simply agree.

originally recited in the synagogue.⁵¹ If so, this might be the case with *Shalom Aleikhem* as well.

Siddur Avodat Halev also points out that there is a brief mention of greeting angels on Friday night in a book of customs from thirteenth-century Italy, and it is also recorded as the practice of a Tosafist from Regensburg.⁵² Thus *Shalom Aleikhem* is not as great an innovation as is typically thought.

* * *

When you look at the widespread text of *Shalom Aleikhem*, the first stanza refers to *malakhei ha-sharet* and the three subsequent ones refer to *malakhei ha-shalom*. One early edition is available online at hebrewbooks.org, an edition from 1650. This is the reading there. Perhaps this was the reading in all early editions.

This sudden switch is very puzzling. The explanations I have seen are not satisfying. Also, there are some *siddurim* that have *malakhei ha-sharet* throughout.⁵³ But I am sure these are later than the 1650 edition. I have also heard of a custom to recite *malakhei ha-shalom* throughout.

It is also interesting that the *Ribbon Kol Ha-Olamim* prayer ends with a brief summary of *Shalom Aleikhem*. It has *ha-shalom* throughout. See the *Complete ArtScroll Siddur*, p. 356. I also noticed this reading in the *Seder Tikkunei Shabbat* from 1650. This is some evidence that the original reading in *Shalom Aleikhem* was *ha-shalom* throughout. Yet, as I stated above, the *Shalom Aleikhem* text in this same siddur has *malakhei ha-sharet* in the first stanza and *malakhei ha-shalom* in the three subsequent ones.⁵⁴

* * *

---

51. *U-vati le-veitekha* (= I have entered your house). See Jacobson, p. 126.
52. *Siddur Avodat Halev*, p. 420.
53. Scherman, p. 14.
54. I am willing to suggest that perhaps the author started with *malakhei ha-sharet* to indicate that he was basing his prayer on the passage at *Shab.* 119b, but otherwise felt that phrase too confining.

I would also like to share one homiletical explanation. At first, when the angels begin to enter, we do not know yet if they are going to bless us, as the Talmud states that one of the angels is an evil angel. But after they enter fully

Some early editions of *Seder Tikkunei Shabbat* instruct to recite each of the *Shalom Aleikhem* stanzas three times. In the context of *Kiddush Levanah*, ARI recited the phrase *Shalom Aleikhem* three times. The recital of the phrase three times in *Kiddush Levanah* is mentioned in *Soferim* 10:2, without explanation. ARI explained the three-time recital in *Kiddush Levanah* as a method of removing *kitrug* (= spiritual prosecution). Most likely, ARI's followers extrapolated that it would be a good idea to recite each of the stanzas in the *Shalom Aleikhem* prayer three times as well.[55]

* * *

The early editions of *Seder Tikkunei Shabbat* also typically include the recital of *Eshet Ḥayil* on Friday night. The recitation of this section (Prov. 31:10–31) was probably also introduced by Kabbalists from Tzefat. They understood the woman being referred to as the *Shekhinah*.

* * *

Mitchell First is an attorney and Jewish history scholar, has now authored five books and many articles, and is a regular columnist for the *Jewish Link* newspaper. He feels worthy of angelic escort.[56]

4. *Anim Zemirot*: Origin and Insights

I am basing this essay in large part on the book *Anim Zemiros* (2020) by Rabbi Elchanan Adler, a Rosh Yeshiva at Yeshiva University-RIETS.[57]

A well-known poem is *Shir HaYiḥud*. This lengthy poem was

---

and are able to see how prepared we are, then we are confident that they will bless us and we can refer to them as *malakhei ha-shalom*.

55. This is sensible since the basis for the origin of the prayer is the passage at *Shab.* 119b and an attempt to protect us from something similar to the *kitrug* of the evil angel.

56. I would like to acknowledge the assistance of R. Arie Folger and Efraim Palvanov with this essay.

57. This book is a revision of his earlier book in Hebrew on our topic, *Tzvi Tifarah*.

divided into seven parts, spread over the seven days of the week. (Now we limit our recital to Rosh Hashanah and Yom Kippur.) It is widely agreed that *Shir HaYihud* was composed by either R. Yehudah He-Hasid (d. 1217) or his father R. Shmuel, or someone in their circle. (This is the circle of early Hasidei Ashkenaz in Germany.)

Most likely, *Anim Zemirot* (also known as *Shir HaKavod*) was authored in this same circle, and perhaps by R. Yehudah or his father R. Shmuel. In support of the former, there is a statement in a manuscript from the year 1489 that attributes it to R. Yehudah. In support of the latter, the poem includes the phrase *tikar shirat rash be-einekha* (= may the song of the poor man be dear in Your eyes). It has been suggested that perhaps the word רש here alludes to R. Shmuel being its author.

R. Adler writes: "It is commonly assumed that *Anim Zemiros* was originally composed to serve as the conclusion for the *Shir HaYichud* and was intended to be recited together with it."[58] I.e., on each day of the week a section of *Shir HaYihud* would be recited, followed by *Anim Zemirot*.

But we have no sources that describe how long such a custom persisted and whether it expanded outside of Hasidei Ashkenaz in Germany.

The earliest mention of *Anim Zemirot* as a liturgical custom is in a work that compiles the customs of Maharil (R. Yaakov Moelin, Germany, d. 1427). The context of the *Anim Zemirot* reference is the night of *Yom Kippur*. The compiler writes: "After they finished reciting *Shir HaYichud*, they recited the Mourners' Kaddish, and afterward he [the Maharil] began to intone *Anim Zemiros* in a sweet voice, followed by *Adon Olam*."[59]

R. Adler writes that "over time the custom developed to recite *Anim Zemiros* on its own, either every day or on Shabbos and festivals." But he admits that we lack the sources to track its precise development in the Ashkenazic world. (It did not enter the Sephardic rite.)

---

58. Adler, p. 31.
59. Adler, p. 32, citing *Minhagim, Hilkhot Leil Yom Kippur* 13.

The poem was first printed in 1535, in Istanbul, in a *siddur* entitled *Tefillah LeDavid*.[60]

Ismar Elbogen, in a leading work on Jewish prayer written in the early twentieth century, wrote that starting with the publication of a certain *siddur* in 1549, *Anim Zemirot* appears thereafter in all *siddurim* of the German-Polish rite.[61] Unfortunately, he does not say where it appears. But we do have the testimony of R. Yoel Sirkes (d. 1640) that the *kadmonim* (= earlier authorities) established that it should be recited every day after the *Kedushah* prayer in *U-Va Le-Tziyon*.[62] So perhaps daily recital was the widespread custom.

Due to the objections of several authorities, the custom of daily recital has slowly diminished:

- R. Mordechai Jaffe (*Levush*, d. 1612) wrote that its recital should be limited to *Shabbat* and *Yom Tov*, based on the idea that enormous praises of God should not be recited frequently.[63] Daily recital reduces them to the level of the mundane, whereas they need to be seen as lofty. He cites the Talmud's criticism (at *Shab*. 118b) of one who recites *Hallel* daily.
- According to the Vilna Gaon (d. 1797), the prayer should not even be recited on Shabbat but should be limited to *Yom Tov*.[64] No reason is stated but most likely his reasoning was the same as R. Jaffe.
- *Arukh Ha-Shulḥan* (d. 1908) calls *Anim Zemirot* a *shir kadosh* and therefore appropriate for recital only on *Shabbat* and *Yom Tov*. Only those are the days that are infused with holiness.[65]
- *Likkutei Mahariaḥ* (R. Yisrael Ḥayim Friedman of Rakov, d. 1922) also advocated limiting the recital to Shabbat and *Yom Tov*. The

---

60. Adler, p. 31. I assume this was a *siddur* that followed the Ashkenazic rite. I do not know in what context it was printed in this work (i.e., daily or holiday, and beginning or end of the service).
61. "All" is obviously not a good word to use. Adler (p. 32), citing this same work, writes "many." *EJ* (3:22) had written "most."
62. Adler, p. 32–33, citing *Baḥ*, *OH* 132. *Baḥ* gives a reason for this specific location.
63. Adler, p. 33, citing *Levush*, *OH* 133.
64. Maaseh Rav 53.
65. *OH* 286:6.

poem needed to be recited slowly and deliberately, and this will not occur when people are rushing to work.⁶⁶
- In more modern times, Rav Joseph Baer Soloveitchik was also against its daily recital. He only recited it on Yom Kippur.⁶⁷

The poem is now absent from the daily rite in *The Complete ArtScroll Siddur* (Ashkenaz edition), published in 1984.

R. Adler adds: "In some communities, *Anim Zemiros* is not even recited on the festivals, but only on the night of Yom Kippur, as was apparently the original custom. In some communities, it is also recited before Shacharis on Rosh Hashanah and Yom Kippur."⁶⁸

* * *

I will now share some insights on the first few lines of the text of *Anim Zemirot*.

The first line is: *anim zemirot ve-shirim e'erog, ki eilekha nafshi ta'arog*. The last phrase means: "Because for You my soul yearns." The root ערג with the meaning "yearn" only appears two times in *Tanakh*, at Ps. 42:2 (*nafshi ta'arog eilekha Elokim*) and Joel 1:20.⁶⁹ The poem ends with the similar phrase: *ki nafshi ta'arog eilekha*.

In the first line, ושירים אארוג means "weave songs." When you realize how the author composed this poem, integrating and adapting verses and midrashim, you understand that "weave" is the perfect word here.

אנעים is from the root נעם which means "pleasant." In the first two words, the author is adapting a phrase from 2 Sam. 23:1, where David is described as: *ne'im zemirot Yisrael*. The meaning of this Biblical phrase is much debated.⁷⁰ In the poem, the phrase *an'im zemirot*

---

66. Adler, p. 34.
67. See Zvi (Hershel) Schachter, *Nefesh Ha-Rav* (1994), p. 162. In a post on thelehrhaus.com, Yaakov Jaffe explains Rav Soloveitchik's opposition to *Anim Zemirot* and some other prayers as follows: "they are too anthropomorphic in nature, or describe the Creator on the same level as human beings and not as significantly greater and beyond." See Jaffe's post of June 22, 2017.
68. Adler, p. 35.
69. This root also occurs in *Tanakh* four times with the meaning "to make a garden or flower bed." The two ערג roots are probably not related.
70. Rashi writes that the meaning is that in the Temple, Israel only sang songs authored by David. The Soncino commentary offers a different interpretation:

means either: "I will pleasantly (sing or compose) songs" or "I will (sing or compose) pleasant songs."

The third line begins *middei dabri bi-khevodekha* (= when I speak about Your glory). The phrase *middei dabri* is from Jer. 31:19: "Is Ephraim my favorite son, a child of delights? As often as I speak of him [*middei dabri bo*], I remember him more and more...." מדי derives from the root די. It literally means "from what is sufficient."[71] From this, it came to mean "as often as."

With regard to *homeh libbi el dodekha*, הומה is an interesting word. To quote from S. Mandelkern,[72] "its essence is a natural noise that living things emit at a time of activity and feeling." I no longer have a TV but I recall the sound Homer Simpson made when he anticipated his favorite meal: "HMMM! Rump roast!" This is our הומה, which is clearly an onomatopoeia.

In *Tanakh*, its root המה is sometimes used in connection with מעי (intestines, belly), which emit noises. See, e.g., the continuation of Jer. 31:19: המו מעי. Eventually the word expanded to reflect feelings of longing and arousal without an accompanying sound.[73] In *Anim Zemirot*, it is used with the heart. *Dodekha* means "your love."[74] So our entire phrase means "my heart longs for Your love."

* * *

A few final thoughts:

- R. Adler writes that we do not know the origin of the custom for *Anim Zemirot* to be recited by a pre-bar mitzvah child.[75] As a possible explanation for the custom, he cites the modern work *Netiv Binah* (vol. 2, 1968): "Aside from the fact that we want

---

"[Literally] 'the pleasant one of the songs of Israel,' which many modern scholars prefer to render as 'the darling of the songs of Israel,' i.e. the favourite subject of popular songs and poems." There are many other interpretations.

71. Klein, p. 319.
72. P. 333.
73. In the *Amidah*, we have *yehemu rahamekha*, referring to the arousal of God's mercy.
74. See Song of Songs 1:1: *tovim dodekha mi-yayin* (= your love is better than wine).
75. Adler, p. 39.

children to participate more actively in the prayer services, this deep composition is full of longing for closeness to the *Shechinah* and should ideally be recited by one who has not yet sinned. This resembles the custom for children to begin their study of *Chumash* with the book of *Vayikra*."[76]

- The common practice is for the *chazzan* and congregation to recite alternating stanzas. But the Vilna Gaon had a different approach. R. Adler summarizes it as follows: "the *chazzan* would recite a stanza out loud and the congregation would repeat it; the congregation would then recite the next stanza and the *chazzan* would repeat it."[77]
- Most of *Anim Zemirot* is an acrostic. There are two stanzas that begin with *resh* and two that begin with *tav*. The latter I understand, as sometimes a doubling is used at the end of a section and the two *tav* stanzas here end the acrostic section, even though there are additional stanzas thereafter. But no reason suggests itself for the doubling of the *resh*. R. Adler's book mentions this issue but does not record any explanation.[78]
- God's four letter name only appears once in the poem, in the קשר stanza.

Finally, an interesting historical note: The Jewish Communists in the early twentieth century changed the first four words slightly: *a-aniyyim zemirot, ve-ashirim eherog*. Translation: For poor people, praises, and the rich I will kill![79]

* * *

Mitchell First recalls leading the Riverdale Jewish Center in *Anim Zemirot* at the young age of 6 in 1964, setting the *shul* age record at the time. He has not been following over the decades to see if this record still stands.

---

76. Adler, p. 39.
77. Adler, p 38. But it seems to be a bit more complicated than Adler's brief summary. See *Maaseh Rav* 170.
78. There is a *piyyut* for Purim by R. Yehudah Halevi (12th cent.) which also seems to have two stanzas for *resh*. The *piyyut* is *Adon Ḥasdekha* (also known as *Mi Khamokha*). I thank Michoel Chalk for this detail.
79. I thank David Beryl Phillips for this historical detail.

5. God as Boḥen Kelayot (= Examiner of the Kidneys)

In our High Holiday prayers, we sometimes refer to God as בחן כליות (= *boḥen kelayot*). He examines the kidneys as a way of judging people. This phrase is found, for example, in the *Attah Yode'a Razei Olam* prayer that we recite in the *Amidah* on *Yom Kippur*. Here we have: *u-voḥen kelayot va-lev*.[80] The reference here is to a divine scan of these internal body parts, kidneys and heart, for their thoughts. Why should this be?

It turns out that in *Tanakh*, the kidneys are viewed as a place of conscience, emotions, desires and wisdom. The brain is not mentioned in *Tanakh*.[81] It seems that the functions that we today assign to the brain, the *Tanakh* assigns to the heart and kidneys![82] Therefore, it is the heart and the kidneys that God needs to focus on when judging someone.

Here are the main verses that reflect the view of the kidneys in *Tanakh*:

---

80. The beginning of this prayer (without our phrase) is found at *Yoma* 87b. The expression *boḥen kelayot* is also found in *piyyutim* for the High Holidays such as *Ve-Khol Maaminim she-hu*. See *The Complete Artscroll Machzor: Rosh Hashanah*, p. 490.

81. The rabbinic word for brain, *moaḥ* does appear in *Tanakh* at Job 21:24, but it means marrow of the bone.

At Dan. 2:28, we have the phrase: "Your dream and the visions of your head on your bed." Here are the comments in the Soncino: "This is the only instance in the Bible where psychical experiences are associated with the head. Its usage here is probably to be accounted for by the act of seeing being connected with the organ of sight."

But the book of Daniel is one of the latest books in *Tanakh*. It probably dates to the second century BCE. In light of the additional medical knowledge available at this time (see below), we do not have to adopt the interpretation just suggested.

82. In *Tanakh*, when someone plans to do something, the typical expression is "he said *be-libbo*," not "he said in his head," as we might say today. This expression in *Tanakh* is typically translated as: "he said to himself."

There is some overlap in *Tanakh* between the roles of the heart and the kidneys. Wisdom, for example, is usually represented by the heart but sometimes is represented by the kidneys.

- Jer. 11:20: And the Lord of hosts who judges righteously, *boḥen kelayot va-lev*....[83]
- Jer. 17:10: I am the Lord, *ḥoker*[84] *lev, boḥen kelayot*, and to give every man according to his ways, according to the fruits of his doings.
- Jer. 20:12: And the Lord of hosts, *boḥen tzaddik, ro'eh khelayot va-lev*....
- Ps. 7:10: *U-voḥen libbot u-khelayot Elokim tzaddik*.
- Ps. 16:7: I will bless the Lord who has given me counsel; even in the night my kidneys instruct me.
- Ps. 26:2: Examine me Lord and test me; test my kidneys and my heart. (The Hebrew roots used in this verse are: בחן, נסה, and צרף.)
- Prov. 23:16: My kidneys rejoice when my lips speak with uprightness.
- Jer. 12:2: You are near in their mouth but far from their kidneys.[85]

The kidneys are also mentioned in the Torah in the context of sacrifices.[86] Of course, no reason is given for including them as one of the parts offered. But perhaps their important role in *Tanakh*'s view of humans is a reason they are included.[87]

---

83. According to Rav S.R. Hirsch (comm. to Ps. 73:21), the kidneys are "the organ of baser, sensual desires and passions." The heart is "the seat of higher spiritual emotions and aspirations." In its essay, *TDOT* (vol. 7, p. 181) offers the following: "The mention of heart and kidneys together is presumably meant to characterize the total person by referring to an especially important organ in each of the two major portions of the body: the heart in the chest cavity above the diaphragm and the kidneys representing the abdominal cavity extending below the diaphragm. In addition, this expression combines the most profound feelings of the emotional life, conceived as being localized in the kidneys, with the thoughts of the heart..., in the majority of cases associated more with the rational faculties. Both together represent the total person, who is being tested by [God]."
84. *Ḥoker* means "investigates."
85. Also noteworthy is the post-Biblical passage at 2 Macc. 2:24. Here we are told that a Jewish man was willing to comply with Antiochus' order and offer a sacrifice. To describe how angry Mattathias was at seeing this, we are told that his "kidneys trembled."
86. See, e.g., Lev. chaps. 3, 4, 7, 8 and 9.
87. I admit this is a weak argument as many other body parts of the animal are also sacrificed.

It is interesting to point out that the translators of the King James Bible (1611) made the decision to use the word "reins" instead of "kidneys" whenever *kelayot* was used in a non-sacrificial context.[88] In recent times, Biblical translators often use "mind," "conscience," or "soul" in these instances in order to better capture the flavor of the verse.

In 2010, Rabbi Natan Slifkin wrote a detailed article on our topic: "The Question of the Kidneys' Counsel."[89] What I write in the next few paragraphs is based on it. (I am only summarizing a small portion.)

The Talmud takes all those verses about the importance of the kidney literally. For example, we find the following passage at *Berakhot* 61a: "The Rabbis taught: The kidneys advise (יועצות), the heart understands, the tongue articulates, the mouth finishes...."

The immediately preceding statement in the Talmud (also preceded with "The Rabbis taught") states that the two kidneys had distinct roles: one kidney counsels man *le-tovah* and the other counsels him *le-ra'ah*.[90]

In another passage, the Talmud states that God placed *ḥakhmah* in the kidneys.[91]

---

88. The earlier English translations had made a similar distinction. See Eknoyan (cited below), p. 3470. The terms are essentially synonymous but the distinction helps show that the word has a different meaning in the non-sacrificial contexts.

89. It is available on his site: rationalistjudaism.com. It is also included as chapter eight of his 2020 book: *Rationalism vs. Mysticism*, pp. 316–336.

90. The next sentence in the Talmud is that presumably it is the right one that counsels *le-tovah* and the left one that counsels *le-ra'ah*. This theoretically raises an interesting issue for Orthodox kidney donors today. Which one to donate? One who addresses this is Rabbi Y. Zilberstein, a prominent *posek* in Israel. He discusses a rare case where the doctors told a donor that either one could be donated and he concludes that one should donate the left one. See his *Ve-Ha'arev Na*, p. 173. (I thank Paul Lustiger for this reference.) Normally the doctors choose which kidney is donated and a nephrologist has advised me that probably 90% of the time the doctors choose the left one. One reason is that the length of the left renal vein is longer and easier to cut and re-sew. Of course, the overriding factor is that they always want to leave the donor with the better kidney.

91. *Rosh Hashanah* 26a.

The *Nishmat* prayer that we recite on Shabbat (composed in the period of the Talmud or perhaps in the few centuries thereafter) also deserves mention for giving an important role to the kidneys: "All innards (*kerev*) and kidneys (*khelayot*) shall sing praises to Your Name...."[92]

Medical knowledge in Biblical times was very limited and the view of the heart and kidneys expressed in *Tanakh* is perhaps consistent with what was thought in the ancient Near East in their time.[93]

It was only in the fifth century BCE that Greek philosophers and physicians began to understand that the brain was important.[94] Unlike the heart which beats, the brain is placid. It is understandable that its importance was overlooked in earlier times.[95]

R. Slifkin points out that the Greek physician Galen (second century CE) knew the brain to have a cognitive function. He continues: "It does appear that some of the Sages of the Talmud may have adopted aspects of Galen's view, since we find R. Yehudah HaNasi disputing some people with the statement, 'It appears that he does not have a brain in his head.'... However, the fact of some of the Sages attributing *some* cognitive function to the brain does not mean that they ruled out the heart and kidneys serving to make moral decisions."

92. Also, there is nothing in this prayer about the brain.

93. See the article by physician G. Eknoyan, "The Kidneys in the Bible: What Happened?," *Journal of the American Society of Nephrology*, 16:12 (2005), pp. 3464–3471 (3468). Of course our knowledge of the medical beliefs of the surrounding cultures is very limited.

94. This new view began with the fifth century BCE Greek philosopher Democritus and was expanded upon in this same century by the Greek physician Hippocrates. See J. Changeux, *Neuronal Man* (1985, Eng. translation), pp. 4–5. See also Eknoyan, p. 3469. Thereafter, Plato too (early fourth century BCE) argued that the intellectual part of the soul was contained in the head. But his student Aristotle reverted to the heart-centered view of the soul. He believed that the brain was only of minor importance and that perhaps its role was merely to cool the blood.

Hippocrates and his colleagues also discovered that an injury to the brain caused the motor impairment to be on the opposite side of the injury. See Changeux, p. 5.

95. Archaeologists have discovered a medical text from Egypt from the seventeenth century BCE (which is believed to be a copy of a text written around 3000 BCE). The text includes a description of forty-eight cases of individuals with head and neck injuries and their consequences. The consequences are

By the time of the Rishonim, there had long been knowledge of the importance of the brain and the more limited role of the kidneys. How did our Rishonim deal with the above Biblical verses? I am going to discuss the approach of a few Rishonim. (Rabbi Slifkin discusses several more.)

Ibn Ezra makes the suggestion that those references in *Nakh* to the kidneys are only verses of metaphor. Because the kidneys are hidden within the body they metaphorically represent man's innermost self.[96]

Ramban accepts that the kidneys are the sources of counsel. He explains that the kidneys are included with the sacrifices because they are instruments of *mahshavah* and *ta'avah*.[97] But he was aware that the brain is the seat of the mind. For example, he writes that the *tefillin* of the head are to be facing the *moah*, which is the "chariot of the soul."[98]

Rabbeinu Bahya was aware that the brain has a cognitive function. In order to reconcile this with the *Tanakh* and Talmud, he proposed that thoughts are conceived in the brain but need to descend to the heart and kidneys in order to be transmitted as directions to the body.[99]

---

sometimes elsewhere in the body. It seems from the comments written that the Egyptians did not understand the profound implications of their observations. See Changeux, pp. 3–4.

Also, in mummification in ancient Egypt, there was no concern for preserving the brain. It was discarded. It was mainly the heart that was of concern as it was needed for the afterlife.

96. See his comm. to Ps. 7:10 and 139:13. In the latter, he also mentions that they are the source of sexual desire and that explains why they are called כליות. (See my discussion of the etymology of the word below.) See similarly his comm. to Ps. 16:7 where he writes that the mention of them alludes to *kohei ha-toladah*.

In his comm. to Ex. 23:25 he writes that *hakhmah* resides in the *moah ha-rosh*.

97. Comm. to Lev. 1:9. In Ramban's view, the sacrifice represented the entire person. Every part of the animal offered represented a particular part, desire or impulse of the person. R. Slifkin writes that there was a scientific view at the time that the kidneys were linked to the sexual organs.

98. See *Kitvei Rabbeinu Moshe Bar Nahman*, ed. H. Chavel, (1963), vol. 1, p. 150 (from *Torat Hashem Temimah*). See also his comm. to Ex. 13:16 where he writes that both the *lev* and the *moah* are the dwelling places of *mahshavah*. (This statement is also made in the context of the *tefillin* of the head.)

99. See his comm. to Gen. 1:27 and 6:6.

R. Judah Moscato writes that the kidneys remove certain negative elements from the blood and release it as urine. Once the blood is cleansed, the forces that power the intellect will produce elevated and perfected thoughts.[100] (He does not address the fact that the Talmud describes one of the kidneys as providing harmful counsel.)

R. Slifkin continues with a discussion of more modern authorities, which I am omitting.

He concludes, citing Rambam, Rav S.R. Hirsch, R. Kook and others, that the best approach is not to view the Bible as a book that teaches science. Rather, it is a book that was written so it could be understood by the people in its time. He points out that the phrase *dibrah Torah ki-leshon bnei adam* appears numerous times in the Talmud. Rambam, for example, in his *Guide to the Perplexed*, uses this principle to explain the numerous anthropomorphic references to God. As Rabbi Dr. Isadore Twersky explains, Rambam understood this principle to be teaching that the Bible was written so it could conform to the "imagination (and frequently crude perception) of the multitude."[101] Similarly, R. Hirsch writes that "Jewish scholarship has never regarded the Bible as a textbook for physical or abstract doctrines...the Bible does not describe things in terms of objective truths known only to God, but in terms of human understanding...."[102]

Finally, R. Slifkin points out that we can use the *dibrah Torah ki-leshon bnei adam* principle to explain many other matters found in the Bible that are inconsistent with science, e.g., its earth-centered description of the universe, its description of dew as descending from the heavens, and its description of the *rakia* in the first chapter of Genesis.[103]

* * *

---

100. *Nefutzot Yehudah* (1588), *derush* 9.
101. Twersky, ed., *Studies in Medieval Jewish History and Literature* (1979), p. 239. This is not the exact language of Rambam. It is Twersky's explanation of what Rambam meant. Rambam had written that *ki-leshon bnei adam* means "the imagination of the multitude."
102. *Collected Writings*, vol. 7, p. 57. See also his comm. to Gen. 1:6.
103. Comm. to Gen. 1:6.

The term for the kidneys in *Tanakh* is always in the plural. Scholars usually suggest that כליה (*kilyah*) was the singular.

With regard to its etymology, there is no clear answer. Is it related to כל = "all," symbolizing some kind of multipurpose role of the כליה? Is it related to כלי = "vessel"?[104] This is one of the suggestions mentioned by S. Mandelkern. Rav S.R. Hirsch derives it from the root כלה and its meaning of longing for something.[105] He writes that the kidneys "represent the innermost source of sensuous desires."[106] Ibn Ezra had also suggested this etymology.[107] The essay in *Theological Dictionary of the Old Testament* mentions a few suggestions but then prefers deriving it from the root כל, which it suggests was an onomatopoeic root related to rolling and roundness.[108]

* * *

Mitchell First has always had a longing for kidney beans.[109]

6. *Maoz Tzur Yeshuati*:[110] Authorship and Insights

We do not know who authored this prayer or precisely when it was authored. But the author did inscribe his name in an acrostic in the first five stanzas, מרדכי. There is also a sixth stanza that begins *ḥasof zeroa kadshekha*, generating the acrostic חזק.

There had been a debate about whether the sixth stanza was a

---

104. This word probably comes from the root כול with its meaning "contain, measure."
105. The "long for" meaning of כלה is an expansion from the original meaning: "complete, end." When you long for something you are exhausting yourself and being completely spent. See, e.g., Ps. 84:3: *nikhsefah ve-gam kaltah nafshi*.
106. See his comm. to Lev. 3:4. See also his comm. to Ex. 23:18.
107. See his comm. to Ps. 139:13.
108. Vol. 7, pp. 176–77.
109. I would like to thank Paul Lustiger for asking me about *boḥen kelayot*, which got me interested in this topic, and Daniel Klein for pointing me to the article by Rabbi Slifkin.
110. As you will see from reading the second part of this essay, we should not call the prayer *Maoz Tzur* any longer. We should call it either *Maoz* or *Maoz Tzur Yeshuati*.

later addition. But in recent times, a *siddur* collecting the prayers of R. Eliezer b. Nathan of Mainz (c. 1090–1170) has been published, based on several manuscripts.[111] The sixth stanza is found there, at p. 519 (with an unusual variant, to be discussed below).[112] Probably, it was omitted over the centuries due to censorship.[113] Also, it would be very unusual for a stanza that begins with a חזק acrostic to be a later addition.[114]

Both the first and sixth stanzas attack Christianity. This fits the period of twelfth-century Germany, as Jewish communities in Germany were devastated by the First Crusade (1096) and the Second Crusade (1147).

A detailed scholarly article on the prayer, published in 2014, had suggested it was composed in Germany between 1160 and 1190.[115] But the author did not seem to know of the evidence from the *siddur* of R. Eliezer b. Nathan.

The prayer was not part of the Sephardic ritual until recent times.

The four middle stanzas narrate, in the past tense, events of four persecutions of the Jews: by the Egyptians, Babylonians, Persians, and Greeks (= Syrian Greeks).[116] Regarding the first and sixth stanzas,

---

111. *Siddur Ha-RAB"N* (Bnei Brak, 1991). I thank Rabbi Mordy Friedman for sharing this important source with me.
112. I am here disagreeing with *The Complete ArtScroll Siddur*, p. 784, which (like many others) had taken the position that the stanza was a later addition.
113. Either by non-Jewish authorities or by Jewish self-censorship. It did not appear in print until 1702. See Y. Melamed, "Ma'oz Tsur and the 'End of Christianity,'" thetorah.com (2016).
114. See Melamed, n. 5 and *EJ* 11:910. The fact that this acrostic is contained within one stanza (and not three) reflects the style of Germanic and Italian *paytanim* (see Frankel, next note, p. 13), and not Sephardic *paytanim*.
115. See A. Frankel, "Ha-Zemer Al Hatzalat Vermayza ve-Zeman Ḥiburo shel 'Maoz Tzur'", *Ha-Ma'ayan* 208 (2014), pp. 9–21.
116. For a story of Chanukah rescue in the modern period, I would like to share that Ismar Schorsch (Chancellor of the Jewish Theological Seminary for two decades) writes that he has always felt a special affection for the holiday of Chanukah. He explains that in 1938, shortly after *Kristallnacht*, Rabbi Dr. Joseph H. Hertz was able to quickly secure his family a visa to England and they flew out of Germany in haste on the first day of Chanukah. Ismar was three years old at the time. His father was fond of recounting that the family lit the

to quote one scholar, they "are both written in the *present* tense and complement each other, and thus express the mindset and wishes of the poet at the time of the composition of the hymn."[117]

The earliest reference to the prayer in a work of *halakhah* is found in the *Leket Yosher*, who was a student of R. Israel Isserlein. The latter was the author of *Terumat Ha-Deshen* and lived in Germany and Austria in the fourteenth century. *Leket Yosher* writes that his teacher, after reciting *Ha-Nerot Hallalu*, would sing *Maoz Tzur Yeshuati*.[118] He adds that sometimes it would be recited בדילוג. This means that his teacher would skip certain parts. (Perhaps he meant the sixth stanza.)

Maoz Tzur Yeshuati is not mentioned by either R. Caro or R. Isserles in the *Shulḥan Arukh*.

In the first stanza, we have the following: "Prepare the house of my prayers and there I will offer a thanksgiving offering. When you have prepared the slaughter for the barking (מנבח) enemy,[119] then I will conclude with a psalm song for the dedication of the altar." The root נבח only appears one time in *Tanakh*, at Isa. 56:10. It is referred to as something that dogs do, so it is translated as "barking." We know from the writings of R. Ephraim of Bonn (twelfth century) that references to an enemy who is נבח are references to Christianity.[120]

The last stanza has the phrase *deḥei admon* (= push away the red one). Esau is called *admoni* at Gen. 25:25. In rabbinic literature, Esau symbolized Rome and Christianity. The precise term *admon* was used for Esau by R. Eleazar Ha-Kallir (c. 600 CE) in several *piyyutim*.[121]

---

first night's candle in Germany and the second night's in England. Ismar's only memory of Germany was that dramatic flight out of it. See his "A Meditation on Maoz Ẓur," *Judaism* 37 (1988), pp. 459–464.

117. See Melamed.
118. *OH, Hilkhot Ḥanukkah*, sec. 24.
119. This is not mild language!
120. See Frankel, pp. 18–19. Frankel also writes that this word alludes to the statements of Christians in the Jewish-Christian debates. "Prepare the slaughter" is based on Isa. 14:21.
121. One is cited by Rashi at Gen. 30:22 (without mentioning Kallir by name).
   Many have suggested that *admon* referred to the German Emperor Frederic Barbarossa who ruled from 1152–1190. "Barbarossa" means "Redbeard" in

In medieval Hebrew, *tzelem* is a reference to the cross. The four words that begin *dehei* can be translated as "Reject Esau [who stands in the] shadow of the cross."[122]

An issue is whether the prayer was written for Chanukah. An alternative view is that it was composed for some other purpose and included an overview of Jewish history and was then borrowed into the Chanukah ritual due to the *Yevanim* paragraph. But because the first stanza includes the word *hanukat* (and incorporates it into its climactic ending), and the historical section of the prayer ends with the story of Chanukah, it is very likely that the prayer was written for Chanukah. This is much more likely than the alternative scenario.

Regarding the melody, see the detailed discussions in the *Jewish Encyclopedia* (1901–06)[123] and the *Encyclopaedia Judaica* (1972).[124]

* * *

A few insights on the phrases in the prayer:

Maoz Tzur Yeshuati: A combination of the words *tzur* and *yeshuah*, or its related word *yesha*, is found four times in *Tanakh*. For example, at Ps. 89:27, we have *ve-tzur yeshuati*.[125] This strongly suggests that the words *tzur* and *yeshuati* in our prayer should be read as one phrase.[126] The meaning of the phrase is "rock of my salvation."

Italian. (In Germany, he was called something similar: "Rotbart.") He was named "Barbarossa" by the northern Italian cities which he attempted to rule.

It is possible that *admon* refers to Edom (= Rome/Christianity) but also alludes to Barbarossa. See *Siddur Avodat Halev* (2018), pp. 953–54 (citing David Berger).

122. This is the view of Melamed. An alternative view is that *tzalmon* here is a synonym of צלמות, traditionally understood as "shadow of death." (But "shadow of death" is probably not its correct interpretation in *Tanakh*. צלמות really means "darkness." See Klein, p. 549.)

When Rabbi Jonathan Sacks translated this line for his editions of the *siddur*, he translated *dehei admon* as "thrust the enemy," concealing the clear allusion to the enemies' identity in the Hebrew.

123. Vol. 8, pp. 315–316.
124. Vol. 11, pp. 910–911.
125. The other three cases are: Deut. 32:15: *tzur yeshuato*; Ps. 95:1: *tzur yisheinu*; and 2 Sam. 22:47: *tzur yishi*. Also, both Ps. 62:3 and 62:7 have *tzuri vi-yeshuati*.
126. The phrase *maoz tzur* is not in *Tanakh*. We do have combinations of

Maoz is a noun. Fortunately it appears many times in *Nakh*. Sometimes it refers to a specific physical structure. See, e.g., Judges 6:26 ("build an altar... at the top of this *maoz*"). Usually, it means "place of refuge" in a more abstract way. See, e.g., Joel 4:16: "God will be a מחסה to His people and a מעוז to *Bnei Yisrael*." מחסה means "refuge, place of refuge" and *maoz* is parallel to it.

What is the root of this word מעוז? There are two possibilities. One is the verb עוז with its meaning "to seek refuge."[127] The other is the verb עזז with its meaning "to be strong."[128] S. Mandelkern, in preparing his concordance, looked at all of the occurrences of מעוז in *Tanakh* and decided that all or almost all derived from the "seek refuge" meaning. Therefore he put them all in the root עוז.

But the truth is that the word *maoz* is a bit more complex. A small number of times it appears in a context with other "strength" words. See, e.g., Dan. 11:1. On those occasions and perhaps a few others, it can be interpreted as a noun with a strength-related meaning, so it would belong in the root עזז. Other times it probably indicates both meanings simultaneously.[129]

For our purposes, it is sufficient to know that most of the time the word is a noun built on the "refuge" meaning, and means "place of refuge" (either physical or spiritual).[130] That should be its presumptive meaning in our prayer. Translating it correctly is *The Koren Siddur* (translation by Rabbi Jonathan Sacks) which translates our three words as "Refuge, Rock of my salvation."[131] Also translating these words this way is *Siddur Avodat Halev*.[132]. (When these works write

---

maoz and *tzur* at Ps. 31:3: *le-tzur maoz* and at Isa. 17:10. But neither of these has our order.

127. In the Torah, its only occurrence is at Ex. 9:19 (in the context of the plague of hail) in the command form העז.

128. Usually, that last *zayin* drops. But one sees it, for example, at Ps. 24:8: עזוז, and at Ps.145:6: ועזוז.

129. See, e.g., *BDB*, p. 732. Every time you look at the word *maoz* in *Tanakh* you have to decide which of the two meanings is being used, or if it is perhaps being used with a double meaning.

130. See e.g., *Daat Mikra* to Ps. 27:1 and 31:3.

131. (2009), p. 898.

132. (2018), p. 952.

"refuge," they mean "place of refuge.") The *Encyclopaedia Judaica* entry (11:910) has "Fortress, Rock (of My Salvation)." "Fortress" is also an appropriate translation, based on the physical meaning of *maoz*.[133]

The *Complete ArtScroll Siddur* does not have a good translation here. They have "O mighty Rock of my salvation."[134] But *maoz* is a noun, so it does not mean "mighty," and as we have seen, *tzur* most likely attaches to *yeshuati* and not to *maoz*.[135]

Sometimes we have words like מָעֻזִּי (my *maoz*) in *Tanakh* and the Masoretes put a *dagesh* in the *zayin* pointing us to a strength-related meaning, or at least to a double meaning. (The *dagesh* indicates that we should interpret the word as if another *zayin* is there.) But when one looks at the word in context, one sees that one does not always have to agree with their *dagesh* suggestion.[136]

It should be evident from all of the above that if *maoz* is a noun and the next two words are a separate phrase, we should refer to the prayer as *Maoz*, or as *Maoz Tzur Yeshuati*, and not as *Maoz Tzur*.

Malkhut eglah: This phrase is based on Jer. 46:20: "*Mitzrayim* is a

---

133. An alternative English word to "fortress" is "stronghold." But since underlying most of the occurrences of *maoz* in *Tanakh* is a "refuge" meaning and not a "strength" meaning, it is better to avoid translating it with an English word related to "strong."
   It did occur to me that perhaps the adjacency of our word *maoz* to the phrase *tzur yeshuati* implied that it is the "strength" meaning of *maoz* that is being emphasized in our phrase. Then I looked at the *Daat Mikra* commentary to the phrase *ve-tzur yeshuati* at Ps. 89:7. They do not understand the import of the phrase here as the "strength" of a rock. Rather, a *tzur yeshuah* is a rock that serves as a shelter and fortress. Assuming they are correct, "refuge" and "fortress" would seem to be the best translations of *maoz* in its context in our prayer.
134. P. 783.
135. Earlier, in their separate historical work *Chanukah* (1981), p. 130, they did mention "Fortress, Rock of my salvation" as one possible translation.
136. An example is Jer. 16:19 where God is described as *uzzi u-ma'uzi u-menusi be-yom tzarah*. Our word מָעֻזִּי is between a strength-related word and a refuge-related word. The Masoretes put a *dagesh* in the *zayin* of מָעֻזִּי here, pointing us to a strength-related meaning. But others, such as Malbim, give מָעֻזִּי here a refuge-related meaning.

very fair *eglah*." Most take the view that *eglah* symbolizes beauty.¹³⁷ Perhaps the reference in this verse is to the beauty of the land or its produce. *Daat Mikra* cites Judges 14:18 where Samson referred to his wife with this idiom. It is also interesting to note Rashi's comment at 2 Sam. 3:5, where the verse refers to a wife of David named *Eglah*. Rashi writes that this is a reference to Michal who was beloved to David.

An alternative approach to the verse in Jeremiah is that of Malbim who points out that Egyptians used to worship the bull.¹³⁸ Alternatively, Targum Yonatan, cited at *Yoma* 32b and followed by Rashi, views the *eglah* as symbolizing מלכות.

Kim'at she'avarti: This could be interpreted in two ways: 1) "just as I passed into this area" (= a short time) or 2) "I had almost perished." The phrase comes from Song of Songs 3:4. It has the first of these meanings there.

Ve-karev ketz ha-yeshuah: On a literal level this means something like: Bring close the end of time with its salvation. But I have seen the suggestion that it also alludes to the meaning: Bring close the end of the "Jesus-people."

Mei-umah ha-resha'ah: This is what we recite today: "Take revenge… from the evil nation." Based on the *admon* reference in the stanza, the implication is that we are asking for revenge on the Christians. But our earliest text of *Maoz Tzur Yeshuati*, the *siddur* of R. Eliezer b. Nathan, has the revenge being taken on *malkhut Yavan ha-resha'ah*!

* * *

We are all used to thinking that Chanukah represents a struggle between the Jews and the Greeks. Of course, we are overly influenced by the term *Yevanim* used in the liturgy and in the rabbinic sources. (I remember in my youth imagining our ancestors battling the Greeks at sea!) The truth is that the struggle was only with the "Seleucid Greeks," the ones located in Syria and ruled by the Seleucid dynasty.¹³⁹ For

---

137. Also, some see in the name רבקה a connection with מרבק, a word associated with cattle.
138. While this is true (e.g., the worship of Apis bulls), the ancient Egyptians worshipped many different animals.
139. When my son Daniel was attending Yale (after two years at Yeshiva

example, after the death of Mattathias and Judah, leadership of the Jews in Israel passed to Judah's brother Jonathan. I Maccabees 12:10 refers to Jonathan's offer to renew ties of "brotherhood and friendship" with the Spartans (= Greeks on mainland Greece)![140]

* * *

Mitchell First knows that it is always important to understand precisely who are our friends and who are our enemies!

7. *Ve-Heishiv Lev Avot al Banim:* What did Malachi Mean?

As we all know, we read from Malachi 3:4 to 3:24 as the *haftorah* on *Shabbat Ha-Gadol*. In our tradition, Malachi was the last prophet. He lived in the early Second Temple period.

Here is the first half of the last sentence in his book (3:24): *ve-heishiv lev avot al banim, ve-lev banim al avotam*. The party doing this is Elijah.

The simplest interpretation is that the verse refers to a reconciliation between fathers and children. See, for example, the translation in the Soncino: "And he shall **turn the heart of the fathers to the children, And the heart of the children to their fathers...**" The Soncino translation is a reprint of the 1917 Jewish Publication Society of America translation. ArtScroll's *Chumash* (Stone edition) adopts such a translation as well with minor modifications.[141]

A weakness with this translation is that the verse uses the word על, not אל. The Even-Shoshan concordance lists 4004 occasions of the words על and ועל in *Tanakh*. (I am not counting other variants like מעל.) It writes that in 28 of these occasions the meaning is אל (= to).[142]

University), he had a Greek roommate. Around the time of Chanukah, his roommate asked him about the meaning of the holiday. Fortunately my son was clever enough to tell him that it commemorated a battle against ancient "Syrians."

140. I thank Efraim Palvanov for this reference.

141. P. 1221: "He shall restore the heart of fathers to children and the heart of children to their fathers."

142. There is at least one occasion where the על is changed to אל with a *ketiv/kri*. This is at 1 Sam. 20:24.

Admittedly this is only a small percentage. Nonetheless, it is not a totally insignificant one.

I will now mention two other interpretations that are widely offered. But in my view, the weaknesses with them are more severe.

The Return to God Approach

The *avot* and *banim* are returning in *teshuvah* to God. This is the view of Rashi and many Rishonim. In this view, על means "with." על can certainly mean "with." It is one of its many meanings.

But there are two problems with this approach. First, God is not mentioned in the verse. השיב appears many times in *Tanakh*. Nowhere else does this word alone imply a return to God. Second, the repetition: *lev avot al banim, ve-lev banim al avotam* is also a weakness. Why should the phrase be repeated? Nothing is added by the repetition if *al* means "with."[143]

One can tweak this approach and translate *al* as *al yedei* (= by means of). Rashi is one who does this. This way the first phrase is referring to fathers who are caused to return by their sons and the next phrase is referring to sons who are caused to return by their fathers. But I doubt that *al* is used anywhere else to mean *al yedei*. But in any event, this is still not a solution to the first problem, the lack of mention of God.

The Return to the Covenant and Values of the Forefathers Approach

In this approach *avot* means our forefathers: Abraham, Isaac and Jacob.[144] Elijah is going to cause "the bonding of the current generation of post-exilic Israelites to the Mosaic covenant of their ancestors," as one scholar has put it. In other words: "faithless descendants" to "faithful ancestors." Interpreting *avot* as our forefathers is reasonable and this message is consistent with other passages in the book such as 3:7.[145]

---

143. Admittedly, one can claim that the repetition is merely there for emphasis.
144. This position is taken in the Anchor Bible edition of Malachi (1998), pp. 374 and 388. More briefly, it is taken in *Sefat Emet, Parashat Va-Yera*, sec. 661.
145. "From the days of your fathers you have turned away from my ordinances and have not kept them; Return to me and I will return to you...."

But does this approach fit the language *ve-heishiv lev avot al banim, ve-lev banim al avotam*? If this was the proper interpretation, the order should be the reverse: Elijah is going to come and cause the descendants to return to the values of the forefathers and then the forefathers accept them.

So I think we have to stick with our initial approach: fathers and children returning to one another. The only issue is whether we read it literally and try to suggest some type of interfamily strife that was prevalent at the time (as some scholars do) or whether we read it metaphorically as reflecting societal strife in general. As examples of the latter, Mishnah *Eduyot* 8:7 cites our verse for the idea that Elijah will come *la'asot shalom ba-olam*, and Rambam, in his commentary on this Mishnah, understands the specific teaching to be that Elijah will remove the שנאה that there is between *bnei adam*.

Finally, there is another approach: to interpret the verse as having a double meaning and implying both the "interfamily reconciliation" approach and the "return to God" approach. For example, Michael Fishbane, in the *The JPS Bible Commentary: Haftarot* (2002), views the plain sense of the verse as implying that "Elijah will work to bring harmony between the generations, reciprocally."[146] But then he adds: "Healing between parents and children is...part of the nation's reconciliation with their God, and the textual ambiguity imbeds a profound and double-edged point."[147] But since God is not mentioned in the verse, I do not think there is any textual ambiguity here.

Additional Notes

1. The book of Malachi gives no background information about him. His father's name is not mentioned. His location is not mentioned. The king in whose time he prophesized is not mentioned. The book begins only: "The burden of the word of the Lord to Israel by

---

146. P. 365.
147. Ibn Ezra writes something similar to Fishbane: The *avot* and *banim* are returning to one another, so that *kullam yihyu lev ehad* when they return to Hashem. See similarly the *Pentateuch* of Rabbi Dr. Hertz, p. 1008. (These comments, in the *Haftorah* section, are not by Rabbi Dr. Hertz but are adapted from the Soncino commentary.) See also the Soncino commentary itself on our verse.

Malachi." But from the ideas that he expresses, (e.g., his criticisms of the sacrifices), one can see that the Temple has already been rebuilt. Most likely, Malachi is the prophet's name (and does not just mean "my messenger") and is an abbreviation of מלאכיהו.[148]

2. An interesting attempt at a plain sense interpretation is offered by R. Eliezer of Beaugency (twelfth cent., found on AlHatorah.org). Elijah will make sure that fathers teach the laws of the Torah to their sons, as stated in Deut. 11:19: *ve-limmadtem otam et bene-ikhem*, and children will ask questions to their fathers, as stated in Deut. 32:7: *she'al avikha ve-yagedekha*.

3. We know from verses in Ezra, Nehemiah and Malachi that there was much marriage to foreign women in that period. The Maggid edition of I Kings offers the following interpretation: "the children born to mixed marriages, and raised in the tradition of their pagan mothers, shall be restored to their fathers, who will teach them to follow God!"[149]

4. A very creative interpretation is given by Abarbanel: The reference is to Elijah reviving the dead: Sons who lost fathers and fathers who lost sons will see them revived!

5. I mentioned above that ArtScroll's *Chumash* (Stone edition), published in 1993, follows the "fathers to children" approach. But the ArtScroll *Tanakh*, published in 1996, follows the "return to God" approach: "And he will turn back [to God] the hearts of fathers...."[150]

6. Regarding the meaning of the word על, we have to praise Avraham Even-Shoshan for giving those lists of meanings with verse citations at the beginning of every entry. Even though he is often only guessing the meaning (sometimes he lists the meaning with a question mark) and many of his thousands of interpretations are wrong, nonetheless he was willing to undertake this Herculean task and surely got it correct 98% of the time. His meaning lists

---

148. *Daat Mikra*, intro., p. 7.
149. Alex Israel, *I Kings: Torn In Two* (2013), p. 272.
150. Similarly, the Conservative movement's Ḥumash, *Etz Hayim*, mentions both of these approaches in its commentary (p. 1298) and cannot decide which to prefer.

enable anyone to see quickly with what meanings a word is used in *Tanakh* and which meanings are frequent and which are rare.

* * *

Mitchell First hopes that the last sentence that he writes before he retires as a columnist and writer will be a clear one.[151]

8. *Ha Laḥma Anya:* Which *Matzah* is it Referring to?

"*Ha laḥma anya di ahkalu avhatanah be-ara de-Mitzrayim.*" Which *matzah* is this phrase referring to? The *matzah* that was eaten at night with the sacrifice? The *matzah* that the Israelites ate thereafter while leaving? Or the *matzah* that they perhaps ate during the years they were slaves?

In an article in *Links to Our Legacy* (2021),[152] I pointed out that there is no evidence from any Biblical verses that the Israelites ate *matzah* while they were slaves, unless one interprets the ambiguous *leḥem oni* phrase at Deuteronomy 16:3 to allude to this. Of course, one can still suggest that *matzah* was a food staple of the Israelite slaves without any verses.[153]

Regarding the possibility that it refers to the *matzah* that the Israelites ate while leaving, here is some further background. At Exodus 12:37 we are told that, as the first step in their travels, the Israelites went from *Rameses* to *Sukkot*. Then verse 39 refers to their baking their *matzot*. If we look at Numbers 33:5–6, we see that they

---

151. I would like to acknowledge the article in *Ḥakirah* vol. 30 by Dr. Yaacov Krausz which got me interested in this issue.
152. Pp. 87–91. I later expanded this article and it will be published in *Ḥakirah* vol. 32 (2022) under the title: "Did the Israelites Eat Matzah While They Were Slaves?"
153. In *Links* and in *Ḥakirah* I discussed a famous view attributed to Ibn Ezra (but not found in any of his commentaries) that the Egyptians fed *matzah* to the Israelites. It is reported that he suggested this based on an experience he had when he was fed *matzah* while in some type of captivity in India. This story is brought down in *Orḥot Ḥayyim* (thirteenth cent.) and *Abudarham* (fourteenth cent.) and was widely cited thereafter. It is recorded in M. Kasher, *Haggadah Shelemah*, p. 5 (Heb. section).

first traveled from *Rameses* to *Sukkot* and then to *Eitam*. *Eitam* is described as being on the edge of the *midbar*. So we can understand that the location of this *Sukkot* would still be considered within *Mitzrayim*.[154] The interpretation "the *matzah* they ate while leaving" is therefore a possibility.

Some parts of the Haggadah are taken from the Mishnah. Others derive from the Talmud or other early rabbinic sources. But the *ha laḥma anya* (= HLA) sentence is nowhere else, so we do not have a context for it. It is not found in the earliest *haggadot*, but scholars believe it originated in Geonic Babylonia.[155]

After that lengthy introduction, which *matzah* do we think HLA is referring to?

David Henshke, a professor of Talmud at Bar Ilan University, wrote an extensive work on the rituals of Pesaḥ, entitled *Mah Nishtannah?* He takes the position that HLA certainly refers to the *matzah* that the Israelites (supposedly) ate while they were slaves.[156] He views the author of the passage as having interpreted the ambiguous *leḥem oni* phrase of Deut. 16:3 as teaching that the Israelites ate *matzah* while they were slaves. Henshke cites Abarbanel who takes this approach and had pointed out that the language *be-ara de-Mitzrayim* implies a continuous type of eating, and not a one-time event.

I agree with Henshke. I would add that if the statement was referring to any other *matzah*, it would have been phrased differently. E.g., it would have specified: "that they ate with the sacrifice in *Mitzrayim*," or "that they ate while they were leaving *Mitzrayim*."

But there are some Rishonim who interpret the passage as a

---

154. See *Haggadah Shelemah*, p. 5, n. 13. There are other locations called *Sukkot* in *Tanakh*.
155. See, e.g., D. Henshke, *Mah Nishtannah?* (2016), pp. 238–39, and S. and Z. Safrai, *Haggadat Ḥazal* (1998), p. 111. It is not found in the earliest *haggadot* that reflect the *seder* of *Eretz Yisrael*. Nor is it in the Haggadah in the *Siddur Rav Saadiah Gaon* (tenth century) which is our earliest Haggadah that reflects the Babylonian ritual. It is found in the Haggadah text in *Seder Rav Amram Gaon*. (Although R. Amram lived in the century prior to R. Saadiah, the editions of this work are based mainly on manuscripts from the time of the late Rishonim, and many additions were made over the centuries in these manuscripts.)
156. P. 238.

reference to the *matzah* eaten with the sacrifice.¹⁵⁷ Henshke suggests that they only gave this interpretation because there is no evidence that the Israelites ate *matzah* while they were slaves. These Rishonim could also argue that HLA was introduced near those *kol* phrases, the latter of which reads: *kol di-tzrikh yeitei ve-yifsaḥ*, a reference to the Passover sacrifice.

There are other versions of HLA which have a text like: "that our ancestors ate when leaving the land of *Mitzrayim*." These versions were also meant to solve the problem that there is no evidence that the Israelites ate *matzah* while they were slaves. But most likely these versions were later changes to HLA and not the original reading.¹⁵⁸

* * *

Unlike Ibn Ezra (see n. 153 above), Mitchell First has never been fed *matzah* while in captivity.

---

157. See, e.g., *Meyuḥas le-Rashbam*, in the *Torat Ḥayyim* edition of the Haggadah, pp. 13–14.
158. Henshke, p. 238.

History

1. The History of the City of Acco

After someone in our family in Israel was in Acco, my wife Sharon suggested to me that I write about it. This city was always a big blank in my mind, so I thought it would be a good idea. It is only mentioned one time in *Tanakh* and I thought the topic would be easy. But was I wrong! It turns out that Acco is one of the oldest continuously inhabited cities on the earth! Also, due to its excellent anchorage area for ships, it has been constantly fought over by armies of the world. To write the history of Acco is to write the history of the Middle East from 2000 BCE and forward! (Acco is like Forest Gump. It constantly appears in important moments!)

Acco is at the northern end of the Bay of Haifa, fourteen miles north of Haifa. In Biblical times, it furnished the best anchorage for ships of all the harbors in the region. (Other ancient harbors in the region were Joffa, Dor, and Ashkelon.)

In its one occurrence in *Tanakh* (Judges 1:31), we are told that the tribe of Asher was not able to drive out the inhabitants of עכו and Tzidon and a few other cities.

But what about prior to *Tanakh*? About 1 mile east of the modern city of Acco, there is archaeological evidence of a site from around 3000 BCE. This seems to have been a farming community that perhaps endured for a few centuries before it was abandoned. But Acco was resettled during the Middle Bronze Age (2000–1550 BCE) and has been continuously inhabited since then.

It is mentioned (as "Akka") in Egyptian Execration texts from around 1800 BCE.¹ These are texts that list enemies of Egypt. A symbolic damaging ritual would be performed on the writing with the intent to cause harm to the enemy.

Thereafter, it is listed as one of the cities conquered by the Egyptian king Thutmose III in the mid-fifteenth century BCE. We also have a letter from the 14th century BCE where its governor wrote to his ruler in Egypt professing loyalty. But Egyptian rule over Acco was lost later in this century. It was regained under Seti I and his son Rameses II, to be again lost in the twelfth century BCE.

As stated above, the *Tanakh* states that the Israelites could not conquer the city. One view is that it remained an independent Canaanite city for the next few hundred years.² But Yohanan Aharoni, a leading scholar of the geography of ancient Israel, believes that Acco was under Israelite control in David's reign. He also notes that 1 Kings 9:11 states that Solomon gave twenty cities in the Galilee to King Hiram of Tyre, and he believes that Acco was one of them.³

Around 725 BCE, Acco joined Sidon and Tyre in a revolt against the Assyrian ruler Shalmaneser V. Later, it submitted to Sancheriv but it revolted against Ashurbanipal. He took revenge on the city with a massacre in about 650 BCE.

Persian rule in *Eretz Yisrael* began in the sixth century BCE. The ancient historians Diodorus and Strabo record that Cambyses (son of Cyrus) conquered Egypt after amassing his army on the plains near the city of Acco.⁴

Alexander the Great conquered ancient Israel from the Persians. After his death, his generals divided his empire among themselves. At first, Acco came under the jurisdiction of the Egyptian Ptolemies. Ptolemy II renamed the city "Ptolemais" in the 260s BCE. The city was mainly known by this name until the Arab conquest in the early

---

1. Acco is mentioned in writings from Ugarit in an early period as well.
2. See *EJ* 2:222.
3. See his *The Land of the Bible: A Historical Geography* (1979, Eng. trans.), pp. 17–18. 1 Kings 9:12, in a very odd passage, reports that Hiram did not like this gift of twenty cities. Perhaps this undermines Aharoni's suggestion, as I would presume that Hiram would have been happy to receive the port city of Acco.
4. In 2018, archaeologists unearthed remains of what might have been this site.

seventh century CE. This is how Josephus, I and II Maccabees, and Greek and Roman writers refer to it.⁵

Antiochus III conquered the city for the Syrian Seleucids around 219 BCE, taking it from the Egyptian Ptolemaic dynasty. His son, the one who persecuted the Jews, founded a Greek colony in the city. It was called "Antioch in Ptolemais."

(Please forgive me for now skipping the Roman and Byzantine periods.)

The Arabs conquered the city in the early seventh century CE. But in 1104, the Crusaders captured it from the Arabs following the First Crusade. It remained in their hands until 1187 when it was taken from them by Saladin.

But a few years later, in 1191, the Christians were able to recapture it, with the forces of the Third Crusade led by King Richard I of England (the Lion Hearted) and King Philip II of France. (This was at a cost of 100,000 men.)

After the victory, the city was given over to a certain order of Knights ("the Order of Saint John") by whom it was held for 100 years and it was given the name "Saint Jean d'Acre."⁶

In 1164–65, Rambam (d. 1204) spent about one year here, after leaving Fez (in Morocco). He spent the rest of his life in Egypt.

In 1170, Benjamin of Tudela found 200 Jews in Acco.

Around 1260, a large number of disciples of R. Jehiel b. Joseph of Paris moved to Acco, and a yeshiva was opened there.⁷

Nahmanides (d. 1270) stayed in Acco initially when he arrived in 1267. Very soon, he went to Jerusalem and made some efforts to build up the tiny Jewish community there. But he then returned to Acco in 1268 and became the leader of its Jewish community.⁸

---

5. The Talmud refers to our city as תלבוש. See, e.g., *Sotah* 34b and *Yoma* 10a. This is a rough equivalent of "Ptolemais." The interchange of the "b" and "m" sounds is common.
6. "Acre" is the French way of writing "Acco."
7. As to R. Jehiel himself, he set out for the land of Israel but did not reach it. It appears that he was forced to return to France due to failing health. See E. Kanarfogel, *The Intellectual History and Political Culture of Medieval Ashkenaz* (2013), p. 329.
8. See *EJ* 12:776.

In 1291 the city was conquered by the Mamluks, who massacred most of its Christian and Jewish inhabitants.

The Ottomans conquered the city in 1516.

The Italian kabbalist Moses Ḥayyim Luzzatto had a difficult life and spent his last three years in Acco with his family. He and his family died in a plague there in 1746.

In 1799, Napoleon's forces landed here and attacked the city, but his forces were defeated by the Ottomans who were aided by British forces.

After the British defeated the Turks in 1918, they used the ancient Crusader fortress as a high-security prison to hold and execute members of the various Jewish underground groups.

On May 4, 1947, members of the Irgun broke into the prison. Though only few Jews escaped, the audacity of the raid was a serious blow to British prestige.

The British chose to develop Haifa as their port. This contributed to Acco's decline in the twentieth century.

Finally, Acco is the holiest city to the Bahai, a religion that commenced in the nineteenth century.[9]

* * *

Regarding the original name of the city, its meaning is uncertain. A Jewish legend is that when the ocean was created, it expanded until Acco and then stopped: עד כה (= until here). A Greek legend is based on the Greek word *akē* that means "healing." Their legend is that Hercules found curative herbs at the site.

Acco's old city is a UNESCO-recognized heritage site with many remains from the Crusader period. Acco's present day population is about 50,000, made up of Jews, Muslims, Christians, Druze, and Bahais.

* * *

---

9. The founder of the faith spent many years in Acco, after the Ottoman rulers put him in prison there in 1868. After decades of strict confinement in the prison, he was finally allowed to live outside the prison in a home. He died in 1892. The home where he lived in his final time (outside of Acco but near it) is the place to which the Bahai turn in prayer each day. Another Bahai holy site is a tomb in Haifa. The Bahai religion did not start in the land of Israel. It started in Iran and elsewhere in the Ottoman empire.

The reason my relative was in Acco recently? Covid-19. Israel had designated it as an area for Covid-19 quarantines! This is consistent with my original point: Acco is like Forest Gump. It constantly appears in major events in history!

2. Moses' Raised Hands at Exodus 17:9–12

At the end of Exodus 17, we are told of a battle between *Bnei Yisrael* and Amalek. Moses said to Joshua: "Choose us men and go out, fight with Amalek; tomorrow I will stand on the top of the hill with the rod of God in my hand.... It came to pass when Moses held up his hand, Israel prevailed, and when he let down his hand, Amalek prevailed." We are further told that Aaron and Hur[10] helped him keep his hands up and that the final result was that *Bnei Yisrael* were able to defeat Amalek here.

By what method were our ancestors victorious here? On the simplest level, it seems that the rod of God had supernatural powers when raised up by Moses' hands, and that this is what caused the victory.

But many sources read additional ideas into the verses to explain what happened. On the other hand, there are other sources that deny any supernatural event here at all.

With regard to the former:
- The idea that *tefillah* played a role is found in the Targumim. See, e.g., Targum Yerushalmi (Neofiti): "Whenever Moses would raise his hands in prayer, the House of Israel would prevail and be victorious but when he would withhold his hands from prayer, the House of Amalek would prevail..."[11] (Many of our later commentators also read "prayer" into the raising of the hands.)
- The idea of **looking at God and putting their trust in Him** is read in by many sources as well. Here is what is found in the *Mekhilta*: "When [Moses] lifted his hands towards Heaven, Israel would look upon him and put their trust in He who ordered Moses to do so;

---

10. On the identity of that mysterious figure Hur, see H. Angel, *Cornerstones* (2020), pp. 174–78.
11. See AlHatorah.org on Ex. 17:11. See also Targum Pseudo-Yonatan on this verse and Targum Onkelos to 17:12.

then God would perform *nissim* and *gevurot* for them." Similar is the Mishnah in *Rosh Hashanah* (3:8): "As long as Israel was looking up and subjecting their hearts to their Father in Heaven, they were winning. If not, they were falling."[12]

With regard to those who seem to deny any supernatural event here at all, here are a few examples:

- Rashbam writes that the way of war is that when soldiers see a raised banner, they are strengthened but when it is cast down, they typically flee and get defeated.
- Bekhor Shor writes that when Moses saw that the Israelites needed more soldiers, soldiers would see the raised arms and arrive. When Moses' arms were down, the soldiers would lose their strength as they would believe they were not doing well in the battle. As to the rod, it functioned as a sign. Typically, when an army is doing well, the sign is raised by a leader so that all should know they are succeeding, When the army is not doing well, the sign is lowered to indicate that more men are needed to come and help.
- Hizzekuni writes that Moses stood on the top of the mountain so that his men could see him and be strengthened by seeing him, as the way of soldiers is for one of their leaders to stand in a high place and hold their flag to encourage them. When the soldiers saw that the flag was low, they believed that their leader had died and they fled.
- Rav S.R. Hirsch: "[I]t is not any magic power in the staff but the אמונה which is expressed and brought to the minds of the people by the uplifted hand, the giving oneself up with complete confidence to God that achieved the victory.... [It was] the confidence in God of the People, which the Leader inspired, [that] led to victory."

It is surprising that these sources and others go out of their way to disregard the simple meaning of the verses that a supernatural event involving the rod of God took place.[13]

---

12. Perhaps the *Mekhilta*, with its statements about *nissim* and *gevurot*, is a later expansion of the Mishnah. Alternatively, perhaps the Mishnah is an abbreviation of the *Mekhilta*. It is hard to tell.

13. Perhaps the denial of the miracle was motivated by the fact that the rod of

In the *Mekhilta*, near the above-mentioned passage, there is a disagreement between two Tannaim about what kind of men were supposed to be chosen by Joshua. In one view, it is *gibborim* and in the other view it is *yirei ḥet*. Perhaps these two Tannaim were disagreeing about whether the story was describing a supernatural event or not.

* * *

One source that takes the position that this was a supernatural event is S.D. Luzzatto. He writes: "Since this was their first war, and Israel was not yet trained for battle, it was necessary to strengthen their hearts to trust in God, and therefore it was necessary that they be saved by way of a miracle.... Although it might have seemed that [Moses'] intention was to pray, this was not so, for the spreading forth of hands [in prayer] is to be distinguished from the raising of the hand with the staff. If Rashbam were correct in comparing Moses' action to the raising of a battle standard, then they ought to have placed Moses' staff on a tall pole and led it before the people.... [T]heir salvation was from God and by way of a miracle, like the other signs and wonders that Moses performed."[14]

Another such source is *Daat Mikra*. This source first writes that looking at the raised rod encouraged the fighters. But then it writes that additionally (not "alternatively"): "The rod of God, raised towards the above, acted like a vessel that pulls to itself from the above *koḥot shel gevurat nitzaḥon ba-milḥamah mi-ḥutz la-derekh ha-teva....*"

Luzzatto and *Daat Mikra* are plain-sense commentaries. But here when the plain sense of a story is that a miracle is involved, they do not hesitate to adopt such an approach.[15]

* * *

God should have its supernatural powers whether it is raised or not raised. Or perhaps it was motivated by the fact that the Israelites had just been criticized for complaining about a lack of water and were probably, on a plain sense level, not viewed as deserving of a miracle.

14. Translation taken from the edition of D. Klein, pp. 248–49.
15. The story ends with Moses building an altar and calling it *Hashem Nissi*. The meaning here is "God is my banner."

The word נס never means "miracle" in *Tanakh*. This is a later meaning of the word. See *Daat Mikra* to Ex. 17:15 and my article in *Links to Our Legacy*

In a famous passage, Herzl wrote (in 1895): "'A flag, what is that? A stick with a cloth rag?' No, a flag, sir, is more than that. With a flag you can lead men where you will – even into the Promised Land. Men live and die for a flag; it is indeed the only thing for which they are willing to die in masses, provided one educates them to do it. Believe me, the policy of an entire people – especially one that is scattered all over the world – can only be made out of imponderables that float high in the thin air. Do you know out of what the German Empire sprang? Out of reveries, songs, fantasies.... Bismarck merely had to shake the tree which the visionaries had planted."[16]

* * *

Mitchell First often has both arms raised while holding on and riding the subway.

3. The *Urim* and the *Tumim*

The phrase *Urim Ve-Tumim* is not in the Torah. When the two objects are mentioned together in the Torah, *et ha-Urim ve-et ha-Tumim* is used twice.[17] I have followed this in choosing the title.[18]

"The *Urim* and the *Tumim*" are first mentioned at Exodus 28:30. Unfortunately, there is no description of what they look like or how they were made and operated. The verse reads merely: "You shall put *et ha-Urim ve-et ha-Tumim* into the *ḥoshen ha-mishpat* (= breastplate of judgment); they shall be on Aaron's heart...."

We learn from additional verses that the *ḥoshen* (= the above

---

(2021), pp. 64–67. (I realize there are many authorities who disagree with this statement and give it a "miracle, very wondrous sign" meaning in certain verses. Nevertheless, I agree with the view of *Daat Mikra*.) This name for the altar does not contradict the interpretation that a miracle was involved.
16. M. Lowenthal, *The Diaries of Theodor Herzl* (1956), p. 22.
17. Ex. 28:30 and Lev. 8:8.
18. The terminology is slightly different at Ezra 2:63 and Neh. 7:65. I cited Ezra 2:63 in the text above. In the verse in Nehemiah, there is no *lamed* on the second word. The reading is לאורים ותמים.

ḥoshen ha-mishpat[19]) was folded so it looked like a pouch and that on the outside it had twelve precious stones. Each stone had the name of one of the tribes engraved on it.

It would seem from Exodus 28:30 and Leviticus 8:8 that "the *Urim* and the *Tumim*" were objects that were separate from the *ḥoshen*. (It is also clear from the phrase לאורים ולתמים at Ezra 2:63 that these objects were separate from one another.)

The balance of the references to the *Urim* and *Tumim* are as follows. At Num. 27:21, we are told that Joshua will ask questions to God via the High Priest and his *Urim*. (This would be in contrast to Moses who spoke directly to God.) Ezra 2:63 and Neh. 7:65 mentioned a genealogical issue that awaited resolution by the High Priest with the *Urim* and the *Tumim*. (The implication was that there was no such item available in their time.[20]) 1 Sam. 28:6 records that Saul was afraid of the nearby Philistines and asked God what to do. But God did not answer him via "dreams, nor the *Urim*, nor prophets." There is also a reference at Deut. 33:8 in the blessing to Levi: *Tumekha ve-Urekha*...

* * *

So what precisely were "the *Urim* and the *Tumim*?" (I am going to abbreviate this now to: "UT.")

Two different views are found in the Geonim and Rishonim. In one view, the UT is the writing of God's name. This writing was then placed inside the *ḥoshen*, which functioned as a pouch. Once the writing was there, the letters on the stones would be able to light up and convey the answer to the question posed. This is consistent with the plain sense of verses Ex. 28:30 and Lev. 8:8 which refer to the UT as something placed into the *ḥoshen*. One of the many who take this view is Rashi. This view is found long before him in Targum Yonatan.

Many others such as R. Sherira, R. Hai and Rambam have a very different view. They take the position that UT is another way of referring to the twelve stones themselves.[21] (In this view, the *ḥoshen*

---

19. Probably the *ḥoshen* was also called the *ḥoshen ha-mishpat* because "the *Urim* and the *Tumim*," the decision-making objects, were connected with it.
20. See Tosefta *Sotah* 13:3.
21. For Rambam, see *Kli Ha-Mikdash* 10:11. See also the commentary of Avraham son of Rambam to Ex. 28:30.

is the breastpiece encrusted with the stones.) This is a difficult read in Ex. 28:30 and Lev. 8:8, but there are sensible reasons to adopt this approach.[22]

Based on *Yoma* 73b, it seems that UT is able to give messages with multiple letters, as many different letters could shine.[23] *Urim* refers to UT's ability to make the answer lucid and *Tumim* to the fact that the answer was complete, i.e., would not change.[24]

Many scholars take an entirely different approach to the UT. They think the UT were merely two small lots (stones? wood?) that would provide only "yes/no" or "innocent/guilty" answers.[25] I will now explain how they arrive at this conclusion. (The lots had to be small, so they could fit in the *ḥoshen*.)

One way to get more clues about the UT is to look at the times in *Tanakh* that a question is asked to God with the *ephod*. This may be a way of referring to the UT, since the *ḥoshen* was attached to the *ephod*.[26] At 1 Sam. 23:11, David asks two questions to the *ephod*: 1) will these men deliver me into the hand of Saul? and 2) will Saul come down? From the way these questions are phrased, it is evident that they are phrased to get only a "yes/no" response. Even though the responses are stated at verse 11 and 12 to be ירד and יסגירו, the actual responses may simply have been "yes." See similarly 1 Sam. 30:7-8.[27]

---

22. The arguments for this approach are set forth by Rabbi Dr. Hertz and by *Daat Mikra* in their comments on Ex. 28:30. Both of these sources first argue for the approach of Rashi and then give the arguments for the other approach (and seem to prefer the latter). For the identities of those who take each approach, see *Torah Shelemah* on Ex. 28:30. See also his *Miluim* section (in a later volume), sec. 11, for further discussion.

23. The names of the twelve tribes do not include all twenty-two Hebrew letters. But the Talmud states that the names of the Patriarchs and another phrase were also on the *ḥoshen*, so all letters were included. Once the letters shined, the priest would have to rearrange them into words. According to another view, the letters actually jumped up and fused on their own.

24. *Yoma* 73b. For some different etymological explanations of UT, see the end of the seventh chapter of J. Talmud, *Yoma*.

25. See, e.g., *EJ* 16:8-9 and *TDOT*, vol. 2, p. 453.

26. Ex. 28:28. The Soncino commentary on 1 Sam. 23:9 believes the reference here is to the UT. See similarly *Daat Mikra* to 1 Sam. 23:2: David asked with "*Mishphat Ha-Urim.*"

27. But more likely the episodes at 1 Sam. 23 and 1 Sam. 30 are not referring to

Sometimes questions are asked to God without mentioning the instrument used. See, e.g., 1 Sam. 10:21 and 2 Sam. 5:23. Perhaps these involved the UT as well. See, e.g., the commentary of Radak to the former.

In the view of most scholars who take the two lots approach, *Urim* is the "negative" answer, coming from the root ארר = curse. It also could mean "guilty." *Tumim* is the positive answer, with its meaning like "perfection." It also could mean "innocent."[28]

Scholars also make the claim that the UT were merely two lots (and only able to give simple answers) from the many additional words found in the Greek translation of 1 Sam. 14:41.[29] This verse and 14:42 already have words like הבה תמים and הפילו. Also, these verses have וילכד (= was taken) two times and this too is a word used in the context of lots.[30]

One problem with the two lots approach (which were perhaps both thrown in some way, or one picked from the *ḥoshen* in a random manner) is that it does not explain why someone would ask and not be answered. See, e.g., 1 Sam. 28:6. So perhaps the manner of its use

---

the *ephod* attached to the UT, but to a more general *ephod* that could be used to ask a question. See *Daat Mikra* to 23:2, n. 4 and note that Saul is the one in possession of the UT at the time. See 1 Sam. 28:6. The *Daat Mikra* commentary suggests that perhaps in the times of permissibility of *bamot* there were "*kamah ephodim*" and note that at 1 Sam. 23:6, the priest Evyatar came with "*ephod*," not "*ha-ephod*." Nevertheless, analyzing the form of the questions asked to an *ephod* is still somewhat relevant to the form of the questions that could be asked to the UT.

28. I have also seen the suggestion that *Tumim* is short for תאומים (= pairs).

29. A portion of what is in the Greek is: "If the guilt be in me or in my son Jonathan...give Urim. But if this guilt is in your people Israel, give Thummim." For the full Greek text, see *EJ* 16:8. See also *Daat Mikra* to 1 Sam. 14:41.

The *EJ* essay takes the position that our Hebrew text is corrupt. Generally, I would have no reason to consider such an approach. But I have written elsewhere about a few sentences that seem to be missing from the eleventh chapter of 1 Samuel. These sentences came to light from a Dead Sea text. See my *Roots and Rituals* (2018), pp. 72–74. The 1 Samuel text is also problematic at 1 Sam. 13:1. See the Soncino commentary.

For evidence of an Assyrian parallel to the view of the UT as two lots, see *Vetus Testamentum* 20 (1970), pp. 495–96.

30. See 1 Sam. 10:20. See also Josh. 7:14.

was not so simple. (Or perhaps there was a third lot which was blank.) Also, the answers at 1 Sam. 10:22 and 2 Sam. 5:23 are too long. One also has to explain the use of the plurals *Urim* and *Tumim* for each. But sometimes important objects in *Tanakh* are referred to in the plural (e.g., God as *Elokim*).

According to Mishnah *Sotah* 9:12, when the *Neviim Rishonim* died, the UT were בטלו. The implication here is that they were functioning for at least part of the First Temple period. Tosefta *Sotah* 13:3 states that they functioned until the destruction of the First Temple. Consistent with this, Ezra 2:63 implies that the UT were not functioning at that time.[31]

The coat of arms of Yale includes אורים ותמים with a Latin translation: *Lux et Veritas* (= Light and Truth.)

* * *

Of course the literature on this topic is voluminous. Aside from the sources I already mentioned, here are a few more sources that should be reviewed: S.D. Luzzatto to Lev. 8:8, *Brown-Driver-Briggs*, pp. 22 and 65, *Vetus Testamentum* 14 (1964), pp. 67–74, *Encyclopedia Mikrait*, vol. 1, p. 181, *The Living Torah*, p. 248, and the anonymous article at thetorah.com of Feb. 5, 2014.[32]

* * *

Mitchell First has been told that there was once a Jewish society at Yale that had shirts made with a picture of a bagel, and the slogan: "Lox et Veritas." Also, a law firm founded in Boston in 1933 by Jewish lawyers (who were largely not accepted at white-shoe law firms at the time) became known as the "Lox et Veritas" firm. (I thank Ira Friedman for this tidbit!)

---

31. Interestingly, Josephus, in the last decade of the first century C.E., writes that they "ceased to shine two hundred years before I composed this work..." See *Antiquities* III, 218. In the few paragraphs just before this, he gives his understanding of the UT. (He equates the UT with the stones themselves.)

32. "The Urim VeTumim." Also, for illustrations, see M. Levine, *The Tabernacle* (1969), pp. 133 and 137.

4. Archaeology and the Assyrian Kings

We have many inscriptions of the kings of ancient Assyria (Iraq). It is interesting to compare some of them to what is written in *Tanakh*.

1. At 2 Kings 18:9, we are told that in the fourth year of the Judean king Hezekiah, the Assyrian king Shalmaneser besieged the city of Samaria (= *Shomron*)[33] and its king Hoshea for 3 years. The next verse states that Samaria was taken at the end of three years. Finally, verse 11 mentions the places that the king of Assyria carried the Israelites to.

   These three verses imply that Shalmaneser was the king who captured Samaria. (See similarly 2 Kings 17:3–6). But we have an inscription from the next king Sargon II stating: "I surrounded and captured the city of Samaria; 27,290 of the people who dwelt in it I took away as prisoners."[34]

   A widespread explanation is that Shalmaneser began the siege, and Sargon II concluded it and captured Samaria after the death of Shalmaneser. (Shalmaneser reigned from 727–722 BCE. Sargon II reigned from 722–705 BCE. He is not mentioned in this chapter. He is only mentioned once in *Tanakh*, at Isaiah 20:1. From Assyrian sources, we learn that he was not the son of Shalmaneser.)

2. 2 Kings 18:13–15 tells us about the next king: Sanḥeriv, son of Sargon II. In the fourteenth year of Hezekiah, he came against the fortified cities of Judea and took them. But he did not take Jerusalem. The *Tanakh* tells us that Hezekiah was willing to pay a tribute to Sanḥeriv in the amount of 30 ככר of gold and 300 ככר of silver. (This was an extremely large tribute. Verse 18:16 reports that Hezekiah had to cut off gold from the doors and doorposts of the Temple.) It has been suggested that Sanḥeriv was taking the tribute as a temporary measure while he prepared for his ultimate advance on Jerusalem.

---

33. The earliest references in *Tanakh* to *Shomron* are references to a mountain or city, and not to a region. This city was built by King Omri in the ninth century BCE and became the capital of the northern kingdom.

34. D.W. Thomas, *Documents from Old Testament Times*, (1958), p. 60.

Here is a small portion from the annals of Sanḥeriv: "But as for Hezekiah the Jew who did not bow in submission to my yoke, forty-six of his strong walled towns and innumerable smaller villages in their neighborhood I besieged and conquered.... He himself I shut up like a caged bird within Jerusalem....."[35] Sanḥeriv then mentions a payment by Hezekiah of "30 *kakkaru* of gold and 800 *kakkaru* of silver." (Ok, a difference on a "small" detail from the number in *Tanakh*.) Another inscription has: "I laid waste the wide district of Judah and made the overbearing and proud Hezekiah, its king, bow submissively at my feet."[36] Implicitly agreeing with *Tanakh* (see below), the Assyrian records nowhere claim that Sanḥeriv destroyed Jerusalem.

3. At 2 Kings 19:37, we are told that Sanḥeriv was killed by two of his sons, Adramelech and Sharetzer. An Assyrian inscription has him being killed by one son, who is not named, during a rebellion. Based on further inscriptions, the Assyrian names of the sons involved were *Arda-Mulissu* and *Nabu-shar-usur*. The instigator of the rebellion was the former.

Material about Sanḥeriv is found in three places in *Tanakh*: 2 Kings chaps. 18–19, Isa. chaps. 36–37 and 2 Chron. chap. 32.

* * *

Now let us look at the end of the Sanḥeriv story in *Tanakh*. The year is 701 BCE. Sanḥeriv was ready to invade Jerusalem, but a miracle occurred. According to 2 Kings 19:35, an angel of God went into the Assyrian camp at night and killed 185,000 men. There is no explanation given about how they were killed. With his army gone, Sanḥeriv withdrew.

The fifth century BCE. Greek historian Herodotus tells the following story in his *Histories*, at II, 141. "King Sanacharib" and his army were ready to battle the Egyptians. But at night a multitude of field mice swarmed over the Assyrian camp and devoured their quivers and bows and the handles of their shields, and they fled the next day unarmed.

---

35. Ibid., p. 67.
36. Ibid., p. 68.

Is this a different event than what is described in *Tanakh*? Or is this just the story in *Tanakh*, in a different version? Scholars are divided on this issue.

Herodotus also wrote that, prior to the planned attack, the Egyptian priest had gone to the temple shrine and bewailed to his god the peril which threatened him. His god appeared to him in a dream and told him to have courage. "Myself will send you champions," said the god. This reminds us of what is found in *Tanakh*: at 2 Kings 19:1 Hezekiah went to the Temple to pray. He also sent messengers to the prophet Isaiah and Isaiah assured him that God would save him. See 2 Kings 19:6–7 and 20–34.

But one piece of evidence that we are not dealing with the same story is the continuation of the story in Herodotus: "And at this day a stone statue of the Egyptian king stands in Hephaestus' temple, with a mouse in his hand, and an inscription to this affect: 'Look on me, and fear the gods.'" This sounds like Herodotus is recording a story that truly occurred in Egypt and not just a legend that may have occurred anywhere. But with Herodotus (the "Father of History," also known as the "Father of Lies") one can never be sure.

* * *

The comparison between the story found in Herodotus and the story in *Tanakh* reminds me of the story in our Haggadah where five Sages (but not R. Gamliel) are *mesubin* in בני ברק and talking about *yetziat Mitzrayim* the entire night until their students come and tell them it is time for the *Shema* of *shaḥarit*. This story is not found outside the Haggadah. But in the Tosefta (*Pes.* 10:8) we have a story of R. Gamliel and the elders who were *mesubin be-beit Beitus ben Zunin be-Lod* and were studying *hilkhot ha-Pesaḥ* the entire night until *kerot ha-gever*. They then raised up [the closed windows], gathered together and went to the *beit ha-midrash*.

Are these stories of two different *sedarim* where there were different topics for the *seder* night? Or is this the same story in a different version? We will never know. My hunch is the latter.

* * *

Mitchell First is an attorney and a Jewish history scholar. These are not conflicting traditions.

5. The Unusual Interpretive Approach of Rashbam

I have read hundreds of Rashbam's insights into verses and know him as a *peshat* commentator, one of the earliest in the Ashkenazic world. He lived in northern France in the twelfth century and was a grandson of Rashi. I have also long been aware of his comments at Genesis 37:2: Rashi admitted to him that "if only he [=Rashi] had the time, he would need to revise his commentaries based on the insights into the plain meaning that arise anew every day."[37]

But what I did not know until recently were Rashbam's comments on the first verse in Genesis: "All the words of the Sages and their *derashot* are correct and true." Also, he states elsewhere that when he offers a plain sense interpretation that is different than the halakhic one, it is the halakhic interpretation that overrules the plain sense interpretation.[38]

So the question arises why Rashbam troubled to write a plain sense commentary at all on verses involving *halakhah*. Why bother if he is just going to conclude that the Sages' interpretations override his own?[39]

Of course, it makes sense that he is fully in agreement with the words of the Sages. He took over the yeshiva that his grandfather had led and later opened his own yeshiva in Ramerupt. He wrote commentaries on the Talmud. So what motivated him to write a commentary that he himself would disregard for purposes of *halakhah*?

---

37. There is an interesting podcast by the Rashbam scholar Martin Lockshin at seforimchatter.buzzsprout.com. Lockshin mentions the above comment and suggests (perhaps only facetiously!) that sometimes grandfathers say things to grandchildren that are not meant seriously and are only meant to encourage them!
38. See his comments at the beginning of Exodus, chap. 21. See also Rabbi A. Bazak, *To This Very Day* (2020), pp. 389–90. Bazak points out that the correct text of the end of the Rashbam here is probably *halakhah okeret mikra* = the *halakhah* uproots the verse. See *Sotah* 16a. See similarly the note in the *Torat Ḥayyim* edition.
39. If he was on the Supreme Court, he would definitely not rule as an "originalist." He might write interesting footnotes about original intent but then he would disregard them!

Here are some famous examples of interpretations by Rashbam that differ from the ones accepted in the Talmud:

- According to Ex. 21:6, if a Jewish slave wants to extend his servitude, he submits for an ear piercing and he is allowed to serve his master לעלם. The Talmud (*Kidd.* 21b) interprets this to mean "until the jubilee." But Rashbam takes the word literally to mean the slave's entire life.
- According to Ex. 21:9–10, a man is obligated to provide a wife with *she'eir*, *kesut*, and ענה.⁴⁰ The first two words probably mean "food" and "clothing." As to the last word, a widespread view of the Sages interpreted it as a reference to marital relations based on the "time" meaning of the root ענה.⁴¹ But Rashbam interprets the word to mean "dwelling," similar to the word מעון. In Rashbam's plain sense interpretation, the obligation to provide marital relations has been completely eliminated.⁴²
- The Sages interpret Ex. 13:9 as a reference to arm and head *tefillin*. But Rashbam reads the verse metaphorically as instructing the Israelites to preserve the memory of the Exodus **as if** it were imprinted on their arm and as an adornment on their head. (A non-observant scholar once joked that he wore the "*tefillin* of Rashbam"!⁴³)

---

40. The context of the particular case is a woman who is a slave, but *Daat Mikra* interprets *ke-mishpat ha-banot* (verse 9) as *ke-dinan shel benot Yisrael*. Similarly, the *Pentateuch* of Rabbi Dr. Hertz interprets it as "to be treated like a freeborn girl who marries." Accordingly, verse 10 is providing the standard obligation of husband to wife.
41. See, e.g., Mishnah *Ketubot* 5:6.
42. It is possible to interpret *onatah* with a meaning related to "dwelling," and then decide that it refers to marital relations. See, e.g., Rosenmueller and Gesenius, cited in S.D. Luzzatto, and the first interpretation presented in *Daat Mikra*. (Note also the euphemism in English: "cohabitation.") But Rashbam does not do this.

For an extensive discussion of the etymology of the word *onah*, see M. Lockshin, "Onah: A Husband's Conjugal Duties?," thetorah.com, Jan. 27, 2002.
43. I am not in any way claiming that Rashbam did not wear *tefillin*. I am only presenting his understanding of the plain sense of the verse. Bazak (p. 393) writes that "it is clear that Rashbam's intention was not to challenge the

- Another Rashbam where he disagrees with the Sages is at Lev. 21:1–4, on the issue of a priest defiling himself for his deceased wife.

Aside from what motivated Rashbam to write plain sense comments on matters of *halakhah*, the other issue that must be addressed is why Rashbam believed that interpretations that seem to be essentially rabbinic in origin take precedence over the plain sense of the biblical passages.

Scholars have pointed out that Rashbam did not seem troubled by the inconsistency in result between *peshat* and *derash* interpretations.[44] In the mind of Rashbam, *peshat* was one category of interpretation and *derash* was another.

As to what motivated Rashbam to write plain sense interpretations on matters of *halakhah*, Yonatan Kolatch writes: "The Sages derived halachot and derashot from peshat problems in the text, such as extra words or sentences or unusual expressions. Chazal viewed these 'aberrations' as concealing information revealed by derash. Thus, to appreciate Chazal's midrashic interpretations, it is imperative first to understand the peshat."[45]

Kolatch also writes regarding the *tefillin* passage: "While the legal ramifications of a 'sign upon your arm' may require the wearing of tefillin, there may be another level beyond the letter of the law – a metaphorical level, in which the spirit of the law demands a constant awareness of God."[46]

But we still do not have an explanation for matters like the complete redefinition of the obligation of *onah*.[47]

---

commandment of wearing *tefillin*." As I stated above, Rashbam states clearly elsewhere that when he offers a plain sense interpretation that is different than the halakhic one, the halakhic interpretation overrules the plain sense interpretation.

44. By the latter, I mean interpretations based on *derashot* using traditional *middot*.
45. See his *Masters of the Word*, vol. II (2007), p. 97.
46. P. 115.
47. It would be interesting if Rashbam wrote a work of *halakhah* related to marriage and if he wrote there that a husband has an underlying moral – but not halakhic – obligation to provide living quarters for his wife. But there is no such work or passage.

Ephraim Kanarfogel writes that "in the medieval Jewish mindset in general, and especially within medieval Ashkenaz, *peshat, derash, remez* (and perhaps even *sod*) were equally valid ways of ascertaining and presenting the truths of the Torah, given the possibility of multiple interpretations and exegesis inherent within the Torah itself.... Thus Rashbam and others could engage in 'enlightened' *peshat* and other critical forms of biblical interpretation while maintaining their roles as leading Tosafists and talmudists..."[48]

But why would Rashbam take the position that the Sages' halakhic interpretations, based on their use of traditional interpretive *middot*, were controlling? After all, aren't the resulting interpretations essentially rabbinic ones?

An interesting suggestion was made by Mordechai Cohen, a professor at Yeshiva University.[49] Cohen suggests that both Jews and Christians in the time of Rashbam viewed the Bible as "essentially a cryptic text, the deeper meaning of which lies beneath its surface" and "both assumed that the deeper meaning of the Bible is the more important, even truer, one." Cohen suggests that Rashbam believed that, in using traditional midrashic interpretive methods, the Sages were not drawing their own creative inferences, "but were actually discovering the deep intention implanted in the Bible by God himself."[50]

But Rashbam repeatedly writes that he is looking for the *omek peshuto* (= the deep plain sense) of the verse when he gives his plain sense interpretations (that are going to be overruled).

To be consistent with Cohen, we would have to suggest that the motivation for Rashbam's commentary was to help us understand the deep plain sense. That way we can better understand the distinction

---

48. See his *The Intellectual History and Rabbinic Culture of Medieval Ashkenaz* (2013), p. 31. This is part of a section called "Multiple Truths and Interpretations." There are sometimes contradictions between Rashbam's interpretation of a Biblical verse in his Talmud commentary and his interpretation of the same verse in his Torah commentary. But Rashbam was probably not bothered by such contradictions. He was taking a different approach in each commentary.
49. See his "A New Look at Medieval Jewish Exegetical Constructions of *Peshat* in Christian and Muslim Lands: Rashbam and Maimonides, in *Regional Identities and Cultures of Medieval Jews*, eds. J. Castaño, et al. (2018), pp. 93–121.
50. P. 115.

between that and the other sense that God wanted, the one that is hidden and must be drawn out by exegetical methods. This distinction is obviously a subtle one.

* * *

Mitchell First recently heard a lecture that pointed out that with regard to legal verses in the Torah, it is sometimes Moses Mendelssohn who is agreeing with the Sages' interpretations, and Rashbam who is disagreeing!

6. Rashbam: Life and Works

Most of this essay is based on Ephraim Urbach, *Baalei HaTosafot* (1980), and Yonatan Kolatch, *Masters of the Word*, vol. II (2007).

1. R. Shmuel son of Meir was born around 1080 and died around 1174. (Both dates are uncertain.) He lived most of his life in Ramerupt, in northern France. His mother was Rashi's daughter Yocheved. His brother was Jacob b. Meir, also known as Rabbeinu Tam. Their father Rabbeinu Meir was a founder of the Tosafist movement.

    Upon Rashi's death in 1105, Rashbam took over the leadership of Rashi's yeshiva in Troyes, but he later returned to Ramerupt and opened his own yeshiva there.

    In 1147, on the second day of Shavuot, Crusaders came and attacked the Jewish community of Ramerupt. Rabbeinu Tam, also living there at the time, was attacked and almost killed.

2. As to Rashbam's livelihood, Kolatch writes: "Like many Jews in northern France, Rashbam made his living as a wine and wool merchant. He had flocks of sheep, and his daughter...supervised the kashrut of their milking."[51] This daughter is the only child of his that we know about. Kosher milk had to be supervised to prevent the addition of milk of dubious origin.

    The following story is told about the milking of his sheep: "I saw that Rabbeinu Tam was very irritated with Rabbeinu Shmuel, who

---

51. Kolatch, pp. 91–92.

had many sheep, and they were a bit far from the Jewish houses and kept on the property of a non-Jew. Rabbi Shmuel used to send his daughter Merona to supervise. But by the time she got there, half or all had already been milked."[52] (Surely, the two brothers loved and respected one another. This is just one weird story.)

3. Aside from his commentary on the Torah, it is believed that Rashbam wrote on the entire *Nakh*. His commentary on Esther and fragments of his commentary on Ruth and Lamentations have been published.

Kolatch mentions commentaries on Job, Ecclesiastes, and Song of Songs that have been attributed to Rashbam, but he adds that Rashbam's authorship of these is questionable. Critical editions of these commentaries have been published. Also, in 1984 Moshe Sokolow published a manuscript that included Rashbam's comments to Zech. 14:7 and Jer. 32:12, as well as part of his commentary to Deuteronomy (see below). Rashbam's commentary on Psalms, starting with chapter 42 and covering most of the rest of the book, has also been discovered in recent years in a manuscript in the National Library of Russia.[53]

4. Rashi often gives multiple interpretations in his commentary on the Torah. But Rashbam, in his commentary on the Torah, consistently limits himself to one explanation. Also, while Rashi often says, "I do not understand" in his commentary on the Torah, Rashbam never makes such an admission. (Of course, perhaps he just did not write when he was not sure.)

5. In the first two centuries after it was written, Rashbam's commentary was cited by many. (On the other hand, there were many who it seems to have never reached, such as Naḥmanides, R. Baḥya, Baal Ha-Turim, and Abarbanel.) It seems to have been unavailable from the fourteenth century until it was first printed in Berlin in

---

52. Urbach, p. 46.
53. The commentary on the first forty-one chapters in this manuscript is that of Rashi. The website AlHatorah.org has been continually adding Rashbam's commentary on the various books of *Neviim* and *Ketuvim*, with references as to where each comment came from.

1705, after Rabbi David Oppenheim found a manuscript among many other rotting documents in a synagogue attic in Worms.[54] In the mid-eighteenth century, Mendelssohn and his colleagues often cited Rashbam in their *Biur*. It has been suggested that Rashbam's commentary may have been ignored in the earlier period because his divergence from the interpretations of Ḥazal was not appealing to those generations. Of course, this is just speculation.

6. The manuscript that Oppenheim had found and printed was missing the first 17 chapters of Genesis, and *Parshat Pinḥas*, and from Deut. 33:4 until the end. (It had been eaten by rodents on both ends!) Some of the missing sections have been found: 1) the commentary to Genesis chapter 1 (almost all of it) was published by Abraham Geiger in 1854, and the commentary to Deuteronomy chapter 34 was published by Moshe Sokolow in 1984.

The website AlHatorah.org has been attempting to reconstruct the missing comments of Rashbam on Genesis chapters 1–17. The individual who runs the site, Hillel Novetsky, did his PhD thesis on this topic. The *Mikraot Gedolot* on the AlHatorah.org site divides the reconstructed interpretations into two categories: 1) almost definite, and 2) questionable. The latter are presented in brackets. The site has notes to briefly explain the basis of each reconstruction and refers the reader to the pages in Novetsky's dissertation for the extensive analysis.[55]

---

54. He was the chief rabbi of Nikolsburg and later of Prague. He was a tremendous bibliophile and his exceptionally large book collection became an important part of the Hebrew section of the Bodleian Library in Oxford. He delayed for many years before publishing the Rashbam manuscript he found. He initially thought that Rashbam may not have intended this commentary for the public.

55. A copy of the dissertation can be obtained from the site. On what basis did Novetsky do his reconstruction? Part is based on Rashbam's other writings that refer to his comments on the missing chapters. Also, there are citations by others to Rashbam's comments on the missing chapters. Also, a significant portion of Ḥizzekuni (thirteenth cent.) is taken from Rashbam (although Ḥizzekuni almost never cites his sources). Most importantly, Novetsky used a Tosafist compilation containing both *peshat* and midrashic interpretations

7. Rashbam's commentary did not appear in the *Mikraot Gedolot* until 1885! The first edition of the *Mikraot Gedolot* was published long before, in the early sixteenth century.

8. We all know of Rashbam's commentary on the tenth chapter of *Pesaḥim*, and on *Bava Batra*, starting on p. 29a (after Rashi's comments end). As to *Bava Batra*, there is evidence that Rashbam wrote even on the earlier pages.[56]

   With regard to *Pesaḥim*, there is a commentary by Rashi on the tenth chapter. So why do we have Rashbam as well? Based on a variety of clues, Urbach suggests what happened. Rashi wrote drafts of a commentary to this chapter. But once he saw Rashbam's commentary, he decided it was not necessary to finish his own.

   Rashbam wrote commentaries on many other tractates. We know this because of mention of these in other Rishonim. AlHatorah.org has part of his commentary on *Avodah Zarah*. Rashbam also composed works of *halakhah* that have not survived (on topics like the laws of *Yom Tov* and the laws of slaughtering).[57]

9. The Tosafot commentaries typically refer to Rashi as *peirush ha-kuntres*. *Kuntres* means "pamphlet."[58] This term was used

---

that has survived in two manuscripts. Although this compilation rarely cites Rashbam by name, Novetsky found that its *peshat* interpretations incorporate large amounts of Rashbam without attribution. Much detective work was done by Novetsky in analyzing unattributed material and suggesting which of it probably derived from Rashbam.

Rashbam sometimes discusses verses from Gen. 1–17 and the other missing sections in his commentaries on the Talmud. But Rashbam has a different method in these commentaries. In his Talmud commentaries, he is not searching for the *omek peshuto* of a verse. We cannot assume that what Rashbam wrote in his Talmud commentary about a verse would be what he would have written in his Torah commentary. Also, when any commentator writes an interpretation in a Talmud commentary, a main motivation is to interpret the verse in a way that makes it fit with the flow of the *sugya*.

(The reason Hizzekuni almost never cites his sources is that he wants his readers to evaluate the suggested explanations unbiasedly.)

56. Urbach, p. 49.
57. Urbach, p. 57.
58. The word קונטרס derives from the Latin *commentarius*. So obvious (but not until it is pointed out!).

because Rashi's students copied his comments into pamphlets. There are Tosafot on *Pesaḥim* and *Makkot* that refer to Rashbam's commentaries with this same phrase: *peirush ha-kuntres*.[59]

10. Aside from being a Bible and Talmud commentator, Rashbam was a communal leader as well, authoring *takkanot* and *gezerot*. Also, hundreds of Rashbam's legal decisions in all areas of Jewish law appear in the responsa of Rosh and Ra'avya, among others.[60]

* * *

Like Rashi, Mitchell First is willing to write that he does not understand something. Like Rashbam, he tries to write only when he has something to add. (If this is contradictory, it is no less contradictory than the interpretive approach of Rashbam that I addressed in the previous column.)

7. An Important Manuscript of Rambam's *Mishneh Torah*: Huntington 80

The manuscripts of the *Mishneh Torah* (hereinafter: MT) that have survived today are of three different types: Yemenite, Ashkenazic (German) and Sephardic (Spanish). There are differences between these types. For example, the Yemenite ones may not include later corrections by Rambam after various laws were questioned and he made changes. The Ashkenazic manuscripts include the later corrections by Rambam, but contains many inaccuracies. The rabbis and copyists in Ashkenaz thought it permissible to make subtle changes in style and language, as long as the content of the law remained unchanged.

Perhaps the most important manuscript of the MT is one at the Bodleian Library at the University of Oxford. This manuscript only contains the first two sections of the MT (*Madda* and *Ahavah*). But at the end, it has Rambam's signature, with the following statement: "corrected against my own book, I Moses, son of Rabbi Maimon of

---

59. Urbach, pp. 49 and 54.
60. Kolatch, p. 91.

blessed memory." This manuscript is known as Huntington 80. One can view it online at digital.bodleian.ox.ac.uk.⁶¹

This manuscript is viewed as the most reliable because of the above attestation that it is consistent with Rambam's own original. Rambam had his own copy and made changes over the years (e.g., fixing errors or changing his text if he changed his mind). The attestation is implying that this manuscript reflected what was in Rambam's own copy, including the changes he made. (Ok, there is no date on the attestation and perhaps Rambam made changes after that.) The exact Hebrew words that Rambam wrote prior to his signature were: הוגה מספרי. (Those two Hebrew words mean: "corrected against my book." But they do not say that it was Rambam himself who checked it against his own book. See my quote from Joel Kraemer's work, below.)

Unfortunately, there are several pages after Rambam's signature, including the section containing his year-round *nusaḥ ha-tefillah*. So one can argue that the attestation did not include this material.⁶²

At the beginning of the manuscript, the following is written (in the same handwriting as the attestation, so presumably it is also by Rambam): "This work belonged to a pupil who was very clever, who studied the law day and night for its own sake....⁶³ This student commanded... [in his will] that the copy in question should always remain in the custody of the *Bet Din*, that it should be neither sold nor otherwise disposed of, and that no man shall ever own it, but that it shall be ready and available to all students to correct their copies by this copy.... Whoever wants to correct his copy shall borrow it from *Bet Din* and shall leave *Bet Din* a deposit... [that will stay there] until he corrects his copy and returns it. It is a *mitzvah* to fulfill the instructions of the deceased..."⁶⁴

How did the Bodleian library acquire this manuscript? They

---

61. The signature is at page 165r.
62. Probably, this material was added by the scribe after the attestation was written. Perhaps the manuscript of the *Mishneh Torah* that the scribe originally copied from did not have this section. Then he found it in a different manuscript of the *Mishneh Torah* and added it.
63. Rambam here gives the student's name and tell us a bit more about him and that he died young.
64. See L. Dukes and H. Edelmann, *Ginzei Oxford – Treasures of Oxford* (1851).

bought it from Robert Huntington, who was an expert in ancient Mideastern scholarly matters and became a chaplain to a company of merchants from England who were working in Aleppo, Syria. He stayed in the area for about 11 years and made it his business to acquire ancient manuscripts. Our manuscript was probably originally owned by descendants of Rambam who moved from Egypt to Aleppo. (See below.) After acquiring it, Huntington sold it to the Bodleian library with 645 other manuscripts in 1693. Neither he nor the library understood its significance at the time of the sale.

We have a reference to a similar authorized copy elsewhere. Someone wrote to R. Samuel ibn Tibbon requesting him to forward a copy of the MT whose text matched one corrected by the Rambam himself and on which Rambam wrote, "This copy of the *Mishneh Torah* is corrected (though not in my presence) by the copy which I wrote, I Moses the son of Maimon the Sephardi."[65]

Does that mean that manuscript Huntington 80 was also corrected outside the presence of Rambam? Joel Kraemer, in his comprehensive work *Maimonides* (2008), writes: "copies would be checked against the autograph original by a scribe or by Maimonides himself, who would certify that a copy has been collated with his codex."[66] So it would seem that in the case of Huntington 80 it is possible that it was not Rambam himself who did the checking.

Additional Notes:

1. Another important manuscript in Rambam's handwriting that survives is his commentary on the Mishnah. Maimonides corrected his own copy of the commentary throughout his lifetime, since his view on many matters changed over the years. What has survived in Rambam's handwriting are five out of the six Mishnah sections. (Rambam's son Abraham even made corrections on the manuscript after his father's death, fulfilling his father's intentions.)

    Three of these surviving volumes are ones purchased by Hun-

---

The necessary pages can be viewed at the post of onthemainline.blogspot.com of Nov. 24, 2011.
65. Ibid.
66. P. 171.

tington and an older colleague and sold to the Bodleian library. According to Kraemer (p. 168), Rambam had a fifth-generation descendant in Egypt, Nagid David II ben Joshua (1335–1415). When he moved from Cairo to Aleppo, he brought with him manuscripts that were family heirlooms. Later, descendants of his sold the three volumes of the Mishnah commentary and the signed MT to some private individuals. Eventually, they were sold to Huntington. (The other two volumes of the Mishnah commentary came to light in Damascus in 1907–08. They are now in Hebrew University.)

2. We now have many more handwritten items from Rambam. They came from the Cairo Genizah. According to Stefan Reif, the head of the Genizah Unit in Cambridge from 1973–2006, there are 120 documents from the Genizah in Rambam's handwriting.[67] (In contrast, as Kraemer points out, not even one handwritten manuscript from Shakespeare, who lived four hundred years after Rambam, has survived.) The synagogue in Cairo with the *genizah* space in its attic (= the Cairo Genizah) was only a short walk from Rambam's home.

3. Another interesting find from the Cairo Genizah in Rambam's handwriting are a few pages from his earlier draft of the MT. (The few pages found are from the laws of hiring and the laws of borrowing and deposits. It seems from these few pages that this earlier draft was organized a bit differently than the MT that we have today.)

4. This is a good place to remind everyone that משנה in the phrase *Mishneh Torah* is based on the phrase *mishneh ha-torah* at Deuteronomy 17:18. Thus it is spelled in English with an "e."

* * *

This essay is based mainly on Kraemer's work, *Maimonides* (2008), pp. 168–71, and the post at onthemainline.blogspot.com of Nov. 24, 2011.

* * *

---

67. Stefan Reif, quoted in *The International Jerusalem Post*, July 9–15, 2021, p. 26.

Mitchell First's book *Links to Our Legacy* (2021) has a correction page regarding a few matters in his prior book *Roots and Rituals* (2018). Like Rambam, his views sometimes evolve. But unlike Rambam, his handwriting is unreadable.

8. The Mashhadi Jews of Northeastern Iran

I recently read a fascinating book about the history of the Jews in Iran and of the Mashhadi Jews in particular: *Concealed: Memoir of a Jewish-Iranian Daughter Caught Between the Chador*[68] *and America.* It was published in 2020 and authored by Esther Amini.

If you think your life is difficult, your perspective will change and you will be exceptionally grateful once you read this book. The author's parents grew up in a remote region of Iran. A large part of this book is about what life was like for the community of Mashhadi Jews there.

The author's mother was born in 1925. She had been forced to live as an underground Jew in the city of Mashhad, a Shi'ite stronghold and pilgrimage site with a long history of maiming and massacring infidels. "Head bent, breathing through a black *chador*, peering through an eyeslit, she slunk through alleyways, faceless and shapeless, passing as Muslim."

* * *

Around 1502, the various Iranian states had united. At that point, *Shia* became its official religion. *Shia* placed great emphasis on ritual purity. Jews were not allowed to enter public baths and were forbidden to step outside their homes when it rained out of fear that their impurity might wash off and contaminate a Muslim!

A nineteenth-century source writes that if a Jew entered a shop for any reason, should his hand touch the goods, he was forced to buy them at any price that the seller chooses. Even in twentieth-century Iran, when making a purchase in a store, a Jew had to place his coins in

---

68. The *chador* is that long black garment that covers a woman's head and body.

a basin filled with water and let the storeowner take them out. This was a ritual cleansing of all currency coming from the hands of Jews.

Another nineteenth-century source wrote that, "at every public festival... the Jews are collected and a number of them are flung into the hauz or tank, that the King and mob may be amused by seeing them crawl out half-drowned and covered with mud."

Mashhad, in northeastern Iran, is its most religiously fanatical city, where a ninth-century *imam* was buried. Millions of Shi'ites visit to worship at his shrine. How did Jews end up there?

An eighteenth-century ruler of Iran invaded India and in 1746 he built a treasury outside Mashhad to store his plunder. He ordered Jewish leaders from an area near Teheran to choose 40 families known for integrity to move to Mashhad to guard his treasury. (In another version, the king moved many families to Mashhad and not all were Jewish.) The author writes that in 1747 her ancestors on both her mother's and father's sides were among the Jewish families selected to move. Just as they arrived, this ruler of Iran was assassinated. The "chosen" were now the "cursed." These Jews were stuck in Mashhad, unprotected by the ruler who had brought them there.

In 1839, there was a devastating pogrom. Some Jews received death by lashes. Others were decapitated in public squares. Mobs burned the synagogue and destroyed Torah scrolls. The Jews who were not killed were given an ultimatum: Convert to Islam or die. Many fled. 300 families agreed to convert, but in secret they maintained their Judaism. This was the practice into which her parents were born. Posing as Muslims, their fathers chanted from the Koran in public, while in their basements they taught their sons Torah.

As part of the charade, her mother would buy meat from a Muslim butcher. (She would give it to street beggars.) The Jews had their own secret *shoḥet*. The author writes that "the tougher life was above ground, the more cohesive they grew underground." Staunchly against marrying outside their faith, they also were opposed to marrying outside their Mashhadi community. Her father told her that the more they were cursed, beaten and hung, the more they studied Torah. But they lived fearfully as prey, waiting for the next wave of predators. The Muslims of Mashhad knew who the "secret" Jews were. On any day an *imam* could declare that there should be a pogrom against them.

One of her father's duties was to periodically bribe the local *imam* to prevent such an occurrence.

For women, the underground Jewish ghetto in the city of Mashhad was a culture of "forced marriages, child brides, birthing children, illiteracy, and fear of the outside world."

It was important for a woman to marry young, because if she was raped, no one would ever marry her. Also, if a Muslim knocked on the door to claim a girl for marriage, parents could honestly reply: "She is taken."

At her parents' marriage, her father was 34 and her mother 14. Her father decided to marry his mother after seeing her from afar. Before the marriage, he had never spoken to her. Her mother did not want this marriage but her opinion was ignored.

During World War II, her parents moved to Teheran. But food shortages and unemployment were just as severe there. In 1939, at the age of 15, her mother had her first child. A few years later, she bore another son. One day in Teheran in 1946, the teacher accused her child of misbehaving. The teacher stuck a poker into an open fire and pressed it against the child's ear and screamed: "Dirty Jew." The author writes that this attack did more than sear her brother's ear. "It seared Mom's soul and incinerated all ties to her ancestral home." She realized that it made no difference whether they lived in insular Mashhad or modern Teheran. She decided to leave Iran forever and go to America where her brother was. Esther's father agreed reluctantly, hoping that once she got to America, his wife would not like it. He had tremendous fears of how he would make a living in the U.S.

It was hard to get a visa from Teheran, so they were advised to move to India first. They lived there for many months and finally a visa came through. (Esther's mother ceremoniously burned her *chadors* upon leaving Iran!)

Most of the book is not about life in Iran, but about Esther's life in America and how she was able to thrive in public school and in Barnard, and about her life thereafter. (She eventually became a psychotherapist.) But in her youth, her old-fashioned father resented every book that she read and every year she was in school. He believed that literacy and education made her less desirable as a wife. Also, that it made her less beautiful and even barren! (No female in either of her parents' families knew how to read or write.) Her mother, who grew up in a duplicitous life in Iran, continued lying in different ways in America. Both parents arrived in America extremely scarred.

Finally, a great story is the day Esther moved into the dorm at Barnard. Over and over, she had assured her father that college was not a den of iniquity and women went there to educate themselves. But what happened when she came with her parents to her dorm room for the first time and opened the door? You can guess. Her naked roommate and her male companion were extremely embarrassed, and her father stormed off in anger.

* * *

Mitchell First's first book (*Jewish History in Conflict*) was largely about the kings of ancient Persia. With this book, he has learned much about modern Persia.

9. Bukharan Jewry and the Dynamics of Global Judaism

Did you ever wonder if there really was a single Jewish people? What do we in the United States have in common with Jews from exotic places? In 2012, Alanna Cooper, an educator with a PhD in cultural anthropology, authored a book on this topic (published by Indiana University Press). While the book is focused on Bukharan Jews, what motivated the author were the larger questions about Jewish peoplehood. The title of the book was: *Bukharan Jews and the Dynamics of Global Judaism*. (In my opinion, the title should have been: The Dynamics of Global Judaism: Case study: Bukharan Jews.)

The term "Bukharan Jews" refers to the Jews in two adjacent countries: Uzbekistan and Tajikistan. These countries are very far east. Tajikistan borders on China. These two areas were part of the Soviet Union before it collapsed in 1991.

The Jews in these areas lived mainly in two cities: Bukhara and Samarkand. Perhaps their origin lies as early as the exile of the Ten Tribes. Probably the Jews moved eastwards over time, as merchants on trade routes. Our first reference to the Jews in Samarkand is a reference by the twelfth-century traveler Benjamin of Tudela. He mentions 50,000 Jews there. (This number may be an exaggeration.) Our first reference to the Jews in Bukhara is a thirteenth-century Arab chronicler. These Jewish communities spoke a language called Judeo-Tajik, one of the many variants of Tajik, a Persian language.

Bukhara was only one city in Soviet Central Asia, but at the beginning of the twentieth century the general term "Bukharan Jewry" became applied to all the Jewish communities there. (This happened only as a result of a fundraising project that the communities undertook to build their own neighborhood in Jerusalem.)

In 1989 there were still 50,000 Bukharan Jews living in Soviet Central Asia. But as soon as the USSR dissolved, these Jews began emigrating to Israel and to the U.S. Today, no more than several hundred remain behind.

The author first had contact with former members of this community when she taught at a yeshiva in Queens in 1993. The yeshiva presented the story of Bukharan Jewry as a rescue of a lost Jewish community and of bringing them into the Torah fold, but the Bukharan students had a very different take on what happened. She was very intrigued by their stories. Her students advised her that she should travel there before the community died out, and she did.

What intrigued her most was the curious sense of familiarity that she, an American and Ashkenazi Jew, felt among them. She writes that she was "easily and readily welcomed into the homes of people from another cultural world, whose historical experiences had been utterly different from my own, and who were total strangers, except for the fact that we commonly identified as Jews. And once inside their homes, synagogues and schools, I was struck by the ways in which their religious practices and categories felt so foreign to me, and yet so familiar."[69]

The author writes: "Is there a single Judaism and Jewish people? And if so, how might these entities be defined in light of the great diversity of Jewish forms that developed across the far reaches of the diaspora?"[70] (She points out that these questions arise in the other world religions as well.)

---

69. P. xii.
70. Ibid.

The author points out that Jewish history has traditionally been written as if there was an agreed-upon definition of "center" and "periphery." The groups in the "center" followed certain accepted texts and are characterized as followers of "Rabbinic Judaism." The groups considered to be on the "periphery" are viewed as Jews that either lost, forgot, misread, misunderstood, or ignored these texts. But the author suggests that the categories "center" and "periphery" are not givens, and evolve through political struggles and economic forces.

A very interesting chapter explains how biased definitions of center and periphery influenced the way that the history of Bukharan Jewry was written. A main event in this history was the arrival of an emissary from Israel at the end of the eighteenth century. The version of the story that was told by modern historians, and which came to be accepted, depicts the emissary as having found these Jews to be religiously ignorant and on the brink of assimilation. Through the emissary's work, they were reeducated and reconnected with the Jewish world. But there is another version of this story which was told among Bukharan Jews themselves. In this version, Bukharan Jewry had long been connected to parts of world Jewry prior to the emissary's arrival. They had great Torah scholars in every generation. They followed the customs of the Persian Jews, which were similar to the customs of the Jews of Yemen. But because those modern historians who wrote the history of Bukharan Jewry and the emissary episode had their own biased view of the way Jewish history should be written, the alternative version was ignored.

In 1897, Elkan Adler, son of Britain's chief Rabbi, traveled to Bukhara and Samarkand and acquired books from them, many printed hundreds of years earlier. From his list of books acquired, we can see that these Jews had connections with the rest of world Jewry.[71]

As an alternative to the "center vs. periphery" model, the author suggests that we can perhaps look at Jewish history differently, with an *edah* model. In this model, we can view Judaism as composed of different tribes.

---

71. See E. Adler, "The Persian Jews: Their Books and their Ritual," *The Jewish Quarterly Review* 10 (1898), pp. 584-625.

Another interesting section raises the issue of what happens when a portion of Bukharan Jewry moves to Israel? Does the leader of Bukharan Jewry in Israel suddenly become the leader of world Bukharan Jewry and the person that diasporan Bukharan Jewry is supposed to turn to?

At the conclusion of the book, the author provides a few metaphors to help understand how Jews scattered across the world maintained themselves as a single people. One metaphor imagines the Jewish people as a rope. The rope contains diverse strands, all bound together, but each runs only for some portion of its length. Another metaphor imagines a tapestry. The tapestry is made up of interconnected threads of many colors, some of which "run through almost the whole" while some "are threads that hang loose, were snipped off, or morphed into a different form." The author proposes a different metaphor, a conversation metaphor. Over all periods, Judaism is a continuing "conversation." "As this conversation unfolds across great distances and historical eras, every given moment carries each preceding moment with it. Laden with historical baggage, it becomes so intimately connected to each party's sense of who they are in the world, that abandoning it becomes almost unthinkable."[72]

* * *

Mitchell First limits his travel to reading books. He once lived for many months on *Reḥov Ha-Bukharim* in Jerusalem. He had no idea of the interesting background to this street name!

10. The Fascinating Life of Judah Touro (1775–1854)

Touro College is named for Judah and his father Isaac. Judah had a very interesting life story, connected with major events of American history.

Judah's father Isaac was from Holland. In 1762 he was chosen as the *chazzan* at the Portuguese congregation in Newport, R.I. This was the first official synagogue in the Americas.

Due to the impact of the Revolutionary War in Newport, the family

---

72. P. 261.

had to move to New York in 1780, when Judah was 5. (Isaac was a Tory, siding with the British.) Thereafter, the family moved again to Jamaica, in the British West Indies.

After Isaac died in 1783, his wife moved back to the U.S. with her four children to Boston to live with her brother. She died in in 1787, and Judah and his siblings were raised by this uncle, a wealthy merchant. The uncle trained Judah in his business and Judah undertook voyages for him.

But in 1801, at the age of 26, Touro decided to leave Boston. He had wanted to marry his uncle's daughter, but his uncle refused him permission.[73]

Judah chose to go to New Orleans. He opened a store there. His timing was fortuitous. The city was in Spanish hands at the time of his arrival, but it was soon transferred to France and in 1803, Louisiana was sold by Napoleon to the U.S. as part of the Louisiana Purchase. Judah was ideally positioned to capitalize on the subsequent commercial boom. He traded in goods sent by his contacts in New England and then invested his profits in ships and New Orleans real estate, and became very wealthy.

He enlisted in the army in the War of 1812. In 1815, in the Battle of New Orleans,[74] a cannonball smashed his leg, ripping off most of his thigh. He required more than a year to recover. The doctors had thought he would not survive. He was nursed back to health by a close friend who he later made the executor and residual beneficiary of his estate. The wound left Touro with a limp and upper leg damage.

After the war, Touro resumed his business interests in shipping, trade, and real estate. He lived a simple life in a small apartment. "I have saved a fortune by strict economy," he said, "while others had spent one by their liberal expenditures." He never married.

The first synagogue in the state was founded in New Orleans in

---

73. Perhaps he felt the need to move far away where there would be no reminders of this very sad episode.
74. The Battle of New Orleans was fought on Jan. 8, 1815. On our side, it was led by Andrew Jackson, who would become the seventh President of the United States. It took place about two weeks after the signing of the treaty which formally ended the war. But news of the agreement had not yet reached the U.S. from Europe.

1828, but Touro did not join as a member, although he did provide it with some financial assistance. It was a small synagogue, composed mostly of Jews from Ashkenazic backgrounds. (There were probably only about 100 Jews in the entire state at this time.) About twenty years later, Jews of Spanish and Portuguese background decided to found a synagogue and Judah was much more involved in the establishment of this one, as Sephardic ritual was the one he grew up with. (In 1881, the synagogues merged. The united synagogue is named for Touro.)

Having grown up in the North and being an abolitionist, he would sometimes purchase slaves in order to free them.

In 1840 he gave $10,000 to Boston to complete the long-languishing Bunker Hill monument, whose construction had begun years earlier. At the dedication ceremonies in 1843, Daniel Webster, American's greatest orator at the time, praised Touro and fellow funder Amos Lawrence: "Amos and Judah – venerated names, Patriarch and prophet press their equal claim. Like generous coursers running 'neck to neck,' each aids the work by giving it a check. Christians and Jews, they carry out one plan. For though of different faith, each is in heart a Man." Lawrence was a wealthy philanthropist who was not Jewish. His father had fought at Bunker Hill.

Judah Touro's lasting fame was as a philanthropist. He contributed $40,000, an immense sum at the time, to the Jewish cemetery at Newport.

In New Orleans, he used his business profits to buy and endow a cemetery, and to build a synagogue, an almshouse and an infirmary for sailors, as well as a church for a minister whom he greatly admired. The infirmary became the largest free hospital in Louisiana, the Touro infirmary.

He was a major contributor to many Christian charities in New Orleans, as well as to such varied causes as the American Revolutionary War monument at Bunker Hill, and the relief of victims of a large fire in Mobile, Alabama. In a New Orleans fund-raising drive for Christians suffering persecution in Jerusalem, he gave ten times more than any other donor.

He donated $20,000 to the hospital in New York City that is now known as Mt. Sinai Hospital. This led to its opening in 1855.

Though he gave liberally to charitable objects during his entire life, the provisions of the will of Touro, who died unmarried, disposed of over half a million dollars in charity, an enormous sum in those days. It included gifts to both Jewish and non-Jewish causes. No American Jew had ever given so much to so many agencies and causes; nor had any non-Jew done so much in such varied ways.

Among the larger bequests were $80,000 for founding the New Orleans Almshouse, endowments for nearly all the Jewish congregations of the country (twenty-three congregations in fourteen states), bequests to the Massachusetts General Hospital, and to the Boston Asylum of Orphan Boys, and the Boston Asylum of Female Orphans, and one for the preservation of the Jewish cemetery at Newport, and for the payment of the salary of the leader of the synagogue in that city. $50,000 was left in trust to Moses Montefiore to help the Jews in Israel. Montefiore used this to build the first Jewish residential community outside the Old City, *Mishkenot Sha'ananim*.[75]

Touro's will also included a $5,000 gift to his cousin who he had wanted to marry decades earlier. She had never married anyone else.[76]

Touro lived in New Orleans for more than 50 years. As mentioned above, the Touro Infirmary and the Touro Synagogue are named

---

75. When the area was dedicated, the dedication stone originally had only Montefiore's name on it, listing him as the sponsoring philanthropist. When Montefiore saw it, he asked that it be changed to give Touro the main credit. It was changed and it now has both their names, with Touro's name first. Other communities in Jerusalem built with funds from Touro but named for Montefiore due to the latter's work include: Yemin Moshe, Kiryat Moshe, Zikhron Moshe, Ohel Moshe, and Mazkeret Moshe. I thank Jeffrey Glazer for these insights.

Neither Montefiore nor Touro had any children. Both dedicated much of their lives and energy to philanthropy and the public good (but Montefiore had more of a focus on the Jewish world). (Unlike Touro, Montefiore did marry.)

76. Touro wrote his will about two weeks before he died. It turns out that his cousin had died a few days before, but Touro did not know. She had been living in Virginia. They had never seen each other again after Touro's departure from Boston. It is possible that a lovers' correspondence had been carried on between them over the many decades. We will never know because, at Touro's request, his voluminous correspondence was burnt after his death. His motivation for burning his correspondence was to protect the identity of those who were financially helped by him.

in his memory. Also, a Judah Touro Scholarship is given at Tulane University.

Touro is buried in the Jewish cemetery in Newport which he endowed. He was the final surviving member of the Touro family. On his tombstone are inscribed the words: "The last of his name, he inscribed it in the Book of Philanthropy to be remembered forever."[77]

* * *

As to *Mishkenot Sha'ananim*, it was built in 1859–60 as an almshouse for the poor. It was the first Jewish building built outside the walls of the Old City. Because it was outside the walls, it was viewed as unsafe and Jews were reluctant to move in, even though the housing was luxurious compared to the overcrowded Old City. People had to be paid to live there. A stone wall was built around the compound with a heavy door that was locked at night. The name of the neighborhood was a paraphrase of Isa. 32:18: "My people will abide in a peaceful habitation, with *mishkenot mivtaḥim* and *menuḥot sha'ananot*."[78]

* * *

Mitchell First hopes to be inscribed in the "Book of Jewish Writers."

11. 1827: Russia Begins to Draft its Jews

One of the major events in the history of Russian Jewry was the imposition of military obligations on them by Czar Nicholas the First in 1827. Here is the background, from *The Jews in Poland and Russia*, by A. Polonsky (2013):[79]

"The induction of Jews into the army elsewhere in Europe was part of the process of transforming them into citizens. This was not the case in Russia. Here, military service was not a general obligation but was imposed selectively on different estates and social and religious

---

77. The most thorough biography of Touro is L. Huhner, *The Life of Judah Touro* (1946). In 2020, a children's book was published about him: *Judah Touro Didn't Want to be Famous*, by Audrey Ades. (I thank Daniel Klein for this reference.)
78. The last word comes from the root שאן, meaning "tranquil."
79. Pp. 81–82.

groups. Jews had initially been exempt from military service after the incorporation into the empire of the areas where they lived. They were all classed as merchants from the point of view of conscription and were required to pay a 500 rouble exemption tax. There were occasional discussions over whether they should be drafted, but they were generally felt to be unsuitable as recruits. This was not the view of Nicholas. He was a convinced believer in the value of the army as a school for virtue which could play a major role in the transformation of his Jewish subjects...."

"The quota varied from year to year, but generally the Jews were required to furnish four to eight recruits for every thousand tax souls.... Jews were inducted into the army between the ages of 12 and 25. Those over 18 served for twenty-five years in the regular army; those under 18 served in special cantonist battalions... until they reached the age of 18, when they commenced their twenty-five-year service. Cantonist battalions had [already] existed for other categories of recruits.... Those who served in them were educated in special boarding schools attached to army camps which had first been created in 1805 for the sons of Russian private soldiers."

"Some categories of Jews were exempt.... As was the case with all groups liable for inscription, the local community was collectively responsible for its implementation.... [Jews were to stay] only in Christian homes during their travels and were forbidden contact with local Jews. Jews who completed their military term were eligible to serve in the civil service."

"This was a punitive law and its introduction was the cause of appalling suffering and of major disruption to Jewish life. In all, during the reign of Nicholas I about 70,000 Jews served in the Russian army; between 4.5 and 6.5 percent of Jews in Russia were conscripted. One reason why service in the army was so hated by the large majority of the Jewish community was that... conversion [of those drafted] was openly encouraged.... [P]erhaps at least half of the cantonists [converted]... and a substantial number of adult recruits did so...."

"The involvement of the communal leadership in enforcement of conscription caused enormous shock, undermining deep-rooted traditions of social solidarity. It precipitated a breakdown of communal bonds, which manifested itself in a number of ways, including violent protests against the *khappers* (those who seized people in order to conscript them) and the *kahal*...."

To explain a bit further, the fact that between 4.5 and 6.5 percent of Jews in Russia were conscripted does not sound so terrible. The problem was that every day you did not know if your child would be one of those *khapped* by the *kahal*!

What is most interesting is the response of the Eastern European Karaites.[80] To give a little background, in the centuries after the foundation of Karaism in around the eighth century CE (the foundation of this sect is a complex subject), major Karaite communities flourished in Israel, Turkey, Egypt, and Iraq. Karaites did not arrive in Eastern Europe until the thirteenth to fifteenth centuries. Just like their Rabbinic Jewish brethren, they suffered in the massacres in Eastern Europe of 1648–49.

But what happened in 1827? Two leading Karaites from Crimea, Simhah Babovich and Joseph Solomon Lutski, went to St. Petersburg to petition the Czar to exempt them, and they were successful. The latter wrote an account of their journey. It was intended to be read in Karaite synagogues in Eastern Europe annually in celebration of their success. It was written in a style parallel to the book of Esther. It is called *Iggeret Teshu'at Yisrael*.[81]

The *Iggeret* begins as follows: "In the days of Nicholas the first, the great Czar and emperor (may he live forever!) who ruled all the Russias and other places, in the year 1827 according to the Christians and in the year 5588 since Creation according to us...a royal order was given.... It was a new law to be established for generations to come, one unknown in earlier days. It was the king's express command that letters be sent by messenger to all the officials in his kingdom in which it was explicitly stated that men from among the Jews be taken for military service in equal measure to other nations and tongues under

---

80. Much of what I write now is based on an article by Prof. Daniel Lasker online at *Tablet Magazine*, Sept. 11, 2020, "Inventing the Karaites." Lasker is a professor at Ben-Gurion University and one of his specialties is the study of the Karaites.
81. The Hebrew text with English translation is found in P. Miller, *Karaite Separatism in Nineteenth-Century Russia* (1993).

his rule.... The Jews would not be permitted to buy men of other nations or to give substitutes other than their own nation's sons.... Great was the mourning, fasting and weeping among the Jews when the king's order reached each province.... As the word 'Jews' was written in the text of the decree, and as it was understood afterwards in some places that the decree was to include each and every Jewish sect and did not exclude the Karaites, the officials in the Crimean towns included us Karaites in this decree as well...."

The two Karaites reminded the authorities that since the time of Catherine the Great (see below) the Karaites had been treated as a separate community from the Rabbanite Jews. The fact that the Karaites did not follow the Talmud also helped distinguish them in the eyes of the Russian authorities. Probably, a bribe was involved as well. (Babovich was very wealthy.)

This was not the Karaites' first political success in Eastern Europe. In 1774, the Karaites in Austria were able to obtain preferential treatment from Empress Maria Theresa: they received an exemption from the marriage tax and half of the poll tax that was placed on the Jews. Also, in 1795, the Russian regime imposed a poll tax on the Jews that was double what was imposed on Christians and Catherine the Great granted the Karaite petition for an exemption.

Subsequent to their success in 1827, the Karaites in the Russian empire received full recognition as Russian citizens in 1863. These Karaites continued to minimize any connection to the Jews throughout this century. In the 20th century, they began to deny any connection to the Jews altogether, falsifying their history and changing many of their rituals. They were able to convince the Nazis that they were not Jews and most were spared in the Holocaust.

* * *

Mitchell First is not related to Czar Nicholas the First. One time in his youth, when he was in Europe, making a collect phone call to his parents, the operator thought he identified himself as "Mitchell the First"!

12. On July 3, 1861, the Pasha Gave the Keys of Jerusalem to the Chief Rabbi[82]

On June 25, 1861, the Sultan of the Ottoman Empire died and there was a new Sultan.

Eight days later, on July 3, the chief rabbi of Jerusalem was presented with the keys to Jerusalem and held them in his home for one hour. This is what occurred, according to one account:

"[T]he Jews waited with all formalities on the governor Surraya pasha and requested him to restore to them the keys of Jerusalem, according to a right which they claimed on the death of one sultan and the accession of another. At the same time, they brought forward such proofs of the justice of their demand that the pasha did not refuse it, but referred it to his ordinary council.... Their decision was in favor of the Israelites, the whole council being aware that they were the ancient owners of the country.

"The ceremony was accordingly performed in the following manner. Said pasha, the general of the forces, accompanied by the officers of his staff, and some members of the council, and followed by a crowd of sight-seers, went to the Jews' quarter, where he was met by a deputation of that nation and conducted to the house of the chief rabbi, who received the pasha at the door, and there was publicly presented with the keys. The pasha was then entertained with the utmost respect at the divan of the rabbi; refreshments, coffee and tobacco were served, and then the rabbi (not having a garrison to defend the keys) restored them with many thanks to the general, who was escorted back by the chief men of the Jews to the governor of the city, Surraya pasha, to give an account of his mission, and shew[83] him that none of the keys were missing. So, in 1861, the Jewish nation possessed for one hour the keys of Jerusalem, which were delivered over to them by the Arabs in consequence of the unvarying tradition which they had preserved."

---

82. In this essay, I am summarizing an article from *Hakirah*, vol. 25 (2018) by Meir Loewenberg. It was titled: "Why did the pasha give the keys of Jerusalem to the Chief Rabbi?"

83. This is an archaic spelling of "show."

Why in the world would the Turkish authorities present the keys of the city to the chief rabbi of Jerusalem for even a short period?

The account above was written by the Italian engineer Ermete Pierotti in his *Customs and Traditions of Palestine* (English tr., 1864). He had been working in Jerusalem, hired by the Ottoman authorities as a consultant. He had no background on Jewish laws and customs. He wrote above that the "decision was in favor of the Israelites, the whole council being aware that they were the ancient owners of the country." This is how he understood the ceremony, as reflecting a publicly expressed conviction by the Muslim leaders of Jerusalem that the Israelites were the ancient owners of the country.

After the 1967 war, Pierotti's account was frequently cited about what happened that day. For example, Israel's ambassador to the U.N. cited this account at a Security Council meeting in 1968 and in 1969 Abraham Heschel quoted it to support Israel's claims to the new territories.

But Pierotti's explanation for the ceremony was just based on his mistaken impressions.

Another explanation for the ceremony was presented by James Finn, the British consul in Jerusalem from 1845-1863. In his book, he mentioned the ceremonies of 1839 and 1861. He explained: "For the exercise of this traditional custom they make heavy presents to the local governors, who allow of a harmless practice.... It is a matter of *bakhsheesh* to them... the Jewish feelings are gratified for their expectation of the future is refreshed, and the Jerusalem Rabbis are enabled to boast all over among their people that they suffer [=allow] the Sultan of Turkey to keep possession of the Holy City."[84]

Another explanation was offered by a monk who lived in Jerusalem in the 1860's. He wrote that the ceremony symbolized that the Jews were given permission by the new Sultan to live in Jerusalem and travel all over Palestine.

What is the true explanation for the ceremony? It was stated by Elizabeth Finn, wife of James Finn. (Women always know best!) This is what she wrote in 1869 (in a missionary magazine): " Some of [the

---

84. James Finn, *Stirring Times: Or Records from the Jerusalem Consular Chronicles of 1853-56* (1878), pp. 117-18.

Jews] termed [the custom] "hiring the city," and said that it was done in connection with the laws of Eruv, for Sabbath observances; for that when a city is thus hired as a whole – all within its walls is considered by their law to have become one house – within which they are then free to pass on the Sabbath from dwelling to dwelling, even though bearing slight burdens, without infringing any of the laws for keeping holy the Sabbath-day...."

This *eruv* explanation was corroborated by Rabbi Eliyahu Bechor Chazan who wrote in 1875 that what happened in 1861 was part of the *eruv* procedure. He was the grandson of the rabbi who received the keys in 1861.

* * *

To give further background, the need for an *eruv* in Jerusalem began in the seventeenth century. That is when the Jews began to spread to different areas within the city walls. Prior to that, usually each courtyard had a majority of Jews.

A necessary step for the *eruv* to work was a lease of the city from the Sultan or his representative. It became the custom to enter a lease for a long period like 50 years. But what happened when the lessor dies in the interim? In the middle of the eighteenth century, some began to question whether the lease would still be effective and recommended a new lease on each succession.

None of the eighteenth-century rabbinical authorities in Jerusalem mentioned taking possession of the city keys for any period as part of the *eruv* lease signing. But the Jerusalem rabbinate adopted this stringency in connection with the successions and signings of 1839 and 1861. Prior to this, this stringency had been followed in some Mediterranean cities at the end of the 18th century. (This is reported by R. Ḥayyim David Azulai.)

A problem arose in 1876 when Sultan Murad V was deposed after three months (on a fifty-year lease). The Jewish community of Jerusalem did not have the funds for a second round of *bakhsheesh*. The Ashkenazic rabbinate ruled that no new lease was necessary. The Sephardic rabbinate arranged a lease with a minor official who was willing to do so for a smaller amount of money.

At the end of the nineteenth century, the halakhic status of Jerusalem changed. It was no longer a "walled city." This change occurred because Jaffa gate and the other gates were kept open 24 hours in order to facilitate the interaction with the new Jewish neighborhoods outside the wall. Later, in 1898 a permanent breach was made in the wall near the Jaffa gate to permit Kaiser Wilhelm to enter without dismounting from his horse. By the time of the next Sultan in 1909, obtaining the city keys was no longer relevant. Other means were used for the Jerusalem *eruv*.

* * *

As an attorney, Mitchell First is a believer in giving *bakhsheesh* to the Judge (but it is important to give more than the opposing attorney gives!)

13. The *Navemar*: The "Ship from Hell" That Sailed to the U.S. in 1941

My mother is Judge Lee First. In 1941, as a 13-year-old, she arrived in the U.S. from Europe on a famous boat, the *Navemar*. The story of this journey, well known in its time, deserves to be retold.

* * *

My mother spent her early years in Switzerland. Her father was a rabbi there. But by 1941, things were getting so bad that her parents realized they had to go to America. Her father had two brothers in Brooklyn who had come a few years earlier. They were able to get visas because they were able to document rabbinical job offers. My mother's father was also able to document a rabbinical job offer. (A synagogue would tell the U.S. government that it needed several rabbis!) My grandfather's sisters did not have this option. One was stuck in England with its bombings for the duration of the war.

My mother's parents were able to buy tickets for a voyage from Spain to the U.S. First they traveled to Barcelona, and then Madrid. Finally they arrived at the nearby seaport town. In her first book *Justice is Blonde*,[85] my mother tells the story as she recalls it at age 13:

"To our great disappointment, no ship was in sight. It was then

---

85. Later, she authored a second book: *Life Can Be Fragile, Handle With Prayer*

we learned that the real meaning of *'manana'* was not 'tomorrow,' but more closely, 'someday.' The tomorrows turned into several months.... [In the interim, HIAS put them and the other passengers in a hotel.]"

"Finally, the long awaited vessel arrived, a freighter called the 'Navemar.' We had paid $500 apiece, a fortune in those days, for accommodations that proved to be nonexistent. With over a thousand people clamoring to get on board, those in charge had decided to let their greed override their compassion."

"[The owners] had gutted the inside of the ship, cramming it with bunk-beds – 500 of them in one room for the male passengers and 500 in another for the women. Health conditions were terrible. There was hardly any water, and it was impossible to wash. Because of the poor refrigeration, food spoilage caused illness and even death."

"After a couple of days, we reached Lisbon. My father and several other observant Jews got off and bought fruit, fish, vegetables and some pots and pans. Now, at least, we had our own little kitchen onboard, one that was comparatively clean and safe."

"Then trouble struck our family. My poor father contracted typhoid fever. Despite his severe illness, he remained in the same room with the rest of the men. A doctor who admired my father took care of him as best as he could, given the shortage of medical supplies."

"Many passengers slept on the decks or in lifeboats in order to avoid the crowded quarters below. There was a good deal of illness, and our numbers dwindled every night, as the bodies of those who died were thrown overboard."

"One day, after more than three weeks, the word went reverberating around the freighter: 'We're in America!' Everybody rushed on deck and there she was: the Statue of Liberty!"

"My father would not see this vision with us because he had been taken off the ship and hospitalized when we had docked in Cuba. My mother now arrived in a new land with her three little ones, and her ailing father-in-law, not knowing when and if she'd ever see her husband again."

(2019). The first is mostly a humorous biography. The second is a combination of *divrei Torah* and humor.

"Word about the Navemar had preceded our arrival: 'Hell Ship Arrives!,' the headlines screamed. Not only was there a swarm of reporters around...there was a good many lawyers as well. It seems the bar had heard: a) how much we had paid for our fare, and b) how badly we had been mistreated.... [The lawyers did help us] recover most of our passage money."

"We arrived on Friday towards evening..., close to the onset of the Sabbath.... Luckily a taxi came by and quickly got us to the Boro Park, Brooklyn address where our relatives had settled.... Not one but hundreds of trees grew in Brooklyn.... To me, it seemed like paradise...."

"Our first day in America brought a wonderful surprise. Not only had our family found and rented an apartment for us in Boro Park, they had also completely decorated it and even stocked it with food. It was a fine start for the new life that we faced in our new land."

A few months later, her father, Rabbi Benzion Blech was healthy enough to leave Cuba and join the family.

* * *

I found more about the *Navemar* online:

- This was a freighter ship equipped to carry 28 passengers, but on this voyage carried 1120.
- Most of the passengers slept in filthy cargo areas which had previously carried coal.
- When the ship arrived in Cuba in 1941, "everyone seemed to be fighting everyone else for the privilege of living. The relationships seemed more animalistic than human."
- "It was a nightmare spectacle. Hollywood could have used it for a setting in a new production of Dante's inferno. Old men and women gasping for breath in the insufferable heat, lying motionless on their bunks, while children tossed and cried. Everyone hungry, everyone thirsty, everyone dirty.... The captains on the old slave ships saw that their human cargoes got better treatment than this, and over a half-million dollars in passage money was paid on this ship."

- "The overcrowding was so dangerous that the *Navemar* was labeled 'a flowing Gurs,' referring to the Gurs concentration camp in France.
- The ship was nicknamed the "Nevermore" by passengers.
- Also on the boat was Marc Chagall's daughter and her husband, with a large case of Chagall's work.[86]
- One lawyer named Saul Sperling handled the cases of 251 of the 578 passengers who sued for refunds, damages and injuries.
- After her refugee voyage, the *Navemar* returned to general commerce. On January 23, 1942 an Italian submarine torpedoed her and sank her in the Strait of Gibraltar.

* * *

When my mother came to this country in 1941, she did not know a word of English. But she learned it by going to the movies and eventually excelled in school. After she got married in 1952, my father, who was already a lawyer for a few years, convinced her to go to law school. There were very few women lawyers in those days. Some judges refused to even speak to her because she was a woman! She eventually changed her first name from "Leah" to "Lee" so that at least when she signed letters, people would think it was a male attorney and be more afraid! After practicing law for 20 years, she was appointed to be a Judge in the Workers' Compensation Court in 1975 by Governor Hugh Carey, and she served in this position for many years.

* * *

His mother, presently 93, is still young at heart and tells people she is only "three times 30." At age 91, she won a stand-up comedy contest at a nightclub in Manhattan!

14. Golda Meir: The Early Years

We have a book in our shul library: *My Life* (1976), an autobiography by Golda Meir. I thought it would be interesting to summarize the

---

86. Chagall himself had left Europe on a boat a few months earlier. He returned to France after the war.

early years of her life, based on this book. As we all know, she served as Israel's Prime Minister from 1969 to 1974.

She was born as Golda Mabovitch in 1898. She lived the first few years of her life in Kiev. Her father was a skilled carpenter and cabinetmaker. Because of his skills, he was given permission to live in Kiev, outside the Pale of Settlement where most Jews resided.

Her main memory of Kiev was of a pogrom that was coming, which she understood to mean that horrible things would be done to her family. All her father could do to attempt to protect the family was barricade the entrance to their home with boards of wood. The pogrom never materialized, but Golda always remembered how scared she was. Addressing an Israel bonds conference in 1959, she admitted: "If there is any logical explanation necessary for the direction which my life has taken, maybe this is the explanation – the desire and determination to save Jewish children, four or five years old, from a similar scene and from a similar experience."

Despite being qualified to live outside the Pale, her parents were still very poor. Eventually, her father decided that he would go to America for a few years and make money and then return to Russia. Golda's mother took her 3 children: Sheyna, Golda and Zipporah to Pinsk where her parents were, to live for a few years and wait for her husband to return. (Between the births of Sheyna and Golda, five boys were born who died in infancy!)

She writes that the *shtetl* "reconstructed in novels and films... that gay, heartwarming, charming *shtetl* on whose roofs fiddlers eternally play sentimental music, has almost nothing to do with anything I remember, with the poverty-stricken, wretched little communities in which Jews eked out a living...."[87]

When they arrived in Pinsk, her sister Sheyna was 14 years old (nine years older than Golda). Sheyna was a dedicated member of the Socialist-Zionist movement, and thus doubly dangerous to the police. As Golda explains, "not only were she and her friends 'conspiring' to overthrow the all-powerful czar, but they also proclaimed their dream of bringing into existence a Jewish socialist state in Palestine."[88] Golda remembers hearing the screams of young men

---

87. P. 19.
88. P. 22.

and women being brutally beaten in the police station nearby. Golda's mother begged Sheyna to have nothing to do with the Socialist and Zionist movements. But Sheyna was stubborn. On Saturday mornings, Sheyna would have meetings in the house with all her Socialist-Zionist friends. Little Golda would listen to Sheyna and her friends and try to make out what they were so excited about. Sheyna's group also often met in the home of her friend Chaya Weizmann, sister of Chaim.

The first time Golda heard about Theodor Herzl was in 1904 when someone said that Herzl died. Sheyna decided to wear only black clothes in mourning for Herzl from that afternoon in the summer of 1904 and thereafter. (This did not end until they reached Milwaukee 2 years later.)

Golda recalls that when she and Sheyna would get into a fight, Golda would sometimes (jokingly) threaten to tell the local policeman in the neighborhood about all of Sheyna's political activities!

Eventually Golda's mother could not take the tension anymore, fearing Sheyna's arrest and more pogroms. She wrote to Golda's father and said that they all needed to join him in America. By now, he had moved to Milwaukee at the urging of the Hebrew Immigrant Aid Society. (They were trying to disperse immigrant Jews around the country.) She wrote to Golda's father (in Yiddish): "It doesn't matter if you've saved enough money or not. Believe me, we must come. Now!"

Golda writes: "The preparations for our journey were long and complicated. It was not a simple matter then for a woman and three girls, two of them still very small, to travel all the way from Pinsk to Milwaukee.... And perhaps if we had known that throughout Europe thousands of families like ours were on the move, headed toward what they, too, firmly believed would be...a better life in the New World, we would have been less frightened. But we knew nothing about the many women and children who were traveling then under similar conditions...and we were very scared."[89]

When the family had to cross the border into Galicia, they had to pretend to be others, memorizing false names. (Her father did not have enough money for official government exit permits for his family. He only had enough for fake passports.) Their ship that crossed the

---

89. PP. 27-28.

Atlantic was packed with immigrants from Russia – pale, exhausted and just as scared as her family was. She spent the nights on sheetless bunks and most of the days standing in line for food that was ladled out as though it was being given to cattle. Their ship took them to Quebec. From there, they had to take a train to Milwaukee.

When they finally saw their father, he was beardless and looked like a stranger. The first thing he did was take them on a shopping trip for new clothes. Sheyna refused to wear the new clothes he bought but Golda was delighted by her pretty new clothes.

Golda's mother opened a grocery store. But eight-year-old Golda had to help out in the store and this made her late for school almost every day. (17-year-old Sheyna, on the other hand, generally refused to help out in the store. Her socialist principles, she declared, made it impossible: "I did not come to America to turn into a shopkeeper, a social parasite.")

Golda loved her elementary school in Milwaukee. When she graduated, she was the valedictorian. (Today, the school is called "Golda Meir School."[90])

Around this time, her older sister Sheyna developed tuberculosis and had to go to the "Jewish Hospital for Consumptives" in Denver. Shamai, her boyfriend from Russia, came to America and made his way to Denver, and the two ended up getting married. (As to Golda's younger sister Zipporah, she was renamed "Clara" by her school principal.)

After Golda graduated from elementary school, she planned to go to high school and become a teacher. But her mother felt that she should now begin working in the store full time and start thinking about getting married. Her mother also reminded Golda that getting married was forbidden to women teachers by Wisconsin state law.[91]

Golda began her first term in high school in Milwaukee in the

---

90. When she was Prime Minister, she came back for a visit. She writes (p. 34) that the school "welcomed me as though I were a queen.... [T]hey serenaded me with Yiddish and Hebrew songs.... Each one of the classrooms had been beautifully decorated with posters about Israel and signs reading SHALOM (one of the children thought it was my family name)...."

91. I believe this law, exceedingly strange to us now, was the law in several other states as well!

autumn of 1912. But the fighting with her parents about this choice continued. Also, her mother was attempting to marry her to someone who was twice her age. Golda wrote all of her difficulties to Sheyna, and Sheyna and her husband suddenly invited Golda to come to Denver to live with them and continue school there.

This sounded good, but how was 15-year-old Golda going to leave Milwaukee? She realized that the only solution was not to tell her parents anything and simply leave. She did write them a brief note that they would read the next day. Before she went to sleep, she went over to Clara's bed. She felt very guilty about leaving her without even saying goodbye. She stroked her face and kissed her, but Clara slept through the farewell. Golda knew that she had deeply wounded her parents but leaving was essential for her growth. In the two years she spent in Denver, her father, unforgiving, wrote to her only once. But her mother did exchange letters with her. When she eventually returned from Denver, she no longer had to battle for the right to do as she wanted.

Sheyna and Shamai's home in Denver was a place where many Jewish intellectuals passed through. Golda learned much from the discussions that took place there, all influencing her more firmly to be a Socialist-Zionist. Also, one of the people she met there was Morris Meyerson. He was not Zionistic like Golda. He loved poetry, art and music. They began to date and slowly fell in love.

She then received a letter from her father saying that if she valued her mother's life, she should return home. She agreed with Morris to temporarily separate, and she went back home. This time it was understood that she would finish high school. She did and then in October of 1916 she registered at a teacher's training college. While she was away in Denver, her parents had changed and became more active in the Jewish community in Milwaukee. Many important Jewish and Zionist leaders now passed through their home. More and more, Zionism was beginning to fill her mind and her life.

Morris dreamed of a world in which everyone would live in peace. National self-determination held little attraction for him. But Morris was willing to agree to marry Golda and move to Palestine. His decision was influenced by the Balfour Declaration of Nov. 1917.

Golda writes that "although in years to come the ambiguous way in which it was worded was to be responsible for virtually endless bloodshed in the Middle East, in those days it was greeted by the Zionists as laying the foundation at last for a Jewish commonwealth in Palestine. It goes without saying that the announcement filled me with elation. The exile of the Jews had ended. Now the ingathering would really begin, and Morris and I together would be among the millions of Jews who would surely stream to Palestine. It was against the background of this historic event that we were married on December 24 1917..."[92]

America's involvement in World War I delayed their Aliyah for a few years, since all transatlantic passenger service was cancelled. But eventually in 1921, they were able to make their voyage to *Eretz Yisrael*.

The story of their voyage in 1921, their time in kibbutz Merḥavyah, how Golda was initially viewed as a "spoiled American" there, their leaving the kibbutz due to Morris' health difficulties, the difficulties Golda had with trying to be a mother to their children, a spouse to Morris, and an active member of the Zionist movement, all of this you will have to read about yourself.[93]

* * *

P.S. Sheyna moved to Palestine shortly after Golda and Morris, and Golda's parents moved in 1926. But what about the younger more Americanized sister, Clara? She became a sociologist and married another sociologist. They lived first in Ohio and then in Connecticut. When Golda met Clara's husband for the first time, he made it clear to her that he disapproved of all nationalism and regarded Zionism as an "extremely reactionary movement"! (Nevertheless, Clara did visit Golda in Israel many times over the years.)

P.P.S. My favorite story: When Golda was around 20, she wanted to give speeches in Milwaukee about Labor Zionism. But women were not allowed to speak in *shul*. She decided that the best way for her to reach the Jewish community was to set up a box outside of *shul* and speak there. When her father heard her plan, he was outraged. He

---

92. P. 65
93. Aside from her autobiography, many books have been written about her.

declared: "Moshe Mabovitch's daughter was not going to stand on a box on the street and make a spectacle of herself!" He threatened that he would publicly pull her home by her braid. Golda was stubborn and made her speech anyway. Yet her similarly stubborn father never dragged her away! It turns out that he was so carried away listening to her that he forgot his threat! Golda wrote that she considers that speech the best one she ever made!

* * *

Mitchell First's father used to say that he did so well in school that they named a floor after him: the "First" floor.

15. Yigael Yadin: Archaeologist, Military Man, Politician

I was always perplexed by references to Yigael Yadin. He had so many roles in the history of Israel but I never knew how to put them together. Finally, I read a short summary of his life in a book by archaeologist Jodi Magness, entitled *Masada: From Jewish Revolt to Modern Myth* (2019). This summary weaved all the details together, and I will try to present this summary briefly here (supplemented by some other sources).

Yadin was born in Jerusalem in 1917 with the name Yigael Sukenik. His father Eleazar was an archaeologist. Yigael became a student of archaeology, but also joined the Haganah in 1933.

In 1939, he became the personal aide to Yaacov "Dan" Dostrovsky, the Haganah's chief of staff. Because the Haganah was outlawed by the British, its members used code names. Sukenik chose the name "Yadin" because he liked the allusion at Gen. 49:16: *Dan yadin ammo*.

In 1945, Sukenik resigned from the Haganah and returned to his studies. But just before Israel declared its independence, Ben-Gurion recalled him to the military. He was head of Military Operations during the 1947–49 War, making many of the decisions that led to Israel's victory.

On Nov. 29, 1947, just hours before the U.N. vote, with war about to break out, his father risked his life and traveled to Bethlehem to negotiate a deal for the first three Dead Sea Scrolls. Of course Yigael was torn. As an archaeologist, he knew the importance of these documents. But as a son and as head of Military Operations for the Haganah, Yigael told his father that it was too risky for him to travel to Bethlehem at this tense time. His father ignored him, and was able to obtain these scrolls.[94]

In 1949, Ben-Gurion appointed Yigael chief of staff of the IDF (= the successor to the Haganah). Around this time, Ben-Gurion required high government officials to adopt Hebrew names. From that point on, Yigael Sukenik became Yigael Yadin, adopting his previous code name.

Yadin resigned his military position in 1952 and resumed his academic career, doing his PhD on the War Scroll from Qumran. In 1955, he received his PhD and was appointed lecturer in archaeology at Hebrew University. He received the Israel Prize in Jewish Studies in 1956 for his PhD study. In 1955, he undertook the first of four seasons of excavations at Ḥazor. In 1970, he became the head of the university's Institute of Archaeology.

The Israel Exploration Society mounted a campaign in the early 1960's to explore caves in canyons along the southwest shore of the Dead Sea. Yadin was assigned to the Nahal Ḥever cave and did his work there in 1960–61. It turned out to yield spectacular finds. As Magness explains: He "excavated caves occupied by Jewish refugees from Ein Gedi at the time of the Bar-Kokhba revolt (132–135 CE). The caves had been discovered by Roman troops, and the besieged refugees, trapped and unable to escape, starved to death. Their physical remains and personal belongings including documents remained inside the caves until their discovery by Yadin. Among the documents are letters written by the leader of the revolt himself...."[95]

Yadin's crowning archaeological achievement was the excavations at Masada, which he directed from 1963–65. Thousands of volunteers from Israel and around the world participated in the excavations

---

94. In my last book, I have told this story and also addressed Yadin's own role in obtaining the next four Dead Sea Scrolls. See *Links to Our Legacy* (2021), pp. 198–201.
95. Magness, p. 189. I have written about these letters in *Links to Our Legacy*, pp. 142–48.

in two-week rotations. One year after the excavations ended, Yadin published a popular book on Masada, which became a best seller.[96]

Within a year of the publication of this book, he was recalled to public service as tensions escalated with Israel's Arab neighbors. Shortly before June 1967, he accepted an appointment as Prime Minister Eshkol's special advisor on security affairs. He played a central role in planning a military offensive which led to Israel's stunning victory. He also ensured that Israeli forces secured the Rockefeller Museum in East Jerusalem, where most of the Dead Sea Scrolls were stored. On Yadin's initiative, a special museum in Jerusalem, *Heikhal Ha-Sefer*, was built for the Scrolls.

After the war ended, Yadin returned to academic life, teaching and working on the publication of the Dead Sea text known as the "Temple Scroll." His position as the foremost archaeologist in Israel was enshrined in James Michener's 1965 novel, *The Source*. The pipe-smoking Israeli archaeologist, Ilan Eliav, was modeled after Yadin.

One of the many books he published was *Tefillin from Qumran* (1969).

After the 1973 Yom Kippur War, he returned to public service as a member of the commission charged with investigating the Israeli government's failure to anticipate the war's outbreak. The report issued by the commission led to the resignation of Prime Minister Golda Meir.

In 1974, he returned to academic life. But in 1976, he returned to public life and was the head of a new political party called *Dosh*, an acronym for the "Democratic Movement for Change." This party advertised itself as an alternative to the long dominant Labor Zionist party. The party won 15 seats, but this came at the expense of the Labor party, and enabled Menachem Begin's Likud party to obtain the largest number of seats and form a coalition without Labor or Dosh. Eventually, Dosh ended up joining Begin's government. Yadin was appointed deputy Prime Minister, a position he served in until 1981. He spent his final years engaged in archaeology and academic life. He died in 1984.

Magness was his student between the years 1974–76 and tells

---

96. The book has been translated into many languages.

the following story from July 1976. She took a course with him that spanned 2 years: "Introduction to the Archaeology of the Land of Israel." The entire grade for the course was based on the final exam. She remembers Yadin as charismatic but intimidating. He was always "Professor Yadin," unlike the other faculty members with whom the students were on a first name basis. All the students had been studying frantically for the final exam. But then they heard the news about the Entebbe rescue. As a result, the whole country was walking around with big grins on their faces, and the students entering the classroom for their final exam were as well. She writes: "It was then that Yadin entered the room and strode (as always) to the front. Sternly he asked, 'What happened? Why are you all smiling?' – and then he broke into a big grin himself. It is the only time I remember seeing Yadin smile like that."[97]

P.S. Wikipedia has the following story: He was sometimes forced to deal with thefts of important artifacts, occasionally by prominent figures. In one instance, the thefts were attributed by others to Moshe Dayan. Yadin remarked: "I know who did it, and I am not going to say who it is, but if I catch him, I'll poke out his other eye, too!"

* * *

Like Yadin, Mitchell First leads a multifaceted life, alternating between law and Jewish scholarship. (But without any military achievements.)

16. The Heroism of Kibbutz *Yad-Mordechai*

There is a kibbutz just north of the Gaza strip called *Yad-Mordechai*. It fought valiantly during the War of Independence and its tenacious fighting for six days was able to significantly delay the Egyptian invasion. The kibbutz was on the main road between Cairo and Tel Aviv. If not for that delay, the Egyptian army could have quickly reached Tel Aviv and the other important cities in the north.

In 1965, Margaret Larkin wrote a book about the kibbutz. The book

---

97. P. 191.

is titled: *The Six Days of Yad-Mordechai.* I am going to summarize it here.

Two groups of pioneers from Poland (members of Hashomer Hatzair) came together to found this kibbutz in 1936. It was originally in an area near Netanya. They called it *Mitzpeh Ha-Yam,* because by looking out to the sea, they could watch for the coming of the comrades they had left behind.

After several years the membership grew. They were 140 adults and 43 children, and the few acres of land they had were not enough to support them. With the help of the Jewish National Fund, they found a new site five miles north of the Arab town of Gaza. Here there would be 400 acres of land and both grain and oranges could be grown. As Larkin writes (p. 23): "Rarely did the Jews move onto fertile land in Palestine. Nearly always they had to reclaim the soil from years or centuries of neglect. In some places they drained the malarial swamps; here, sand would be the enemy." They moved to this new site in December 1943.

The new name for the kibbutz would be *Yad-Mordechai.* It was named for Mordechai Anielewicz, the leader of the Warsaw ghetto uprising. He fell in a battle in May 1943. The meaning of the name: "A Memorial to Mordechai."[98]

A few years later came the Nov. 1947 partition plan. As Larkin writes (p. 51): "The foundation of a Jewish State had been their dream and hope since their youth. For this they had severed their ties with their families and with their native land. For this they had remade themselves, the sons and daughters of shopkeepers, into farmers. With their own sweat and energy they had extracted wealth from ruined soil; with high idealism they had created a unique way of life. And now that their efforts were about to be crowned by the establishment of their own state, it seemed that they were not to be a part of it. The new borders, as defined by a Commission of the United Nations, put Yad Mordechai in the Arab state."

When independence was declared in May, they rejoiced, but with

---

98. I have discussed the different suggestions of how the word יד came to mean "memorial" in *Links to Our Legacy,* pp. 37–40.

sorrow. Many of the members thought of Moses: he saw the Promised Land from afar, but after all his years in the desert, he could not enter it.

The "good news" was that since the Arab leaders announced that they would not respect the U.N. decision anyway, the exact partition plan line did not matter much. The Arabs were going to fight all the Jewish settlements. Everyone understood that the settlements must provide centers of resistance, and must hold out until final borders or armistice lines were established.

Interestingly, there was a widespread belief at the time that the kibbutz would not have to face the Egyptian army. Egypt's opposition to the invasion plans of the other Arab countries was known. It was assumed that the kibbutz would only have to hold out against Arab bands of irregulars. In a meeting of the Arab League on April 30th, the Egyptians had refused to commit themselves to the use of their army. Their Minister of Defense had stated: "We shall allow our men and officers to volunteer for service in Palestine and we shall give them weapons but no more." (The reality was that their army was not prepared for war.)

But a few days later his government changed its mind. Larkin writes (p. 83): "The fears of the politicians that a triumphant Trans-Jordan, engorged with the lands of Palestine, would emerge as the leading power in the Middle East had proved stronger than caution." Egypt was fighting in Palestine mainly to prevent King Abdullah from taking more than his share.

Thereafter, one of the members of the kibbutz was able to get into Gaza while pretending he was a Red Cross driver. He spoke to an Egyptian major. The major told him that the next day there would be an attack on Yad Mordechai.

What to do next? Who to evacuate? The kibbutz had not been thinking this way, as they had been assuming that there would be no invasion of the Egyptian army. "Nothing lowers the spirit of a fighter so much as when he sees first steps in evacuation," a Palmach commander once wrote. The kibbutz hastily decided to evacuate the children, the nursing mothers, and the few other women who were more sensitive than most. Some made a point of giving their children their photograph albums (in case the worst happened). The children were evacuated to a nearby settlement ten miles to the east.

On May 19, the Egyptian planes came. Larkin writes that within fifteen minutes they had destroyed much of what had taken the settlers years to build.

When the battle began, the defenders numbered only 113 men and boys, only slightly over half had guns. They were fighting an Egyptian army of about 2000. What happens during the fighting? The phone lines are cut, the kibbutz members cannot communicate with one another. They have to risk their lives and run amidst gunfire to send messages to one another, as they are scattered in different (barely) fortified places in the kibbutz. They have very little ammunition. (Sometimes they obtain new ammunition by taking it from dead Egyptian soldiers.) They did not have enough mines. Instead they put up signs to scare the Egyptian invaders: "Warning-Mines."

They hoped that the Haganah, recognizing the strategic importance of the kibbutz, would send reinforcements and strike or bomb the Egyptian army from the outside. But the Haganah was too overwhelmed. There were too many other isolated points that needed help.

The end result was that after a few days, after suffering 23 dead and 40 wounded, the defenders had to retreat and abandon the kibbutz. During the following days, they tried to convince the Haganah that with more men they could recapture the kibbutz. But the Haganah had other priorities at the time.

But a few months later, on Nov. 5, Israel was finally able to recapture the kibbutz.

In that initial time in May, the Egyptian army had expected to take the kibbutz within a few hours. Instead, they lost their momentum and had to change their battle plans. The Haganah benefited greatly because of the delay and were able to fortify other areas.

Today, there is a memorial statue to Anielewicz next to the destroyed water tower at the kibbutz. He is depicted standing heroically and holding a grenade. There is also a Holocaust museum at the kibbutz: "From Holocaust to Revival Museum." The kibbutz is known for producing honey and olive oil, and supplies about 50% of all the honey consumed in Israel.

I have left out so many details and I highly recommend that everyone read this book.

* * *

Mitchell First is an attorney and Jewish history scholar. (He feels unable to make any biographical jokes related to this war. Please excuse him.)

17. James McDonald: The First U.S. Ambassador to Israel (1948–1951)

It is well-known that very shortly (11 minutes!) after the Jewish state was declared on May 14, 1948, President Truman announced that the U.S. recognized it.

But what happened after that? When was a U.S. (or any country's) ambassador appointed to it? When did full legal recognition come by the U.S.? What were the major issues faced by the State of Israel in that early time?

I came across a book on these topics. It is by James McDonald, who was appointed by Truman on June 22, 1948, to be the first U.S. Ambassador to Israel, serving in this capacity until 1951. The book's title: *My Mission in Israel*. I would like to share some of what I learned.

1. McDonald writes at the beginning of the book that it is going to be a personal report about his experiences as ambassador and that he will rely a lot on his diaries. "I have refrained from retelling the stories of Israel's heroic defense, its improvisation of Army, Navy and Air Force, the miracles of transforming deserts into orchards, the spectacular change of the physical face of the land...." It is evident that he is someone who was in awe of what the Jewish people had accomplished.

2. Here is the background to McDonald and his appointment. McDonald had prior positions in international affairs and had been involved with America's efforts in Palestine for many years. But he had not talked to Truman since the summer of 1946. He had returned to New York in May 1948 after trips to California and South Africa. He and his wife were weary of traveling and were looking forward to some extended quiet time at home. He was 61 at the time. He wanted to write his memoirs and improve his golf game (!).

At 4 p.m. on June 22, Clark Clifford, Counsel to the President, telephoned him out of the blue and offered him this appointment. McDonald responded that he was not expecting this and needed time to think about it. He added that he had "no independent income" to support himself with. One hour later Clifford called again telling him that Truman had made up his mind and wanted to make the announcement the same evening. Clifford assured him that the position would be of the highest rank with appropriate compensation. McDonald reluctantly accepted. The appointment was quickly relayed to someone from the Israeli government and they indicated they would accept him. (Foreign governments always have to be notified in advance in case they object to the choice.) The official announcement of the appointment was made less than three hours after Clifford first telephoned McDonald. McDonald writes: "My family's first intimation of the news came to them from the seven o'clock radio broadcast."

3. In this early stage after Israel's declaration of May 1948, there was only one other country that had an ambassador to it. This was Russia. Russia's representative arrived in Tel Aviv three days before McDonald arrived in August. (Britain, for example, did not recognize Israel until May 1949. In the early period, British officials would write to the "Jewish Authorities," instead of to the "State of Israel" and their letters would be returned unopened!)

4. It was important to Truman to have his own man as the ambassador to Israel, rather than a State Department appointee because of what happened three months earlier. In this famous episode in March 1948, the U.S. Ambassador to the U.N. (without consulting Truman, but with the backing of the State Dept.) announced that the U.S. no longer supported the partition plan of November 1947. This had embarrassed Truman greatly.

5. When McDonald had his first meeting with an official from the State Department regarding his salary, he reported Clifford's promise that the position would be with the highest salary, a class I mission. The State Department official was shocked. The State Department had planned a much lower salary level, a class IV level.

They compromised on class II. (I never realized that there were different levels of missions to foreign countries!)

6. An issue that arose was when the U.S. would give Israel full recognition (de jure recognition) as opposed to mere de facto recognition. Traditionally, for de jure recognition, there needed to be a stable government, a willingness to honor international obligations, and effective control of a recognized territory. The initial Provisional Government of the State of Israel had to prove that it was not merely a *junta*. McDonald understood that there was a disagreement between Truman and the State Department. Truman wanted to give full recognition as soon as possible. But the State Department had doubts about the stability and representativeness of the Provisional Government. (Full recognition eventually came on Jan. 31, 1949, after the first Israeli election.)

7. In July 1948, in order to resolve the continued fighting, U.N. Mediator Count Bernadotte came up with a plan for the Jewish State to give up part of the Negev, even though the Negev had been awarded to the Jewish State in the partition plan. Bernadotte also proposed that the entire city of Jerusalem be placed under the rule of King Abdullah of Jordan (instead of being an international city for ten years). In response, on July 26, the government of Israel announced that "New Jerusalem" was declared Israel-occupied territory, to be under a Jewish military governor. McDonald wrote that "it seemed abundantly clear that my post, if a difficult one, would certainly be an exciting one." (Bernadotte was later assassinated in September 1948 by the Stern gang.)

8. In the summer of 1948, the elderly Chaim Weizmann was still in Switzerland. He had been made President but was still not in the country. In August, on his way to Israel, McDonald went to visit him. After discussing all the current events, Weizmann told McDonald that he was not able to be in touch with the government in Israel and was unclear about the future for him there. As far as he knew, no establishment had been set up for him. Embarrassingly, he had to ask McDonald to remind the officials of the government of Israel to write to him! (Later, McDonald met with Golda Meir.

She apologized for not writing to Weizmann but she said that everyone knew that Weizmann would find Israel unbearably hot in the summer and would not want to arrive until September.) McDonald also discussed the manner of Weizmann's eventual trip to Israel, as he could not arrive in a manner unbefitting a President.

9. McDonald learned that as an ambassador it was important not to bother the busy President with too many queries. "An envoy who wrote too often or at too great length… eventually wore out his welcome and lost whatever influence he might have had."

10. McDonald wrote that he had met Hitler. "I had become convinced that the battle against the Jew was the first skirmish in a war on Christianity, on all religion, indeed on all humanity."

There is so much more in this book. I have only touched on a small portion of the interesting material!

* * *

Mitchell First has no plans for government public service. His public service is writing weekly columns.

18. Insights into Jewish Names and Modern Israel

I base most of this essay on an article by Aaron Demsky, "The Hebraization of Names in Modern Israel," *Brown Journal of World Affairs* 25 (2018).[99]

1. When did Jews begin to have last names (= surnames)? Demsky explains: "The modern history of Jewish surnames begins with the tolerant policies of the Austro-Hungarian Emperor Joseph II, who in 1787 ordered the Jewish masses to take family names. Other eastern European sovereignties followed: the Polish Kingdom in 1797, the Russian Empire in 1804 and 1835, and, finally, the German

---

99. Demsky was a professor of Biblical History at Bar-Ilan University for several decades. He is also the founder and director of *The Project for the Study of Jewish Names*.

principalities. By the early nineteenth century, Jews throughout Europe had adopted family names. This was necessary for imperial states to have an official means of registering their Jewish minority... [T]his development was a positive step toward their recognition as citizens."

There were a variety of categories of European Jewish surnames. They might be based on one's father's name, mother's name, name of a place, physical trait, personality trait, occupation, heritage, and lineage. There were also artificial names, based on some thirty basic words like "gold." Several names are widely viewed as having an acrostical basis, e.g., Katz (*kohen tzedek*) for someone with Priestly lineage, and Segal (*segan le-kehunah* = aid to the priest) for someone with Levitical lineage.[100] A very creative priestly acrostical name is אזולי: *ishah zonah va-ḥalelah lo yikaḥu* (Lev. 21:7).

2. An early figure who Hebraized his European surname was Eliezer Ben-Yehuda. He arrived in Eretz Yisrael at age twenty-four in 1882, and was a major force in the renewal of the Hebrew language. He and his wife vowed that they would speak only Hebrew once they arrived.

This agreement initially bound his wife to silence, as she knew no Hebrew! The family would not hire a servant, despite the wife's ailments, and their newborn son was not allowed to have playmates for several years, so his Hebrew would be "pure." It took a long time before the child began to say any words. The story is also told that, years later, when Eliezer's mother finally came to visit from Lithuania, having not seen him in many years, he refused to speak to her in a language that she could understand![101]

When he arrived from Lithuania in 1882, he abandoned his European name "Perelman," and registered himself as בן־יהודה. (He had used this name before in his literary activities.) His original

---

100. The word סגן appears many times in the later books of *Nakh* (but never in the Torah). It derives from Akkadian. In early rabbinic Hebrew, it usually refers to an aid and deputy to the high priest.
101. He is said to have broken his vow only one time. He spoke French with Baron Edmond de Rothschild on one of the latter's visits to *Eretz Yisrael*.

name meant "Perel's husband." His father's name was Yehudah Lieb. Perhaps his new name was just a reflection of his father's name. But on a deeper level, the name יהודה symbolized the Jewish people and was an appropriate choice for one with a vision of leading a national movement.[102]

One of the first modern words that Ben-Yehuda created was מלון (= dictionary), from the older Hebrew word, מלה.

3. David Gruen arrived in *Eretz Yisrael* in 1906. He chose the name "Ben-Gurion." *Gur* is a young animal in *Tanakh*, usually a lion. Among Ben-Gurion's associates, Shkolnik became "Eshkol," and Shertok became "Sharet."

Shimon Persky took the name "Peres." This is the name of a Biblically forbidden bird. It only appears twice in *Tanakh*. Perhaps it comes from the "break" meaning of this root. It is often identified with the ossifrage.[103] In his youth in Israel, Peres had seen a huge bird called by this name and had been impressed by it.

4. The second President of Israel was Yitzḥak Ben-Zvi. His prior name was "Shimshelevitch." His wife, Golda Lishinsky, chose the new name "Rachel Yannait." She based her last name on the Hasmonean king Alexander Yannai (c. 100 BCE, great-grandson of Mattathias). With that added "-it" ending, she expressed her independence and gave the name a feminine touch.

In 1933, Ben-Zvi wrote an article: "Remove the Foreign Names From Among You." He argued that the foreign surnames testified that the Jews were still strangers in their own land, and called upon the leaders of the Zionist movement to abandon these names. He renewed his call after the Jewish State was created. He believed that Hebrew names would help bind the various communities. To promote the policy, guidebooks on how to Hebraize one's name were published.

---

102. Demsky thinks that Ben-Yehuda was probably aware of the passage at *Eruvin* 53b which states that בני יהודה were meticulous in their language (as opposed to those living in the *Galil*).
103. In Latin, this means "bone breaker."

5. In 1944, an official of the Jewish Agency proposed a detailed plan for the Agency to Hebraize the names of large sections of the Jewish population. For example, he proposed that all with the name "Goldberg" would become "Harpaz." His plan never went into effect. (This official had changed his own name to נמצא־בי. It had originally been "Netsabitski"!)

   On an individual basis, changing one's surname is not as easy as it sounds. Siblings might disagree with your new choice or feel strongly about keeping the family name.

6. In June 1948, the provisional government declared: "The citizens of a Hebrew state cannot continue to appear in personal and public life with foreign names.... A radical change is required." Accordingly, officials, health workers, teachers and youth leaders set about Hebraizing the names of young arrivals, often without their approval and without even attempting a connection. For example, Fairuz, Jean, and Sa'id all might become "Yitzḥak."

7. In the mid 1950's when Ben-Gurion became prime minister and minister of defense, he instituted a requirement to Hebraize one's surname for those representing the young state overseas in the diplomatic corps (and beauty pageants!) and for officers serving in the military. (I believe these requirements no longer exist.) Golda Meyerson became "Meir" but refused to change her given name.

   One notable Israeli leader who did not change his surname was Menachem Begin. Ezer Weizman and Chaim Herzog resisted official pressure to change their names because of the importance of their relatives in the early history of Israel.

8. Many Holocaust survivors wanted to preserve their last names as they were the last remaining members of their families.

9. The most popular first name in Israel for years has been "Muhammad." This is because 20% of the population in Israel is Muslim and in Muslim tradition everyone is obligated to have at least one person in the household with this name.[104]

---

104. The name Muhammad is related to the Hebrew root חמד. It means "praiseworthy" in Arabic.

10. For Jewish Israelis, the ten most popular first names among newborn boys in a recent year were: Ariel, David, Lavie, Ori, Yosef, Eytan, Noam, Daniel, Itai and Judah. For girls: Tamar, Avigail, Yael, Adele, Noa, Sara, Shira, Noyah, Esther and Taliah.[105]

11. Finally, for those who are torn between past and future, a solution is to create a double last name. Examples are the Hebrew linguist Moshe Goshen-Gottstein, the Israeli general Amnon Lipkin-Shahak, and the Rabbis/educators Adin Even-Israel Steinsaltz and Aaron Rakeffet-Rothkoff.

* * *

Mitchell First will of course change his last name to *Rishon* if he makes Aliyah, but perhaps he will choose *Rishon Le-Tziyon*! (I thank Judy Heicklin for this suggestion!)

---

105. Demsky finds it helpful to divide these names into: traditional biblical names, renewed biblical names, and new names.

Hebrew Roots

1. בער: The Multiple Meanings of the Root בער

The puzzle of the root בער has been burning inside me for decades.

1. Six times in *Tanakh* we have a noun with the meaning: "cattle, domestic animal." (Admittedly, in these six occasions, there is a *yod* in the middle: בעיר.)
2. At Ex. 22:4, the root is used as a verb two times and seems to refer to an animal eating. The noun is found here as well. Here is the relevant part of the verse: "When an individual is יבער a field or vineyard, and lets בעירה loose,[1] and it is בער in the field of another..."
3. Many times in *Tanakh*, בער has a "burn" meaning.
4. It also many times has meanings like "destroy," "remove," and "eliminate." See, e.g., Deut. 26:13: *biarti ha-kodesh min ha-bayit* (tithes), and Deut. 21:21: *u-viarta ha-ra mi-kirbekha* (rebellious son).
5. Many times it has a meaning like "stupid, foolish." E.g., Psalm 92: *ish baar lo yeida*.

---

[1] The first part of this verse is awkward when read literally. The way to read this part of the verse is: "When an individual is יבער a field or vineyard, that is to say he lets בעירה loose and it is בער in the field of another..." See S.D. Luzzatto (edition of D. Klein with verse translation from the Italian), pp. 348–349. See similarly *Daat Mikra*. (But see also the different approach to verse 22:4 mentioned in the Targum cited below.)

Most agree that meaning 5 derives from meaning 1. (If so, "brute" might be a better translation than "stupid, foolish.") There are also those who take the opposite view: animals are called בעיר due to being stupid.

But what about all the other meanings? Can we relate them?

With regard to Ex. 22:4, Rashbam and many others see the meaning of the two verbs as animals eating. But since the "eat/feed" meaning is not clearly found elsewhere in *Tanakh*, many see the literal meaning of these verbs as "destroy." See, e.g., Hizzekuni, S.D. Luzzatto, and *Daat Mikra*.

If the meaning at 22:4 is "eat/feed," we can easily see a relation with the noun (= meaning 1). If the meaning here is "destroy," it is hard to view these domestic animals as "destroyers" (although many are willing to adopt this view: animals are destroyers of grass). Most likely, we have two unrelated meanings of בער in the verse: a noun for "animals" and two verbs with the meaning "destroy." The verse is merely using wordplay.[2] (At 22:5, we have further wordplay: the "burn" meaning![3])

Another issue in the root בער is the relationship of the "burn" meaning to the "destroy/remove/eliminate" meaning. Perhaps the "burn" meaning is a separate root entirely. Or perhaps the others are merely expansions from it. Or perhaps the verb fundamentally meant "destroy" and burning is just one type of destruction.

* * *

Let us see how some scholars have dealt with our root בער:

- The *Brown-Driver-Briggs* lexicon puts most of the meanings in the same category but states that the connection is "obscure."

---

2. A more common word for animal could have been used in this verse, but S.D. Luzzatto points out that wordplays help the masses remember the laws.
3. There is another way to look at the relationship between verse 22:4 and verse 22:5. In light of verse 22:5, perhaps all the בער roots in verse 22:4 should be interpreted as burn-related. This view is found in the Palestinian Targum known as Targum Neofiti 1. For an extended discussion of this very different view, see M. Shapiro, *Between the Yeshiva World and Modern Orthodoxy* (1999), pp. 164–68. I thank Ariel Zell for this reference.

- *Theological Dictionary of the Old Testament* includes the following comment: The words with these three letters "present a very confused picture with regard to both etymology and meaning."
- The lexicon of M. Z. Kaddari raises the possibility that "burn" and "remove" are each separate roots. (Also, that "eat/feed" is another separate root, related to the noun.)
- Solomon Mandelkern puts all the בער words in the same entry. He takes the position that the fundamental meaning of the root is "removal and cessation." The "burn" meaning is a type of removal. Animals remove/destroy grass.
- The Koehler-Baumgartner lexicon notes that there is a word in Arabic resembling בער that means "dung."[4] It suggests that this may have been one of the original meanings of the root and that animals are called בעיר due to the dung they produce.
- Ernest Klein does not seem to relate the noun meaning, "animal," to the other meanings.[5] As to the other meanings, he thinks that the "remove, destroy" meaning is an expansion from the original "burn" meaning.

I agree with Klein. I do not think that these kinds of animals should be viewed fundamentally as "destroyers," even of grass, and that we have to live with unrelated meanings in the case of this root.[6] As to his second position, I agree that "burn" is a very concrete meaning and would likely be an original meaning. The only remaining issue (a minor one) is whether the "destroy/eliminate/remove" meaning is a separate one, or as he suggested, an expansion.[7] (The Koehler-Baumgartner lexicon explicitly leaves this issue unresolved.)

* * *

---

4. Also, an Arabic cognate to בער means "camel." In inscriptions of Old South Arabic (from late Biblical times), this cognate means "beast," and especially "camel." See *TDOT*, vol. 2, p. 201.

5. I think there is a typographical error in the first column in the entry for בעיר (p. 79). "II" should be "III." (Klein's work is an amazingly useful one but once in a while there are typographical errors of this nature.)

6. Our Hebrew letter *ayin* is a merger of two different earlier Proto-Semitic letters. This could help explain what happened here.

7. Although we have a verb in English "consume" which would apply to all

Let us look at some traditional commentaries:

- Rashi on Ex. 22:4 takes the position that all the בער words in this verse are related and have a fundamental meaning related to בהמה. But Rashi does not mention the "burn" meaning of the same root (which is found twice in the next verse!)[8]
- Radak takes the same position that Mandelkern later expressed.[9]
- Most creative is Rav S.R. Hirsch (comm. to Gen. 45:17 and 39:9). He views the fundamental meaning of the root as "fire" and suggests that with this all can be explained. He views a Divine fire of life as burning in humans and animals. This motivates all our activities. But, unlike humans, animals do not have the ability to restrain this fire. They are called בעיר because they operate purely on this fire instinct. Every damage done by an animal is based on it following its primal fire instinct. (R. Hirsch would presumably view the "destroy/eliminate/remove" meanings as expansions from the "burn" meaning, although that is not stated here.)

* * *

The multiple meanings of בער present difficulties in certain verses.

For example, at Ezek. 21:36, the prophet is describing a future punishment of Ammon: "I will deliver you into the hands of *anashim bo'arim*, skillful in destroying." Many give *bo'arim* the "stupid men" meaning here. For example, Rashi does this and both Mandelkern and Even-Shoshan list this בער word with the other entries with the meaning "stupid." But another view is that the reference is to men who make fires. See, e.g., *Metzudat Tzion* and *Metzudat David*. (The word אש is found earlier in the verse.) Finally, *bo'arim* can mean "destroyers," parallel to the last word in the verse, משחית.

Finally, another ambiguous verse is 1 Kings 14:10. The end of the

---

meanings including the "burn" meaning, this is too abstract a verb to be an original meaning of the Hebrew root.

8. A note in the ArtScroll edition of Rashi (p. 279) implies that Rashi believed that the two בער words with their fire meanings at verse 22:5 are not related to the בער words of verse 22:4. (In general, Rashi does try hard to relate words with the same root. He is a "meaning-minimalist." See my essay in *Links to Our Legacy*, pp. 107–110.)

9. See his *Sefer Ha-Shorashim*. See similarly Hizzekuni to Ex. 22:4.

verse uses the phrase: *ye-vaer ha-galal.* Is this phrase referring to the "removal" of dung? Or to the "burning" of dung? I will leave it to someone else to research this issue.[10]

* * *

On the subject of בער, Mitchell First is very proud to have written an article for *BAR* (= *Biblical Archaeology Review*) in 2012.

2. גדד: The Root גדד and the Prohibition of *Lo Titgodedu*

There is a root in Biblical Hebrew גדד that means "**cut.**" It often appears in the *hitpael* form where it means "cut oneself" (= self-mutilation).[11]

Biblical Hebrew also has a root אגד that has a "**join/group**" meaning. This root appears four times in *Tanakh*. See, e.g., 2 Samuel 2:25: *agudah eḥat.*

Almost certainly, there is no relationship between these two roots אגד and גדד with their opposite meanings. (But see below.)

Also, thirty-three times in *Tanakh* we have a noun *gedud* that refers to a military unit. Where does this noun come from? There are two ways to relate it to גדד = cut. In one view, it represents military men who invade the land of others. They cut it into sections and make inroads. In another view, it represents military men who were sectioned off from the rest of the Israelites.[12]

* * *

Most interesting is the discussion in the Talmud at *Yevamot* 13b regarding Deuteronomy 14:1. The verse reads: "You are the children of the Lord your God; *lo titgodedu* and you shall not make any baldness between your eyes for the dead."[13]

---

10. There is a good post on our root at balashon.com on Aug. 23, 2020.
11. The *hitpael* form appears one time in the Torah (Deut. 14:1) and a few more times in *Nakh*. The verb גדד also appears two times in the Aramaic part of *Tanakh*, in the book of Daniel. There it is not in the *hitpael*, and it refers to cutting a tree.
12. *BDB* mentions both views.
13. "Between your eyes" is an idiom for "on your head."

The plain sense of *lo titgodedu* is a prohibition on self-mutilation. The Talmud understands it as referring to self-mutilation in the context of grieving, but it is possible that it is a more general prohibition (see below). In any event, aside from this prohibition, the Talmud derives an additional prohibition from this verse: the Israelites are prohibited from dividing themselves into factions.[14] Without getting into the details, the conclusion of the passage at *Yevamot* 13b is that both prohibitions derive equally from this verse (and are derived from those two *tavs* in the word). This is a very odd claim, as the "factions" interpretation does not fit the context of the verse at all. Also, the passage in the Talmud here is giving two interpretations of this verse, but the interpretations do not have anything to do with one another.[15]

What does Rambam do with this *sugya*? In his *Sefer Ha-Mitzvot*, negative prohibition #45, he enumerates both prohibitions under this negative commandment but remarks that the second is *kemo derash*.[16] But later, in his *Mishneh Torah*, he does make it seem that both derive equally from the verse. See *Avodah Zarah* 12:13–14. (Interestingly, Rashi on Deut.14:1 only discusses the self-mutilation interpretation.)

Going back to the plain sense of verse 14:1, the word למת (*la-met*, "for the dead") at the end of the verse does not necessarily relate to the *lo titgodedu* prohibition. Therefore, the prohibition on self-mutilation can be a general one, not related to grieving. It is evident from the story at 1 Kings 18:28 that self-mutilation was practiced even outside of grieving contexts. As set forth in the Soncino commentary there: [Cutting oneself is] "a form of worship common to several cults with the purpose of exciting the pity of the gods, or to serve as a blood-bond between the devotee and his god." See also *Daat Mikra* on 14:1.

* * *

---

14. Rashi writes that the purpose of this prohibition is to avoid giving the impression that there is more than one Torah, while Rambam writes that the purpose is to prevent conflict.
15. See Maharal, *Gur Aryeh* commentary.
16. This is a Hebrew translation of what he wrote in Arabic.

There is one more interesting thing about the passage at *Yevamot* 13b. When the Talmud discusses the "factions" interpretation, it uses the following phrase, in the name of Reish Lakish: *lo taasu agudot agudot.* We mentioned above that גדד is a root that means "divide," while אגד is a root that means "join/group." When deriving a prohibition from *lo titgodidu,* we would have expected Reish Lakish to use a word from the root גדד! Why did he use the word *agudot*? Perhaps Reish Lakish believed that *agudot* was derived from the root גדד, and was just an Aramaic form of this word.[17] There may not even have been a Hebrew or Aramaic word that meant "factions" that was clearly derived from the root גדד in the time of Reish Lakish.

A related issue is how one should translate *lo taasu agudot agudot* in the statement of Reish Lakish. Is the proper translation: "Do not form groups [and] groups"? Or "Do not form factions [and] factions"? Most translations prefer the word "factions," implicitly connecting *agudot* to the root גדד. See, e.g., Jastrow, p. 11, and the ArtScroll edition of *Yevamot* 13b.

* * *

Finally, let us look at the blessing for Gad at Genesis 49:19: *Gad gedud yegudenu, ve-hu yagud akev.* How would you translate it? R. Aryeh Kaplan in *The Living Torah* translates: "Raiders shall raid Gad, but he will raid at their heel." R. Kaplan is translating all three of those words with a "raid" meaning, and has Gad as the object in the first phrase. But there are many other ways to translate this sentence. For example: 1) Raiders shall raid Gad but he will cut off their heel; 2) Gad shall go forward and attack, and he shall attack the [enemy's] heel, and 3) Good fortune will pursue Gad, and he will have good fortune in the end. This last interpretation is based on the "fortune" meaning of the letters גד.[18] For many other possible translations of the blessing to Gad, see *The Living Torah.*

* * *

---

17. It is also significant that *Sifrei* Deut. 96 on *lo titgodedu* cites to Amos 9:6 which uses the word *va-agudato.*
18. *Gad* seems to have been the name of an ancient deity in charge of man's fortune. See Isa. 65:11 and *Daat Mikra* there, *EJ* 7:249, and *Shabbat* 67b.

As an attorney, Mitchell First is a divisive force. But as a scholar, he tries to unite his readers around correct interpretations.[19]

3. הביט: Various Words for "Seeing" in *Tanakh*

Aside from that common verb ראה, there are many other verbs for seeing in *Tanakh*. I am going to focus on the word הביט. Thereafter, I will briefly discuss שקף and שגח.[20]

With regard to the words הביט, הבט and their variants, the underlying verb is נבט.[21] The *Tanakh* does give us one clue that this is the root. One time, out of the sixty-nine times that this verb appears in *Tanakh*, the initial *nun* is there. This is at Isaiah 5:30: נבט.

The Akkadian cognate to our root נבט means "to shine brightly."[22]

* * *

There are a few times where we have both הביט/הבט and ראה in the same phrase.[23] Sometimes, the former is first. Other times the latter is first.[24]

Two fundamental questions are raised by our root: 1) what is the distinction between הבט (in its various forms) and ראה? and 2) why is the former almost always in the *hifil* (= causative)?[25]

Here is an approach. When the הבט verb precedes the ראה verb

---

19. I would like to thank Rabbi Ezra Frazer for suggesting that I write about this root.
20. I am not discussing ציץ, שור, צופה and חזה.
21. The *ḥirik* under that ה tells us that a letter dropped here. If there were no dropped letter, there would be a *tzere* under the ה, as in the word הביא (*heivi*). I discussed the topic of missing *nuns* in *Roots and Rituals* (2018), pp. 176–80.
22. Tawil, p. 232. Tawil suggests that the Akkadian meaning is being used at Isa. 5:30 and Ps. 34:6. Our word is also found in Ugaritic, with the meaning "to shine forth, come into view." *KB*, p. 661. Tawil suggests the following semantic development: "shine forth > come into view > look at."
23. A similar expression in English is "look and see."
24. I am not concerned here with verses such as Num. 23:21, where the two verbs are found spaced far apart in different parts of the verse.
25. There are several verbs in *Tanakh* that mean "to hear." One is קשב. In contrast to a verb like שמע, this root, as a verb, is always in the *hifil*. Its meaning

in the same phrase, the import is often that the person must change his position to the area to be seen.²⁶ See, e.g., Psalms 142:5: *habbit yamin u-re'eh* (shift to the right)²⁷ and Isa. 63:15: *habbet mi-shamayim u-re'eh* (shift down).²⁸

If the context does not imply a change in position, a הבט that precedes a ראה implies concentration before the seeing.²⁹

When ראה precedes הבט, the import of the הבט is also one of concentration.³⁰

ראה is a verb that merely describes what the eyes see, but הבט (with or without a verb from the root ראה) seems to be similar to the English word "focus," either in its meaning of a shift in direction of the head, or its meaning of concentration.³¹

הביט/הבט are usually followed by אל. Probably this is because אל implies a focus. In contrast, ראה is usually followed only by את.³²

Probably, the reason for the *hifil* in the meaning of shifting the direction of the head is that you are "causing the object to come into view." Perhaps the use of the *hifil* then expanded to the concentration meaning as well.

Also, ראה often implies a wider view than הבט.³³ Finally, ראה can be accidental or spontaneous,³⁴ and this is not the case with הבט.

* * *

---

is probably "to incline one's ear." I thank my publisher Rabbi Alec Goldstein for pointing this out to me.

26. S. Wertheimer, *Be'ur Shemot Nirdafim She-Ba-Tanakh* (1924), p. 63. (This is a useful book on Biblical synonyms and is accessible on hebrewbooks.org.)
27. See similarly Ps. 80:15 and *Daat Mikra* there.
28. See similarly Ps. 33:13.
29. See *Daat Mikra* to 1 Sam. 17:42. See also Lam. 5:1 and Isa. 42:18.
30. ראה precedes הבט at Lam. 1:11 and 2:20, and Hab. 1:5.
31. A meaning for הבט as something like concentration is implied in a passage at J. Talmud *Rosh Hashanah* 3:9. This passage is the basis for Rashi's similar comments on Num. 21:8. Also expressing this view are Malbim to Isa. 5:12 and Wertheimer, p. 88. The root does not imply concentration every time it is used, but most of the time this seems to be the case.
32. Malbim to Isa. 5:12 and Wertheimer, p. 88.
33. Kaddari, p. 690.
34. Malbim to Isa. 5:12 and Wertheimer, pp. 63-64.

The verb שקף appears twenty-two times in *Tanakh*. Ten times it is in the *nifal* (e.g., נשקפה), and 12 times it is in the *hifil* (e.g., השקיף).³⁵ In both the meaning is "looking out and down."³⁶ It is often used in connection with looking out a window. See, e.g., Judges 5:28 (mother of Sisera), and 2 Sam. 6:16 (Michal looking at David).³⁷

All *kohanim* know Deut. 26:15. Here, at the end of *Birkat Kohanim*, the *kohanim* recite their silent request that God look down from the Heavens and bless the nation of Israel and its land: *Hashkifah mi-me'on kadshekha min ha-shamayim u-varekh et amkha et Yisrael ve-et ha-adamah asher natatta lanu*....

* * *

The root שגח only appears three times in *Tanakh*, always in the *hifil*. From the reference at Psalms 33:14, we see that it is parallel to the הבט and ראה of the prior verse. But what kind of seeing does the verb imply? At Song of Songs 2:9 we have *mashgiaḥ min ha-ḥalonot, meitzitz min ha-ḥarakim*. In this verse, the context is looking through an opening (the narrow window of an ancient house). At Isaiah 14:16, the context is looking at someone in a pit in *She'ol*. The implication here too may be a narrow area that one has to strain to see.³⁸ Therefore, a reasonable approach to our verb is that it applies to looking through a narrow area. This is the view of Rashi and Radak.³⁹ But many others view the verb שגח as indicating an intense viewing.⁴⁰

Perhaps the extra effort necessary to see due to narrowness, or the intense viewing, would explain why the verb is in the *hifil*.

At Psalms 33:14, the verb refers to God looking *mi-mekhon shivto*

---

35. I have seen the suggestion that there was no *kal* and that the verb arose based on the noun *mashkof*, in one of its meanings. See Kaddari, p. 1140.
36. See, e.g., *BDB*, p. 1054, Klein, p. 679, and *TDOT*, vol. 15, pp. 462–63.
37. *Tanakh* also includes several nouns from the root שקף. Perhaps some or all derive from our verb שקף. See *TDOT*, vol. 15, pp. 462–64. But some or all may derive from a different verb in Aramaic with the meaning "strike." See *BDB*, p. 1054.
38. The King James Bible on Isaiah 14:16 has "narrowly look." This is followed by the Jewish Publication Society of America translation of 1917.
39. See their commentaries on Isa. 14:16.
40. See, e.g., *KB*, p. 1414: "to look at closely and to examine critically," and Rav S.R. Hirsch to Psalms 33:14.

over all the *yoshvei ha-aretz*. Perhaps looking from *mekhon shivto* implies a bit of narrowness in the looking. (After all, the verse is not saying that God is looking from *shamayim*.) If no narrowness is implied here, those who adopt the "look through a narrow area" approach would take the position that the verse would be using a later expansion of the verb's meaning.

* * *

Many of the words that I discuss in this book, including some of the above, have different meanings and connotations in modern Hebrew. In this connection, I would like to share the following story.[41] Nehama Leibowitz and her husband (who was her uncle) made Aliyah from Europe in the pre-State period. Neither was very familiar with modern Hebrew. On their first visit approaching *Yerushalayim*, she saw a road sign on a hilly road that said in Hebrew: "stay in low gear." The story did not say but almost certainly the Hebrew phrase on the sign used the phrase *hilukh namukh*. She was very impressed with the sign. She said to her husband: "How beautiful it is in *Eretz Yisrael* that there are road signs that remind those making the pilgrimage to the Holy City to enter it with humility!" She thought the sign was an instruction to "walk humbly"!

* * *

Mitchell First pleads guilty to lack of knowledge of much of modern Hebrew. But he finds that this lack helps him with Biblical Hebrew as he is not misled by modern meanings.

4. זהר: Is There A Connection between "Light" and "Warn"?

I am always fascinated by words that have disparate meanings but share a common root. For example, the root לחם means both "bread" and "fight," the root שנה means both "repeat" and "change," and the root הלל means both "praise" and "foolish."[42]

---

41. From *HaMizrachi* magazine, April 2021.
42. I discussed the first two in *Roots and Rituals* (2018). I discuss the last in this book. In *Roots*, I also discussed the root קלס, which means both "mock"

Recently, I read an article by Rabbi Reuven Chaim Klein and he mentioned a root with disparate meanings that I had not noticed before: זהר means "light" but it is also the root of "warn."

The early Jewish lexicographers (e.g., R. Yonah Ibn Janaḥ and Radak) do not make a connection between these two זהר meanings. But Avraham son of Rambam does, See his commentary on הזהרתה at Ex. 18:20.[43]

In modern times, one traditional source that connects the two meanings is Rav S.R. Hirsch. Here are his comments on Ex. 18:20: "So הזהיר must mean to light up an object for somebody which otherwise he would not have seen..." His translation of הזהרתה in this verse is "make clear."

Many scholars argue for the relationship as well. For example, the relationship is obvious to S. Mandelkern. He writes that when someone warns another he is *mofia or al derekh ḥaveiro*. E. Klein writes that the "warn" meaning is probably derived from the "shine" meaning but does not discuss it further.[44] The *Brown-Driver-Briggs* lexicon had written that most scholars identify the two roots.[45]

In English, aside from the word "enlighten," we also use "illuminate" and "shed light on" as synonyms for "teaching."

At first I was suspicious of the connection between the two זהר

---

and "praise." I explained there that the meaning in *Tanakh* is always "mock." The "praise" meaning in Hebrew is a post-Biblical meaning derived from the Greek meaning of the word.

43. *Peirush Rabbeinu Avraham Ben Ha-Rambam Z"L Al Bereshit Ve-Shemot* (translation from the original Arabic).

R. Saadiah Gaon probably relates the two זהר meanings as well. This is implied in his commentary to Ecc. 12:12, where he writes (according to the translation) that the essential meaning of the root זהר is *ha-biur ve-ha-giluy*. (His commentary to Ecc. 12:12 is cited in the *Torat Ḥayyim* to Ex. 18:20.) But since *ha-biur ve-ha-giluy* is merely a translation, my evidence can perhaps be refuted. (Whether or not this commentary is by R. Saadiah may be an issue as well.)

44. Klein, p. 195. See also Kaddari, p. 243, and U. Cassuto, *Nesiatah Shel Asherah Be-Kitvei Ugarit, Tarbitz* 20 (1949), pp. 1–7 (7).

45. But it added that the relationship is "possible, but not certain." Also, the essay in *TDOT* mentions the possibility of the development from "make shine, enlighten" to "teach." See vol. 4, p. 42. But it does not evaluate its merit.

meanings. After all, we all know the word אזהרה and it often implies a warning and negative instruction.[46] But it turns out that this word is not in *Tanakh*.

Nevertheless, it is true that most of the instances of the verb זהר in *Tanakh* occur in the context of warnings not to do something. But *Tanakh* has at least one example of a positive instruction, the statement at Exodus 18:20: *ve-**hizhartah** et'hem et ha-ḥukkim ve-et ha-torot, ve-hodata lahem et a ha-derekh yeilkhu vah ve-et ha-maaseh asher yaasun* (= you shall **teach** them the statutes and the laws, and you shall inform them the path that they must walk in and the deeds that they must do"). There is nothing negative in this sentence. So perhaps "warn" is just a later development from an earlier "teach." "Teach" is the way the verb is often translated in this verse.

At Psalms 19:12, we have: *gam avdekha nizhar bahem*. This is another phrase that might reflect the "teach" meaning, as opposed to the "warn" meaning. (Please look at the full context, starting from verse 8. This phrase also might reflect the "light" meaning, see below.)

In the "warn" meaning, the word is always in the *hifil* (causative) or *nifal* (passive). See, e.g., Ezekiel 33:3: הזהיר (*hifil*). I believe this supports the connection I am arguing for. Probably, the literal meaning of the *hifil* is: "to cause light for someone."

There is one weakness to our attempt to relate the two meanings. A widespread view is that the "light" meaning only appears two times in *Tanakh*, in relatively late books: at Ezekiel 8:2 and at Daniel 12:3.[47] But this is not conclusive proof of a late origin for the meaning.[48] Also, it is possible that the "light" meaning is reflected in the word *nizhar* at Ps. 19:12.[49]

Also, many scholars relate the root זהר and its "light" meaning to

---

46. The poetical liturgical compositions known as *azharot* list both positive and negative commandments.
47. The "warn, teach" meaning appears many more times than this.
48. *TDOT*, vol. 4, p. 41 mentions the possibility of evidence for a meaning related to "light" in Ugaritic. This is still an open question.
49. See, e.g., M. Fishbane, *Text and Texture* (1979), p. 88. His translation of the relevant phrase: "Even your servant is made resplendent by them." (See the prior verses for the context, especially the last two words of verse 9.) Fishbane

the root צהר.⁵⁰ The latter root surely underlies the word יצהר, fresh oil, which appears many times in *Tanakh*. It is called this either because it shines, or because it is something that just appeared.⁵¹

* * *

In modern Hebrew, the Balfour Declaration is referred to as *hatzharat* Balfour. That first word הצהרת was invented by Eliezer Ben-Yehuda (d. 1922), as he invented the verb הצהיר with the meaning "to declare, to put something out there for all to see." (At Job 24:11, we have יצהירו, with its original meaning "to make *yitzhar*"!) Without Ben-Yehuda's word, the declaration would likely have been called *hakhrazat* Balfour, based on that older word הכריז.⁵²

* * *

I would like to thank Rabbi Reuven Chaim Klein, whose May 12, 2021 article "Brilliant Prohibitions" on his "What's in a Word?" site taught me about this root זהר and inspired this column.

* * *

Mitchell First needs someone to enlighten him about the mysteries of the Zohar.

5. זמר: The Three Meanings of the Root זמר in *Tanakh*

We all know that the root זמר has a "making music" meaning in *Tanakh*. But three times it is used to mean "cut, prune" in the context

---

also believes that *nizhar* here includes the "warning" meaning. I thank Aryeh Wiener for this reference.

50. See, e.g., Mandelkern, and Klein, p. 542. ז and צ are both sibilants and prone to interchange.

51. Klein, p. 262. The word *tzaharayim* appears many times in *Tanakh* as well, but a widespread view among modern scholars is that its root is "back." See, e.g., Klein, p. 542. Similarly, the word *tzohar* (Gen. 6:16) may derive from a "back" meaning. See Tawil, p. 318. But some scholars do believe that both these words derive from an original meaning related to "light."

52. I learned all of this from the post at balashon.com of Oct. 27, 2006, on the word צהר.

of vines. For example, at Lev. 25:3, we have: *shesh shanim tizmor karmekha*. The other two verses are Lev. 25:4 and Isa. 5:6.

Could these two verbs have a common origin? I will mention two suggestions, but both are unlikely. The first points to the fact that the root מלל has a "cut" meaning (e.g., circumcision) and a "speak" meaning. Perhaps when one speaks, words are cut from one's mouth. This would be the case in singing as well as speaking. But those two different meanings for מלל are probably not related to one another, so there is no reason to relate our two meanings. The second suggestion is that when one cuts branches from the vines, this is done to improve the vines and make them praiseworthy/worthy of singing about.

What about the reference to God as *ozi ve-zimrat*? We all know this phrase from *Oz Yashir* (Ex. 15:2). This phrase also appears at Isa. 12:2 and Ps. 118:14. It is usually translated as "my strength and [my] song."

But *Oz Yashir* includes many words that parallel one another, so perhaps *zimrat* has a meaning parallel to עזי. The Hebrew *zayin* and the Aramaic and Arabic *dalet* often substitute for another (e.g., זהב and דהב and many other examples). U. Cassuto on Ex. 15:2 points out that in Arabic, the root *d-m-r* means "power, help." In the very old language of Amorite (pre-Biblical period), *d-m-r* means "protect." Similar is the meaning of *d-m-r* in South Arabic, a language from the late Biblical period. In Ugaritic, *d-m-r* has the meaning "soldier." For all of these reasons, giving זמר the meaning "power, help, protect" in Exodus 15:2 seems a reasonable approach.[53] Therefore, Cassuto translates the phrase as: "The Lord is my strength and help." *Daat Mikra* also mentions this interpretation as a possibility.[54]

We now have three different meanings for our root זמר in *Tanakh*: 1) make music, 2) cut, and 3) (perhaps) power. (We should not be so

---

53. There are masculine names in the *Tanakh* with this root, e.g., several different individuals named "Zimri." Perhaps these too derive from this "power, help, protect" meaning. This meaning has also been suggested at 2 Sam. 23:1 and Isa. 25:5. See Kaddari, p. 253 and *Daat Mikra* on the first verse.

54. Another approach views the phrase as a "hendiadys" with the meaning "mighty fortress." Note the parallel to the singular *yeshuah* in the second part of the verse. This suggests that *ozi ve-zimrat* reflects only one concept. (On "hendiadys," see my essay later in this section of this book.)

surprised by this. In Arabic there are two different *zayin* letters. Based on this and other evidence, scholars believe that this was the case in Proto-Semitic as well. Ancient Hebrew collapsed two different *zayin* letters into one. I admit it would be better if there would have been three different *zayin* letters originally!)

(On a related matter, we would have expected *ozi ve-zimrati* in the Hebrew at Ex. 15:2. It is often translated as if this last *yod* was there.[55] It is noteworthy that Rashi on Ex. 15:2 is not bothered by the lack of the *yod* and he translates *zimrat* with the "cut" meaning: "The strength and cutting down [of enemies] by God were a deliverance for me.")

* * *

Now let us look at Gen. 43:11. Jacob is telling his sons to bring a present to that leader in Egypt (Joseph): take *mi-zimrat ha-aretz*. Does it mean: 1) most praiseworthy products of the land (from the "sing" meaning)? 2) the improved products of the land (an expanded meaning from "cut off")?, or 3) the power of the land? Rashi, Ibn Ezra and many others adopt meaning number 1.[56] But others adopt meanings 2 or 3.[57]

* * *

Now let us look at animals. At Deut. 14:5, we have *zamer* as a kosher animal. This is the only time this animal appears in *Tanakh*, and the cognate languages are of no help, so its meaning remains unclear. One possibility is a giraffe.[58]

---

55. But what happened to it? One interesting approach is the "double duty" approach. The word after *zimrat* begins with *yod*. That *yod* is actually doing double duty. So even though there is no *yod* at the end of *zimrat*, we have a right to translate it as if it was there. There are many examples of this double duty phenomena in *Tanakh*. That is for another essay. For further reading on this issue, see E. Würthwein, *The Text of the Old Testament* (1979, Eng. edition), p. 107, I.O. Lehman, "A Forgotten Principle of Biblical Textual Tradition Rediscovered," *Journal of Near Eastern Studies* 26 (1967), pp. 93–101, R. Margaliot, *Ha-Mikra Ve-Ha-Mesorah*, pp. 64–70, *Pentateuch* of Rabbi Dr. Hertz, comm. to Lev. 1:1, and S.D. Luzzatto, comm. to Gen. 27:46 and Lev. 1:1.
56. See, e.g., Rav S.R. Hirsch: "take from that of which the land boasts."
57. For meaning 2, see, e.g., Klein, p. 200. For meaning 3, see e.g. Kaddari, p. 255.
58. This possibility is based on the Septuagint translation of *zamer* as a *camelopardalis* (= camel-leopard). This was the ancient term for a giraffe. The

Song of Songs 2:12 has "the time of the *zamir* has arrived." This might mean the time for "singing." Others believe it is a reference to a bird known for its singing. (Note that the continuation of the verse refers to the sound of the turtledove.) Alternatively, it could mean the time for "pruning."⁵⁹

The *Tanakh* also has the word *zemorah* a few times. It means "branch, twig" (from the "cut" meaning). Also, the *Tanakh* has *mazmerah*, a knife for pruning. Finally, there is also *mezameret*, a tool to shear wicks.

* * *

An interesting question is if there is a difference between the two music meanings: זמר and שיר. One often suggested possibility is that the former involved instruments (at least originally) and the latter did not. See, e.g., Ibn Ezra to Ps. 105:2, Radak to 1 Chr. 16:9, *Daat Mikra* to Ps. 1:3, *Theological Dictionary of the Old Testament*, vol. 4, p. 98, and M.Z. Kaddari, p. 254.⁶⁰

* * *

Every morning we say "*Pesukei De-Zimrah*," usually translated as "verses of song." But a beautiful homiletical interpretation has been suggested: verses that help **cut away** the distractions that impede us from properly serving God.⁶¹

* * *

---

giraffe looks like a cross between a camel and a leopard and many believed it was. For a recent extensive discussion of all the possibilities for *zamer*, see Rabbi N. Slifkin, *The Torah Encyclopedia of the Animal Kingdom*, vol. 1 (2015), pp. 288–300. The *zamer* is mentioned only once in the Talmud, at Ḥullin 80a. As R. Slifkin explains, a widespread suggestion in scholarship is that the *zamer* is a type of wild sheep. He writes that this suggestion is perhaps supported by the above passage in the Talmud. He also writes that "[i]t seems that even the Sages of the Talmud were uncertain regarding its identity."

(I have called this animal *zamer* because that is how R. Slifkin refers to it. Technically, its name was probably *zemer*. This is how scholars refer to it. It is only because it ends the verse that it appears in the form *zamer*.)

59. For all of these, see Soncino and *Daat Mikra*.
60. I thank Rabbi R.C. Klein for the first two references.
61. I thank Rabbi R.C. Klein for this idea. He attributes it to R. Elimelekh of Lizhensk and Ḥatam Sofer.

One of the most important archaeological finds in ancient Israel is the "Gezer Calendar," dating from the tenth century BCE. It is a small tablet that describes monthly and bi-monthly periods and attributes an agricultural activity to each. It begins "two months gathering (אסף), two months planting (זרע)." A few lines later it has *yarḥo zemer*, which means "two months pruning."

No one knows the purpose of this tablet. Scholars have speculated that it could be a schoolboy's writing exercise (since the script is crude), or the text of a popular song, or something designed for the collection of taxes from farmers. It was found in 1908 in the city of Gezer, not far from Jerusalem.

* * *

Many years ago, when I renewed my subscription to *Biblical Archaeology Review*, I was given a replica of the Gezer Calendar. I thought I saw the word חדש repeating throughout. This inscription, like all inscriptions from the First Temple period and earlier, is in Old Hebrew. But I was looking at the replica upside down. It turns out that it was ירח and ירחו that were repeating!

6. חול: The Meaning of חול When Contrasted with קדש

Four times in *Tanakh* we have a verse contrasting קדש and חל. One is at Leviticus 10:10. Here is an instruction to Aaron about understanding the difference between קדש and חל, and טמא and טהור.[62]

What is the precise meaning of חל in these verses? And how do we understand the various meanings of its probable root חלל and their relation to one another?[63]

All agree that the verb חלל has a few different meanings.

One meaning is "bore, pierce." For example, Ezekiel 32:26 refers to *meḥuleli ḥerev*. These are people pierced by the sword. The similar

---

62. The other three such verses are in the book of Ezekiel.
63. In contrast, the root קדש has been much discussed. For example, there is a recent book by Rabbi Alec Goldstein about it: *A Theology of Holiness* (2018). Full disclosure: He is also a publisher and his company published this book. What is his company's name? Kodesh Press, of course!

phrase, *ḥalal ḥerev*, appears many times in *Tanakh*. Indeed all those meanings of חלל as dead body in *Tanakh* likely come from the "pierce" meaning.⁶⁴

That musical instrument with openings, חליל (six times in *Tanakh*), also comes from this root. The word חלון = window (an opening in the wall) also derives from this root, appearing many times in *Tanakh*.

What about the word for "begin"? We have ויחל and החל many times in *Tanakh* with the meaning "begin." See, e.g., Genesis 6:1 and 9:20.⁶⁵ Some scholars believe that the root of this "begin" meaning is חלל with its "opening" meaning. But others disagree. (I will discuss this below.)

We also have חלל with a "pollute, defile, desecrate" meaning. For example, the *Tanakh* refers to חלל in the context of desecrating the *Shabbat*, desecrating God's name and desecrating the Temple.⁶⁶ But sometimes the connotation of חלל and its derivatives is more neutral, like "ordinary, non-holy." For example: *leḥem ḥol* (= common bread) at 1 Samuel 21:5. See also Ezekiel 48:15.

The *Brown-Driver-Briggs* lexicon views the "bore, pierce" meaning as one meaning of the root חלל, and the "pollute, defile, desecrate" meaning as a completely different meaning. E. Klein, in his etymological dictionary, takes the same approach. So too does *Theological Dictionary of the Old Testament*. Also, all of these sources believe that the "begin" meaning is, in some awkward way, derived from the "pollute, defile, desecrate" meaning.⁶⁷

But there is a different way to look at the root חלל and to unify and explain all these meanings. Hayim Tawil suggested it in an article included in his collected essays.⁶⁸ Also, the etymology columnist

---

64. See, e.g., *KB*, p. 320. In ancient warfare, killing the enemy was normally a matter of making holes in him with a sword or a spear. See the essay by Philologos (cited below).
65. Also, the related word תחילה appears many times in *Tanakh*.
66. Also, the word חלילה probably relates to this meaning, as it is typically said regarding something reprehensible.
67. See, e.g., *TDOT*, vol. 4, p. 410, for a suggestion.
68. *Lexical Studies in the Bible and Ancient Near Eastern Inscriptions* (2012, eds. A. Berkovitz, S. Halpern, and A. Goldstein).

Philologos suggested it in one of his columns.⁶⁹ I will now present their suggestion.

What is holy is complete.⁷⁰ As Philologos wrote (with slight exaggeration), "it has an overflowing plenitude; it is surrounded by a field of divine energy that can be dangerous to approach or come in contact with." What the verb חלל does, in making an opening, is puncture the completeness.⁷¹

As to the "begin" meaning, this too is an expansion. It is an expansion from the original "pierce, bore" meaning. Every beginning is an opening. It is as if one is making a dent and piercing a hole.⁷²

The above approach which unites all the חלל meanings deserves serious consideration.

It also has ramifications for how we understand the word חל in its contrast with קדש. If there is a separate fundamental root חלל that means "pollute, defile, desecrate," then more likely that is the meaning of חל when it is contrasted with קדש. But now we see that perhaps the fundamental meaning of חלל is only "pierce, bore, puncture." Then חל, in its contrast with קדש, perhaps only means "pierced, punctured, lacking in completeness/holiness." This is not as negative a meaning. In this view, "polluted, defiled, desecrated" would be a later expansion from the "lacking in completeness/holiness" meaning.⁷³

There is a beautiful idea that in this world we have the "holy" (קדש) and the "not yet holy" (חל).⁷⁴ I used to think that this was

---

69. Column of Mar. 31, 2021, mosaicmagazine.com. Philologos cleverly titled his column: "The Holy and the Holey"!
70. Even in English, one mainstream view derives "holy" from "whole." See Goldstein, p. 64.
71. In the above article, Tawil argues that נקב is another word that originated with an "opening" meaning and then expanded to a "defile" meaning. For the latter meaning, see Lev. 24:11 and 24:16.
72. This connection between "begin" and "pierce, bore" was mentioned long ago in Mandelkern.
73. This is perhaps what happened in English as well. Our English word "profane" derives from the Latin *profanus*, which derives from *pro fanum*: "before/outside the temple." I.e., outside sacred grounds. Just like our Hebrew word חול, this English word also has two connotations: "common" and "defiled."
74. I believe it originated with R. Abraham Isaac Kook.

wrong because I thought חל fundamentally meant "polluted, defiled, desecrated." But now this idea can be more seriously considered.

At Leviticus 10:10, the Jewish Publication Society of America, in their translation of 1917, translated *ḥol* as "common." Many other translations take such an approach.[75]

* * *

A few more eye-opening thoughts:

- The phrase *ḥol ha-moed* is not found in *Tanakh*. (It refers to the "ordinary, common" days of the holiday.)
- The word *ḥilonim* for secular Israelis comes from our root.
- Tractate *Ḥullin* is about ordinary meat, not defiled meat.
- Finally, if you think this column is too obscure, I hope you realize that the word for the חלה you eat probably comes from this root. It derives from the חלל = perforate meaning.[76] (If I understood ancient baking, I would better understand why!)

* * *

Mitchell First had always wondered about that Arabic word *ḥalal*. Now he understands that it is cognate to our word *ḥol* and is food that is permitted to be eaten because it is not holy.

7. חרף: The Season חורף and the Marital Word נחרפת

The Biblical root חרף seems to have two branches. One branch is the name of a season. The other is a verb with meanings like "reproach, taunt, scoff" and the related noun חרפה (disgrace, shame). First, we are going to suggest the meaning that underlies the "season" mean-

---

75. See, e.g., *The Living Torah*: "common" and Rav S.R. Hirsch: "laical." See similarly *Daat Mikra*. Also, S.D. Luzzatto translated the entire phrase as "between that which is sacred and that which is not." See the edition of D. Klein. The proponents of this interpretation can argue that the instruction to Aaron is presented as the difference between קדש and חל, and טמא and טהור. חל and טמא are not presented as parallel to one another.
76. Klein, p. 217: "perforated (cake)." See also *TDOT*, vol. 4, p. 417: "ring-shaped bread." Another common occurrence of our root is in the word חלולים (openings) in the *asher yotzar* blessing!

ing.⁷⁷ Then we are going to shed light on that difficult Biblical word נחרפת at Leviticus 19:20.

I. The Meaning of the Word חורף

I live in New Jersey. When I hear the word *horef*, I think: cold.⁷⁸ But our impressions from the U.S.A. about the meaning of חורף in Biblical Israel are, of course, irrelevant.

As to the underlying meaning of the word, the *Brown-Driver-Briggs* lexicon (1906) had pointed to an Arabic cognate and stated that it had the meaning "gather fruit, pluck." In this view, חורף would mean the season of gathering and plucking.

Some of the other etymological sources that I have seen give the Arabic cognate only the "pluck" meaning.⁷⁹ In this scenario, we might have to limit the fundamental meaning to activities involving "plucking." But "plucking" is broad enough to imply "gathering" and "harvesting," as it is the first step in these other activities. So again, based on the Arabic cognate, we could interpret *horef* as the "season of gathering and harvesting."⁸⁰

But there is a better approach to the "season" meaning. In Akkadian and in Aramaic, חרף has the meaning "early".⁸¹ In *Tanakh*, it likely has this meaning at Job 29:4: "As I was in the days of חרפי, when God's counsel was upon my tent."⁸² From this verse and the surrounding verses, it is clear that the reference is to a period when God took care of Job. Thus, the reproach-related meanings do not fit. Therefore most modern scholars interpret the word as meaning "early" here: my early time, my youth.⁸³ Rashi, *Metzudat Tzion*, Malbim and many

---

77. At Gen. 8:22, Psa. 74:17, Amos 3:15, and Zech. 14:8, חורף is mentioned in the same verse as קיץ. The use of the two together sometimes implies the entire year. But this does not mean that we have to find a meaning that spans half the year or anything close to that.
78. In case you are wondering, the word "winter" derives from the meaning "wet."
79. See, e.g., Mandelkern, and *TDOT*, vol. 5, p. 206.
80. See, e.g., Klein, p. 233: "the time of fruit gathering."
81. For Akkadian, see, e.g., Tawil, p. 120. For Aramaic, see, e.g., Jastrow, p. 505.
82. It is well-known that the book of Job includes many Aramaic words and usages.
83. See, e.g., *TDOT*, vol. 5, p. 206, and *KB*, p. 356.

other traditional commentaries had given this interpretation centuries before. They did not know Akkadian but they knew the "early" meaning from Aramaic.

Now that we know that this "early" meaning of the root חרף exists in *Tanakh*, we can interpret the "season" meaning in this light. Accordingly, the essay on the "season" meaning of the root חרף in *Theological Dictionary of the Old Testament* concludes that it means "the early season of the year (that is, of the agricultural year, which begins in the fall)."[84] I.e., it is the season when the seeding/planting takes place. See similarly the Koehler-Baumgartner lexicon: "time for seed and early growth."[85]

In disagreeing with the "harvesting" approach, the above essay in *Theological Dictionary of the Old Testament* cites several verses that suggest that "harvesting" is a theme of קיץ, not חורף. In each of the following verses, קיץ is parallel to קציר: Proverbs 6:8 and 10:5 and Jeremiah 8:20.[86]

An argument can also be made from Proverbs 20:4 that חרף is a season for plowing, not harvesting. A reasonable interpretation of this verse is that it criticizes the lazy one for not plowing in the *ḥoref*: "When *ḥoref* sets in, the lazy one does not plow; he will seek at harvest time and have nothing."[87]

* * *

Over the centuries many other etymologies have been offered for

---

An earlier interpretation by many scholars was "in the days of my autumn," with "autumn" implying "prime." See BDB. As the Soncino commentary had explained here: *Ḥoref*'s "ordinary meaning is 'harvest-time, autumn,' in Arabic 'freshly gathered fruit.' It denotes maturity rather than youth."

84. Naḥmanides, in his comm. on Lev. 19:20, had long ago intuited that חורף was the beginning of the year in an agricultural sense. But he does not suggest that this is what the word meant.

85. P. 356. This is of course a marked contrast to what is probably the common assumption today. The common assumption today is probably what is found in the Even-Shoshan concordance. This source, at p. 402, describes the Biblical חורף with the following three words: *tekufat ha-kor ve-ha-geshamim*.

86. For other evidence of "gathering" as a theme of *kayitz*, see Jer. 40:10 and 40:12.

87. The verse is a bit ambiguous and subject to other interpretations. The first word *mei-ḥoref* can be understood as *ba-ḥoref*. See *Daat Mikra*.

the "season" meaning of the root חרף. Because they are creative, I will mention some of them:[88]

- The season when sharp tools are used. (In the Aramaic of the Talmud and of the Targumim, and in Arabic, there is a word חריף which means "sharp." This word does not appear in *Tanakh*, except as a name. But a widespread view is that the Biblical "reproach" meaning is an expansion from an original "sharp" meaning: "to say sharp things."[89])
- The season when the *avir*[90] is *ḥarif ve-kashe*.
- "On Gen. VIII, 22 we took the underlying meaning of חרף to be abandonment, to be abandoned, from which then חורף would be the time of the year when the earth is completely passive..." See Rav S.R. Hirsch's commentary to Lev. 19:20.
- The time of sowing barley and legumes. These are quick (חריפין) to ripen in a short time. See Rashi on Gen. 8:22.
- The "season" meaning derives from the root ערף which has a meaning "flow" or "flow like rain."[91]

* * *

I mentioned at the beginning of this essay that our root also has meanings like "reproach, taunt, scoff" and the related noun חרפה (disgrace, shame). But if "early" is the fundamental meaning of the "season" root, it is hard to see a connection to these meanings. Since our Hebrew letter *ḥet* is a merger of two different earlier *ḥet* letters, two different and unrelated meanings for our root is not surprising.[92]

11. The Meaning of נחרפת at Leviticus 19:20

At Leviticus 19:20, we have the case of a female slave who is נחרפת to one man, but has relations with a different man. The precise details of the case are subject to dispute. In any event, in this case involving

---

88. My mentioning them does not mean that I take them seriously.
89. See, e.g., Klein, p. 233.
90. This word of course derives from the Greek *aer* (= air).
91. It is accepted that ע and ח sometimes interchange. For example, both the roots עמר and חמר seem to have the meaning "heap."
92. *TDOT* (p. 210) provides some evidence to support the idea that the "season" meaning and the reproach-related meanings originated with two different *ḥet* letters.

a female slave, the female and the male who had relations with her do not receive the death penalty. Rather, verse 20 states that בקרת תהיה, a very unclear phrase, and verses 21–22 refer to a sacrifice that the male must bring for his sin.[93]

Based on the context, Rashi gives the word the meaning "designated" (מיועדת and מיוחדת). He adds: "I do not know a דמיון to this in Scripture."[94] Ibn Ezra suggests a connection to the word חרפה. Naḥmanides suggests the meaning is נערה, based on Job 29:4. Rav S.R. Hirsch suggests a meaning related to חרב.[95] *Brown-Driver-Briggs* suggests the meaning "acquired" based on a cognate in Arabic. Another scholar suggests "plucked" (with an implication of betrothed!).

But a better approach can be suggested. As mentioned above, our root means "to be early" in Aramaic and Akkadian, and in *Tanakh* at Job 29:4, and probably in connection with the "season" meaning of חרף. Based on this, the meaning "assigned in advance" (of redemption or emancipation) has been suggested by some scholars,[96] and the implication would be a form of "betrothal."[97]

Earlier, among our traditional sources, at the AlHatorah.org site on Lev. 19:20, I found a Tosafist commentary who mentions the view that the word means מוקדמת and cites a passage in the Talmud where the root has this meaning. This commentary cites Job 29:4 as well.[98]

* * *

---

93. Death to both is ordinarily the punishment for post-betrothal relations with a different man. The punishment to each in this case is unclear from the verses and depends in part on the meaning of בקרת תהיה.
94. He means that he cannot find another instance of this root in *Tanakh* with such a meaning.
95. As stated earlier, prior to this he suggested an underlying meaning of the root חרף. But when he tried to apply this meaning here, it did not fit the context. So he redefined his underlying meaning of the root חרף in light of the root חרב.
96. See Tawil, p. 120. See similarly *TDOT*, vol. 5, p. 207: "'given *early* (to a man)' or better: 'given an early status.'"
97. *KB* (p. 356), published in 1995, writes that there is an Akkadian cognate, *harupu*, which means "betrothed" and cites to the particular text. But Tawil's work, published in 2009, did not mention this. Earlier, *TDOT*, published in 1986, did not mention any such Akkadian cognate. Probably, the meaning of the Akkadian text is disputed.
98. On the site, this commentary is called קיצור פענח רזא. Also noteworthy is

There is much discussion of our word and the case of the נחרפת in both Talmuds. See, e.g., *Kiddushin* 6a, *Gittin* 43a, *Keritot* 9a and 11a, and J. Talmud *Kiddushin* 1:1. I am not going to summarize these discussions. I will state that nowhere in either Talmud is an interpretation based on the "early" meaning suggested.

A widely quoted statement in the Talmud (*Kidd.* 6a) is that, in the region of Judea, an ארוסה is called חרופה.

III. The Phrases חרפו נפשם and מחרפים נפשם in Our Prayers

Many memorial prayers in modern times refer to soldiers and others involved in security who *ḥerfu nafsham* for the State of Israel.[99] Similarly, there is a more recent prayer composed for the Safety of the United States Armed Forces which praises the U.S. soldiers who are *meḥarfim nafsham* to protect the wellbeing of all of God's creations.[100]

In modern Hebrew, the above idiom means "risk one's life." Where did this idiom come from?

It is clear that it is based on Judges 5:18. Here the tribe of Zevulun is being praised in the song of Deborah.[101] They are described as *am ḥeref nafsho la-mut*.[102] This is the only time in *Tanakh* that the root חרף is used with any form of the word נפש.

Let us try to understand the phrase in the Biblical verse. It is best if we can understand the phrase with an already known meaning of

---

the *Gur Aryeh* commentary on Lev. 19:20. It cites Job 29:4 for the idea that our root means "beginning" and writes that being an ארוסה is *hatḥalat ha-ishut*.
99. See the entry "'*Yizkor*' *le-Ḥallalei Maarakhot Yisrael*" on the Hebrew Wikipedia site.
100. This prayer was composed by Milton Moshe Markovitz (then of Queens, now of Teaneck) at the request of Rabbi Fabian Schonfeld, shortly after the events of Sept. 11, 2001. Hundreds of synagogues in the U.S. have incorporated it into their *Shabbat* and holiday morning services. The text composed in 2001 is included in the volume *Contending with Catastrophe: Jewish Perspectives on September 11th*, ed. M. Broyde (2011), p. 245. A modified version of the prayer is included in *The Koren Siddur, American Edition* (2009), p. 521.
101. The verse seems to imply that this praise applies to the tribe of Naftali as well. This is how it is interpreted in the Soncino and *Daat Mikra*.
102. The last word is vocalized in our tradition as *la-mut* (= to die), as opposed to *la-mavet* (= to death). Compare Isa. 53:12 (*la-mavet nafsho*).

the root חרף.¹⁰³ One can translate this phrase in the verse as a tribe that "taunts himself to die." The implication can be "risks its life."¹⁰⁴ Alternatively, when one risks one's life, one can be said to be undervaluing it. In this way חרף can be related to the "reproach, shame" meaning.¹⁰⁵ Alternatively, in this same approach, one can learn the implication of the phrase as not just risking its life but sacrificing its life.¹⁰⁶

But now we can suggest a new approach, based on the "early" meaning: A tribe that brings itself out early (= eagerly) to die [= being willing to risk or sacrifice its life].¹⁰⁷

Conclusions

Most likely, the underlying meaning of the "season" meaning is the early season of the agricultural year, when the seeding and planting takes place. Most likely, the meaning of נחרפת at Leviticus 19:20 is also based on the "early" meaning. The word likely means "assigned in advance of redemption or emancipation." Finally, the import of *ḥeref nafsho la-mut* at Judges 5:18 remains unclear, but we have offered a new possibility.

* * *

P.S. The etymology of קיץ is another interesting issue. See, e.g., the concordance of Mandelkern and the post at balashon.com of June 5, 2006, for some preliminary discussion. If חורף means the "early" part of the agricultural year, we can speculate that perhaps קיץ means its "end."¹⁰⁸ But this topic deserves much more research.

* * *

103. This is in contrast to the suggestion of Rashbam. In his commentary on Lev. 19:20, Rashbam suggests that the meaning of the root at Judges 5:18 is *masar nafsho*. (He then uses this meaning to support his interpretation of נחרפת as *mesurah u-meyuḥedet*.) But we have no other evidence for the root חרף with the meaning מסר. Thus his interpretation of Judges 5:18 is an unlikely one.
104. See *KB*, p. 355.
105. See, e.g., *Metzudat David*. See similarly *BDB* which relates it to a "despise, scorn" meaning.
106. See *TDOT*, p. 212: "despised his life... the members of the tribe preferred to sacrifice their own lives rather than lose the battle."
107. See similarly Tawil, p. 120, citing an earlier scholar: "a tribe that precipitously exposed itself to death."
108. See, in particular, Amos 8:2.

In the early part of the year, Mitchell First sometimes seasons his food with items that are *ḥarif*.[109]

8. ישן: The Two Meanings of ישן: Sleep and Old

There are two Biblical roots with the letters ישן. One has the meaning "sleep." The other has the meaning "old." An issue had always been whether they were related.

The traditional view had been that the two were related. But the exact nature of the relationship was debated. One view was that the original meaning of the root was "sleep," and that "old" was just a later expansion. For example, the *Brown-Driver-Briggs* lexicon (1906) had suggested that the original meaning of "old" in Hebrew was "withered, flabby, like a lifeless plant with top hanging down, as if in sleep." (This seems very farfetched!)[110]

Another suggestion was that the basic meaning of the root was "be still." This also could explain both meanings in some (unsatisfying) way.[111]

But then the language of Ugaritic was discovered in the early twentieth century in archaeological finds on the western coast of Syria. Ugaritic is an early Semitic language that is closely related to Hebrew.

It turns out that our two ישן roots had different letters in Ugaritic. "Old" was *y-th-n* and "sleep" was *y-sh-n*. So most likely we are dealing with two unrelated roots.[112]

To explain further, our present letter ש has merged two **different** letters that were in the original longer Proto-Semitic alphabet.[113] One

---

109. I had been postponing analyzing this root for decades because of that difficult word *neḥerefet*. I would like to thank Michael Alweis for asking me about *ḥerfu nafsham* and *meḥarfim nafsham*, forcing me to finally confront this root.
110. Klein agrees that the "old" meaning is merely a sense enlargement of the "sleep" meaning (without repeating the strange explanation found in *BDB*).
111. The essay in *TDOT* (vol. 6, p. 439) still prefers this approach.
112. See, e.g., *KB*, pp. 447–48, and E. Horowitz, *How the Hebrew Language Grew* (1960), p. 107. (I highly recommend this very inexpensive book by Horowitz.)
113. Scholars believe that this alphabet had either twenty-seven or twenty-nine letters. See my *Links to Our Legacy* (2021), pp. 111–115.

of the original letters was pronounced "sh." The other was pronounced "th." Eventually, both merged into שׁ in our twenty-two letter Hebrew alphabet.

That our Hebrew שׁ is the result of a merger of two different root letters explains why we do not have to stretch to find a relationship between other words as well such as: *shemen* and *shemonah*, *ḥeresh* (= deaf) and *ḥarash* (= cut, plow), *shelaḥ* (send) and *shulḥan*, and *she'ar* (remainder) and *she'eir* (kin). In all of these pairs, the latter most likely had an original "th."[114] (Usually, it is Ugaritic that helps scholars determine the original Proto-Semitic letter.)

We can also now explain why the Hebrew word for "three" is שׁלשׁ while its Aramaic counterpart is תלת. Both Hebrew and Aramaic share the same twenty-two letter alphabet. The Proto-Semitic letter that was pronounced "th" usually became a *shin* in Hebrew, while it usually became a *tav* in Aramaic. Most likely, this "th" letter was the first and third letter in the Proto-Semitic word for "three."

* * *

On the subject of ישן and its "old, advanced in years" meaning, I will now discuss the words for grandfather and grandmother in modern Hebrew: סבא and סבתא.

If one looks through *Tanakh*, there is no word for either grandfather or grandmother. אמו and אביו are sometimes used for this purpose. For example, at 1 Kings 15:10, אמו seems to mean "his grandmother,"[115] and in the next verse, אביו seems to mean "his grandfather."

In the modern period, the words have gone through some evolution.

The 1943 official dictionary of kinship terms in Hebrew lists grandfather as סב (*sav*) and grandmother as סבה (*savah*). But then it adds that *saba* and *sabta* are permitted as terms of affection, due to their similarity to the word *abba*. Then a smaller line adds that *saba* and *savta* are permitted for general use as well (even when not involving affection).[116]

---

114. See Horowitz, pp. 106–07.
115. See, e.g., Radak, Soncino and *Daat Mikra*.
116. The post at balashon.com (see below) assumes that this smaller line was added after 1943.

Edward Horowitz describes the origin of the word סבא as follows: "It is a word created by the little children in Israel, following closely the word "abba." The children were told to call this relative סב but it was simply much easier for them to link both these older loving male adults with these two similar sounding names: *abba* and *saba*."[117]

The seventeen-volume Ben-Yehuda dictionary (begun by Eliezer Ben-Yehuda in 1910, and continued after his death in 1922 by his wife, son, and other scholars) does not include *sav, saba, savah, sabta,* or *savta*. But one of the definitions of זקן was "grandfather." But זקן could never take off as a word for "grandfather" because it would confuse people who would think it is a reference to advanced age and limited abilities.

The word סב for "grandfather," found in the above 1943 official dictionary of kinship, is based on the Talmud where one can find סבא (*sava*) as "grandfather."[118] This word in the Talmud is related to the Biblical words שב (Job 15:10)[119] and שיבה.[120] These Biblical words mean "old" and "gray hair" but never "grandfather."

In the Talmud, one can also find סבתא (*savta*) as grandmother.[121]

* * *

The latest challenge for modern Hebrew is a word for great-grandparents. The 1943 official dictionary of kinship suggested *av-shilesh* and *em-shileshah*. But people today use *saba-raba* and *savta-raba* (with either א or ה ending.) The more grammatically correct term for great-grandmother would be *savta-rabta*, but this is rarely used today.

* * *

Mitchell First has three grandchildren, the oldest is three. She is not (yet!) interested in these etymological discussions and merely calls him "Zaydie."[122]

---

117. Horowitz, p. 100.
118. E.g., *Ket.* 72b, and *Yev.* 38a and 40b. *Zaken* and *avi av* are also used in the Talmud.
119. See also 1 Sam. 12:2.
120. This word appears many times. See, e.g., Lev. 19:32: *mipnei seivah takum*.
121. E.g., *Bava Batra* 125b.
122. My discussion of *saba* and *savta* has been based on the post on this topic

9. כברת: The Meaning of *Kivrat Ha-Aretz* (Genesis 35:16)

This phrase appears three times in *Tanakh*: at Gen. 35:16 and 48:7 and 2 Kings 5:19.[123]

On first impression, it would seem that the root of the first word is כבר. The root כבר has several meanings in *Tanakh*. The simplest fit would seem to be its meaning of "many." See, e.g., Job 35:16. (It also has the related meaning: "mighty." See, e.g., Isa. 17:12.)

With the meaning "many," we can understand *kivrat ha-aretz* as implying a large distance. Menaḥem ben Ḥelbo,[124] Rashbam, and many others understand the phrase this way.

The problem with the "large distance" approach is that the context of the phrase at 2 Kings 5:19 suggests a short distance.

Another approach to the word is that of Radak. He does not view the initial כ as a root letter. He views the root as ברה with a meaning related to "eating." (See, e.g., 2 Sam. 12:17.) Accordingly, Radak views the phrase as meaning the approximate length of time a traveler travels until his first meal. See his *Sefer Ha-Shorashim*, entry ברה and his comm. to Gen. 35:16. This length of time would probably amount to a considerable distance.

Now I will summarize the famous comments of Naḥmanides (d. 1270) on our phrase. When he first wrote his commentary he was in Christian Spain and he wrote that he agreed with Radak. But near the end of his life, he had to flee Spain, as an eventual consequence of his famous public disputation. The last three years of his life were spent in *Eretz Yisrael*. His commentary continues that once he was there he saw that the distance between the burial site of Rachel and the city of *Beit Leḥem* was short. He wrote that he now retracted what he wrote earlier, and offered the interpretation that ברת here means daughter, as ברת is an Aramaic word for daughter. Naḥmanides wrote that the implication of the phrase "daughter of [a distance of] land" is "a short distance." (The traditional site of the tomb of Rachel is only one mile north of Bethlehem.)

---

at balashon.com of Sept. 2, 2008. I would like to thank Steve Schaffer who first got me interested in this topic.
123. The second and third times, the second word is *aretz*.
124. Cited in Rashi to Gen. 35:16.

A different approach is taken by Ralbag. He realizes that there is one time in *Tanakh* (Amos 9:9) where the word כברה means a "sieve" (= something used for sifting). Based on this, Ralbag believes that the reference to *kivrat ha-aretz* refers to the ploughed area around the city, i.e., its cultivated fields, gardens, and vineyards. The implication of the phrase at Gen. 35:16 would be that only a small stretch of cultivated land separated them from *Beit Leḥem*.[125]

Taking an entirely different approach, scholars today understand the phrase *kivrat ha-aretz* in light of a phrase in Akkadian, the language of ancient Assyria and Babylonia. (Akkadian is a Semitic language, but it is written in cuneiform, unlike the other Semitic languages.) The Akkadian parallel is *bēr qaqqari*. (That second word is the equivalent to the word קרקע.) Accordingly, כברת הארץ should be translated as "approximately one land-mile." The כ means "approximately," and the land-mile was equivalent to a distance of around ten kilometers (= six miles). *Bēr* is the construct form of *bēru*, the Akkadian term for the ancient "mile."[126] *Daat Mikra* is willing to adopt this approach and explains that the Torah here was using an international measure of distance.

(The Akkadian language had the term "land-mile" to distinguish it from another term in their language: "heaven-mile," a measure used for distances in the sky, also with the prefix *bēru*. That is why that second word הארץ was used in our verse. It is otherwise unnecessary, or a word like דרך would have fit better.)

Finally, the context of the phrase at Gen. 35:16 supports the idea that the reference is to a short distance. We are told that Jacob left *Beit El* and it was *od kivrat ha-aretz lavo Efratah* when Rachel began to give birth. Why should Efrat be named if it was still far away? Most likely, it was named because it was not far away. Our insight from Akkadian is consistent with this.

* * *

---

125. See also Rashi on Gen. 35:16 who cites an aggadic explanation based on the "sieve" meaning but admits that it is not a plain sense interpretation.
126. See Tawil, pp. 56–57, C. Cohen, "Elements of 'Peshat' in Traditional Jewish Bible Exegesis," *Immanuel* 21 (1987), pp. 30–42 (34), and N. Tur-Sinai, *Peshuto Shel Mikra* (1962), vol. 1, pp. 58–60.

In case you are wondering why Akkadian, a Semitic language, was written in cuneiform, here is the explanation. The Akkadians settled in Mesopotamia in the third millennium BCE in the area of the Sumerians. The Sumerian language was not a Semitic one and was written in cuneiform. The Akkadians took over the Sumerian writing system, as the Semitic alphabet had not yet been invented. But even after the Semitic alphabetic was invented (probably around 1700 BCE, in the areas of Egypt and Sinai), the Akkadians continued to use only the cuneiform writing system. (A loose contemporary analogy is that I still use AOL as my email address.)

* * *

Going back to our root כבר, I have already mentioned two different meanings to the root: "many/mighty" and "sieve." The root also has a meaning of "intertwining, netting." See, e.g., 1 Sam. 19:13 and 2 Kings 8:15.

There is much debate on whether all or some of these meanings can be related. But it is very hard to connect "many/mighty" and "sieve." (But Rav S.R. Hirsch makes a clever attempt in his commentary to Ex. 27:4: sieving with a *kivarah* is "a real mastering of the material that is to be cleaned through it.")

There are many who try to connect the "intertwining" and "mighty" meanings. For example, perhaps the word started with an "intertwining" meaning and then expanded since intertwined items tend to be strong.

A similar phenomenon occurs with the root גדל. At Deut. 22:12 and 1 Kings 7:17, it has the meaning of "twisted threads," and it has been suggested that here too the "strength" meaning is an expansion. I do not find any of this convincing. I think we have to live with two different unrelated meanings of גדל[127] and a similar lack of relation between the "intertwining" and "mighty" meanings of כבר. But many do connect the "sieve" meaning of כבר with its "intertwining" meaning.

* * *

What about that word כבר? Interestingly, it is only found in Ecclesiasticus. Perhaps it originally meant "length of time" and derives from

---

127. See *TDOT*, vol. 2, pp. 391–92.

the "many /mighty" meaning of כבר. If so, "already" would be a later meaning of the word.[128]

Finally, we have the word עכבר. It appears six times in *Tanakh*. A few of these times it clearly means a small rodent. The balashon.com post of June 5, 2007, tells the story of a woman in Israel who thought that *Allahu Akbar* meant "God is a mouse." An Arab worker in the supermarket corrected her and explained that *Akbar* with a hard "k" (as opposed to *Akhbar*), means "great, big." The above post continues that the language scholar Chaim Rabin believed that the word עכבר for a small rodent did originally come from a "mighty, big" meaning. I.e., the small rodent was called this as a euphemism.[129]

* * *

Mitchell First limits his travel to riding the 167 bus to Manhattan. So far he has not seen any rodents there (unlike in the subway!).

10. כשף: What is the Meaning of מכשפה?

Exodus 22:17 commands that one is not allowed to let a *mekhashefah* live. But what precisely is a *mekhashefah*[130] and what is the meaning of its root כשף?

We have one example of *kishuf* in the Torah, in addition to the general prohibitions at Ex. 22:17 and Deut. 18:10. The one example is Ex. 7:11. Here the Egyptian *mekhashfim* are able to turn their rods into serpents just like Aaron did. So *kishuf* seems to be a form of magic, i.e., an attempt to defy the laws of nature.[131]

Can we see anything like this in the root כשף? After all, words

---

128. See R. Gordis, *Koheleth: the Man and his World* (1951) and Jastrow, p. 609. For more thoughts on this word, see *Daat Mikra* to Ecc. 1:10, n. 22. One of the suggestions made there is that our word is a contraction of כבשעבר (= as in the past).

129. This is only a theory. One does not have to accept it. I remain very suspicious.

130. In all cases but one, Jer. 27:9, the noun has an initial *mem*. I doubt there is a distinction between the noun with the initial *mem* and this one.

131. See similarly *Daat Mikra* to Ex. 7:11: *moftim she-lo ke-derekh ha-teva*.

generally start with concrete meanings, and not with broad meanings like "do magic" or "attempt to defy the laws of nature."

Here are some attempts to understand the root כשף, ones which at least provide some etymological basis for their attempts:[132]

- כשף has a meaning of "cut." There is an Arabic cognate with this meaning. The reference can be to someone who cuts herbs to make a magic brew.[133]
- כשף has a meaning of "cut." There is an Arabic cognate with this meaning. The reference is to self-mutilation, a method of making requests to the gods (see, e.g., 1 Kings 18:28).[134]
- כשף is related to חשׂף with its meaning "reveal." Acts of *kishuf* reveal the hidden or the future.[135]
- כשף is related to שׁוף. At Ps. 139:11, this root seems to have the meaning of "covering." Acts of *kishuf* are activities performed in secret.[136]

Admittedly, all of these suggestions are difficult.[137]

Our word does have a cognate in the ancient Semitic languages of Ugaritic and Akkadian.[138]

Outside of the Torah, there are nine places in *Nakh* where these people who do *kishuf* are mentioned. But the passages are not helpful in determining the precise activity they performed. (Also, the meaning of the term may have evolved over the centuries.)

---

132. This is in contrast to explanations like the one of Ibn Ezra. In his comm. to Ex. 7:11, he writes that a *mekhashefah* alters the way things appear to others, but he does not give any etymological basis for this explanation.
133. See, e.g., *BDB*.
134. See, e.g., *BDB*.
135. This is one of the views mentioned in Mandelkern.
136. S.D. Luzzatto to Ex. 22:17. (Luzzatto is also trying to explain the word אשף, another word in *Tanakh* for "magician.") But *shuf* does not have a "covering" meaning the few times it appears elsewhere.
137. Also worth mentioning is the long etymological discussion by Rav S.R. Hirsch at Ex. 7:11. He relates our word to the roots קשב, ישב and כזב!

An interesting homiletical interpretation of *mekhashfim* is found at San. 67b in the name of R. Yoḥanan.
138. For the former, see *TDOT*, vol. 7, pp. 361 and 363. For the latter, see Tawil, pp. 174–75.

Sanhedrin 7:11 teaches that one is not punished for *kishuf* if one pretends to do *kishuf* to someone but merely deceives him (although such actions are still prohibited). But this Mishnah does not tell us what *kishuf* is! Interestingly, the *Daat Mikra* commentary, at Ex. 22:17, writes that the *Tanakh*, Talmud, Rambam, and Aharonim are all unclear about the precise activity that is considered *kishuf*!

* * *

Several times in *Tanakh* there seems to be a connection between *kishuf* and idolatry. See, e.g., 2 Kings 9:22, and Michah 5:11. Also, at Ex. 17–19, we have prohibitions in the following order: *kishuf*, sexual relations with animals, and sacrificing to idols. Could there be some reason for this grouping?

Umberto Cassuto is able to give an approach that answers these questions. First he explains the prohibition (comm. to Ex. 7:11): "An act of magic is actually an attempt to achieve a given object outside the laws of natural causation, which would otherwise be impossible. The magician believes that he has the power- or others believe so- to compel, by his acts and utterances, the forces of nature and the demons, and even the gods, to do his will. Obviously, there is no room for such views in Israel's religion. The laws of nature were established by the Creator, and it is impossible for a human being to change them in any way; *a fortiori* it is unthinkable that a man should be able to force God to do anything contrary to His will. Consequently, the Torah is absolutely opposed to all forms of magic...."[139]

Cassuto continues (comm. to Ex. 22:17): "Every magical act, even for a purpose that is not evil, is forbidden, since it constitutes an attempt to prevail over the will of God, who alone has dominion over the world." Now we understand why *kishuf* is linked with idolatry. We also understand the connection to verse 19, the prohibition of sacrificing to idols.

But what about 22:18, sexual relations with animals? Cassuto points out that there are many references to such practices in pagan mythology. For example, in Ugaritic poetry Baal had relations with

---

139. U. Cassuto, *A Commentary on the Book of Exodus* (1967, Eng. edition), p. 95.

a cow. In the epic of Gilgamesh, Ishtar had relations with various animals. Rabbi Dr. Hertz comments here that relations with animals "formed part of many ancient heathen cults."

In Cassuto's view, verses 17-19 are one unit representing laws against three idolatrous customs (and all are punishable by death).[140]

Cassuto also points out that in the ancient Near East what was prohibited was only magic intended to harm. In contrast, Cassuto understands the Torah to be prohibiting all kinds of magic.[141]

* * *

A common question is why the prohibition at Ex. 22:17 is in the female form. According to our tradition, a male who engages in the same behavior is equally punished. (See, e.g., the *Mekhilta* on this passage, and *San.* 67a.)

A widespread answer is that the Torah used the female form because most of the individuals who engaged in *kishuf* were women. (This answer is given in both the above sources and in Rashi.) An added suggestion is that the Torah needed to stress that even a woman needed to be killed, since people have more mercy on women.[142] Finally, a third answer is that the word מכשפה does not have to imply only females. Perhaps it is just a collective noun. In the same manner, דגה does not imply only female fish and חסידה does not imply only female stork.[143]

* * *

A few more thoughts:

1. There are many other words in *Tanakh* for those who do mystical activities: חרטם, חבר, אוב, שחר, ענן, נחש, לחש, ידעני, אשף, and קסם. For most of these words, we have a better understanding of their meanings. The terms can be categorized into three groups: magic,

---

140. Similarly, Rambam includes the prohibition of *kishuf* in *Avodat Kokhavim* (11:15). See also *Moreh Nev.* 3:37.
141. See similarly *EJ* 11:703. The cognate to *kishuf* in Akkadian is a term used only for magic intended to harm.
142. See e.g., Rambam, *Moreh Nevukhim* 3:37 and *Daat Mikra* to Ex. 22:17.
143. This view is expressed by R. Yonah Ibn Janaḥ in his *Sefer Ha-Rikmah*. Admittedly, most nouns do not have collective forms.

divination, and astrology. *Kishuf*, at least in its original meaning, seems to have belonged in the first category.[144]
2. At Ex. 22:17, Targum Onkelos translates *mekhashefah* with the Aramaic word חרשא (*ḥarasha*). This means "sorcerer, magician." It probably got this meaning from the "silence" meaning of חרש, and initially referred to those who recited mystical formulas silently or with murmuring.
3. In the translation of the Torah into Greek (third century BCE, Egypt), the word used for *mekhashefah* and its variants is consistently something like *pharmakeia*. This seems to mean either "herbalist" or "poisoner."[145] (In my experience, what is found in the Greek translation is always interesting but there is little chance that it reflects what a difficult word meant originally!)
4. A final question is why the punishment is not expressed as: "She must be put to death." What is expressed instead is: "Do not let her live!" The most interesting answer is provided by Bekhor Shor and Hizzekuni. The phrasing teaches that you are entitled to kill her before she goes to *Beit Din*.[146] If you wait, she will use her magic and escape! (Perhaps twitching her nose like Samantha!)

* * *

As you might have guessed from his last comment, Mitchell First used to enjoy the TV show *Bewitched* as a child.

11. לעט: *Hal'iteni Na Min Ha-Adom Ha-Adom Ha-Zeh* (Genesis 25:30)

Many see a coarse request here by Esau. Is this really the case? Let us analyze the request word by word.

I am basing much of this essay on an article by Joseph H. Prouser

---

144. See *TDOT*, vol. 7, p. 365.
145. Rabbi Dr. Hertz follows such an approach. See his comments on Ex. 22:17 and Deut. 18:10. (At least it has a sound etymological basis, but only to the Greek translation!)
146. For more on this topic, see M. Kasher, *Torah Shelemah, Mishpatim*, sec. 338.

in *Conservative Judaism*, vol. 56 (2004).[147] But I am going to disagree with his conclusion.

1. *Na*: This word is commonly translated as "please" or "now." If the meaning is "please," this is certainly good manners. If the meaning is "now," this is a satisfactory statement as well.[148] (I will discuss the word *na* further at the end of this essay.)

2. *Min*: This word indicates that Esau is only asking for a portion of the item. There is nothing wrong with that. Prouser suggests that Esau is being considerate and leaving for others.

3. *Ha-adom Ha-adom Ha-zeh*:

Admittedly, Esau did not specify what the food item was. This can be evidence of coarseness and inarticulateness. But perhaps (as Nahmanides states) he did not know what the precise food item was.

What about the duplication of the color? This is the only time in *Tanakh* that we have such a duplication.[149] What does it symbolize?

Rashbam suggests that when people are in a hurry, they often double their words. So there is a criticism here of Esau for asking for his food in a hurry. (Another example of duplication as indicating "hurry" may be the angel's intervention to Abraham at Gen. 22: 11: *Avraham, Avraham*. The angel was hurrying to try and spare Isaac from being sacrificed.)

But let us look at some other views of the duplication.

Radak suggests that the duplication merely indicates Esau's intense desire for the item. This is not necessarily a bad quality.

S.D. Luzzatto writes that duplication is used for items that remain separate and do not mix together into a single mass. He cites Ex. 8:10:

---

147. "Seeing Red: On Translating Esau's Request for Soup," pp. 13–20.
148. There is one place in *Tanakh* (Ex. 12:9) where נא means "raw." There is a view that gives it this meaning here. But since this is a unique meaning of the word in *Tanakh*, we should presume that this is not its meaning here.
149. Elsewhere in *Tanakh* we do have words like אדמדם and ירקרק, and there is a disagreement as to whether such forms indicate a lightening or an intensification.

ḥamarim ḥamarim (= piles of frogs). He believes that lentils fit into this category.

Nahum Sarna suggests that the duplication may indicate that the color was "deep red."[150] Prouser suggests that "'deep red' is a thoughtful description of the soup's aesthetic and culinary appeal. Esau is offering his compliments to the chef." Prouser points out that there is a type of wine called *blanc de blanc*. He writes: "Had Esau been dining on lentil stew in a fine restaurant, he might have ordered an accompanying glass of fine white wine – *blanc de blanc* – with no fear that his repetitive language would be construed as inelegant, crude, coarse or impatient. The attentive *garçon* would understand that the request was for a 'light, white wine,' not 'white, white stuff...'"

Note also the duplication at Num. 14:7: *tovah ha-aretz me'od me'od* (= an exceedingly good land).

Accordingly, the duplication does not have to indicate impatience, inability to articulate, or coarseness.

* * *

So far we have seen that, without analyzing the first word, it is easy to conclude that Esau has done nothing wrong. Now let us analyze that first word.

4. הלעיטני:

The root לעט appears nowhere else in *Tanakh*. But the Akkadian cognate to לעט means "swallow."[151] In the Mishnah, it also means "swallow." At Mishnah *Shabbat* 24:3, it is used in connection with feeding camels and calves, although it is the gentlest of the several methods mentioned. The method mentioned is *mal'itin*, which means that food is put in the animal's mouth and the animal swallows it. In the Tosefta, it is also used in connection with feeding animals.[152] In the Talmud, it is sometimes used in connection with feeding humans.[153]

S.D. Luzzatto explains that the sound לע indicates swallowing. This

---

150. N. Sarna, *The JPS Torah Commentary: Genesis* (1989). One source that suggested this long before was Hizzekuni (*adom be-yoter*).
151. See Tawil.
152. See Jastrow, p. 714.
153. See, e.g., *Menaḥot* 98a.

is an obvious onomatopoeia.¹⁵⁴ לעט and בלע both derive from this לע root. Other similar sounding words for "swallow" in Biblical Hebrew are לעו (Obadiah 1:16) and עלע (Job 39:30).

In our verse, לעט, with that initial ה, is in the *hifil*: "cause me to swallow."

Prouser argues that because the word appears only one time, we should be hesitant to translate it in a way critical of Esau and that we should look at the other words used by Esau here to shed light on the word's meaning and connotation.

But the reason the word appears nowhere else is that it is an unusual manner of eating. Moreover, the meaning "swallow" alone is enough to suggest that it is a reference to an uncouth manner of eating. As the commentary in the Anchor Bible writes: "Esau is depicted as an uncouth glutton; he speaks of 'swallowing, gulping down' instead of eating or the like."¹⁵⁵ Similarly, Robert Alter remarks: "It is safe to assume [לעט] was always a cruder term for eating than the standard Biblical one."¹⁵⁶

Thus, although Prouser suggests that a translation of our phrase could be: "Please may I have just a taste of that lovely red soup," I cannot agree.¹⁵⁷ Coarse behavior is likely implied by הלעיטני.

(Here, for example, is the translation of the entire phrase in a coarse manner in *The Living Torah*: "Give me a swallow of that red stuff!")

Prouser concludes his article with the following interesting comment: The translators of this Biblical phrase have "swallowed," uncritically and unflinchingly, the depiction of Esau as a coarse boor.¹⁵⁸

* * *

---

154. In English, we have the word "gulp" for a similar activity. (Its sound even resembles the לע sound.) Most likely this is an onomatopoeia as well.
155. E.A. Spieser, *The Anchor Bible: Genesis* (1981), p. 195.
156. Alter, *Genesis* (1996), p. 129. The interpretation of Rabbi Dr. Hertz is also noteworthy: the word implies "animal-like voracity."
157. Rav S.R. Hirsch's comments also deserve mention. He writes that it is not the food itself but the color that attracts Esau: "It reminds him of the blood of a gasping dying animal that delights his eye when his arrow has found its mark." In his commentary, he paraphrases Esau's statement as: "Quickly give me some of that lovely red stuff!" But his official translation was: "Let me gulp, I pray thee, of this red red pottage."
158. Prouser also argues that Esau's request for a mere swallow might be

On the word נא, an interesting verse is Numbers 12:13, where Moses prays for Miriam to be healed: *Kel, na refa na lah*. Here is the 1917 JPS translation (at the top in the *Pentateuch* of Rabbi Dr. Hertz): "Heal her **now**, O God, I **beseech** thee." The first נא is translated as "now" and the second as "I beseech thee."

In contrast, ArtScroll's *Humash* (Stone edition) has: "**Please**, God, heal her **now**."

Of course, even though the English words "now" and "please" are different, there is not that much difference in meaning between them. נא is perhaps best viewed as an intensifier of a request. Whether it should be translated as "now" or "please" depends on the context.

Finally, interesting is the translation of *The Living Torah*, which seems to drop one of the נא words: "O God, please heal her!" Perhaps the exclamation point at the end is there to reflect the second נא. Or perhaps the initial נא generated the initial "O."

* * *

As his wife will vouch, Mitchell First is always careful to ask for his food with proper etiquette (not exactly!).

12. מופת: What is the Root of *Mofet* (= Wonder, Sign)?

The word מופת or its plural appears thirty-six times in *Tanakh*. Sometimes it refers **to supernatural events/wonders** like the ten plagues. See, e.g., Ex. 11:9-10.[159] Other times מופת refers to a **sign that is a prediction**. For example, at Isaiah 20:3 the מופת is the prophet's walking naked and barefoot, and this predicts and symbolizes a future shameful event that will occur.

Our question is: what is the root of מופת?[160]

---

considered "admirably restrained, especially given his hunger and fatigue." But I am not convinced that "swallow" meant only a request for a small amount. Rashi, for example, believes the word implied a request for a large amount (*shefokh harbeh*).

159. Or Joel 3:3-4.

160. With regard to the parallel word אות, some believe it is related to the root אתה/אתא with its meaning "come." If this is correct, we can easily see that the

As background, the *mem* letters at the beginning of a noun are almost always not root letters. This is because an initial *mem* is typically added to the root letters to turn the verb into a noun. Also, *vav* is almost never the first root letter in a Hebrew word. When one sees a *vav* as a first root letter in a form of a word, this means that the first root letter was really a *yod*. For example, in the root ידע, that *yod* turns to a *vav* in the various forms of the word, e.g., הודיע (= make known). Now we will look at the various approaches to the root of מופת:

1. יפה: As a verb, this means "to be beautiful." S. Mandelkern categorizes our word in this root and (writing in 1896) claims that most scholars agree.

2. יפת: Rav S.R. Hirsch is one who takes this approach to our word. He suggests that this root is related to the root פתה. פתה means "open" in Aramaic and most likely, it has this meaning at Prov. 20:19. R. Hirsch also reads the "open" meaning into the word יפתה at Deut. 11:16 (part of *Shema*). R. Hirsch believes מופת is in the *hifil*, and literally means "to cause to be open." Accordingly, מופת is a sign that forces one to be open to (= take notice of) a teaching. See his commentary to Gen. 1:14 and Ex. 4:21.

   Radak, in his *Sefer Ha-Shorashim*, is another who believes that the root is יפת. He writes that a מופת is a sign whose purpose is to cause one to believe in something that is to occur in the future.

   Most scholars would not agree that there is a root יפת in Biblical Hebrew. There is no other evidence for it. Of course, the response would be our word is evidence for it, thirty-six times.

3. אפת: This approach is taken in the *Brown-Driver-Briggs* lexicon. The suggestion is that מופת is a shortened form of מאפת. This work cites an Arabic word *ifutun* that means both "wonder, portent" and "calamity." Mandelkern also mentions this view. He writes that the Arabic word means *nifla* and *yotzei min ha-kelal*.

---

root implies something that will come true in the future. But other suggestions have also been made for the root. See, e.g., Klein, p. 15: אוה, with a meaning "sign, mark." See Num. 34:10. Alternatively, *TDOT*, vol. 1, p. 167 writes that the etymology of אות is "wholly uncertain," but then suggests it is related to אוה with its meaning "wish, desire."

4. יפע: One who makes this suggestion is S.D. Luzzatto (comm. to Ex. 7:9). We all know the Biblical word הופיע with its meaning "shine forth," which comes from this root. Luzzatto believes that our word is a shortened form of a related word מופעת. The meaning is *mofia ve-galui la-kol* so that, after it, there is no uncertainty. When he translates the word מופת in Italian, the word he uses means "proof."[161] In his Hebrew commentary, he uses the word ראיה, which means "proof."

5. פלא: This is the view of Naḥmanides (comm. to Deut. 13:2). He believes our word is a shortened form of מופלאת (from the root פלא = wonder). He believes that מופת is used when something is done that involves a change of the natural forces of the world.[162] (I initially thought Naḥmanides' suggestion was farfetched. But the more I learned about the root פלא,[163] the more I now take this suggestion seriously.)

* * *

A few other comments:

1. It has been observed that מופת is often used as a description of the events of the Exodus (nineteen out of the thirty-six times).
2. At least one time the same event is described as an אות in one verse and as a מופת in a different verse. At Exodus 4:2 Moses' rod is turned to a נחש and this is described as an אות (see 4:30). Yet at 7:9–10, when Moses does a similar thing in front of Pharaoh (turning his rod into a תנין), the term used is מופת.[164]
3. According to many, there is some overlap between אות and מופת. Every מופת is an אות, but not *vica versa*.

---

161. See the edition of D. Klein, p. 99.
162. Without discussing the root, Malbim says something similar. A *mofet* is something that involves a change of nature and is מפליא for all to see. See his comm. to Ex. 7:3.
163. See the essay below.
164. Seforno (Ex. 7:9) suggests that if the purpose of the sign is to convey a message about the messenger, as in Exodus chapter four (= the reliability of Moses), אות is used. But if the purpose of the sign is to convey a message about the sender, מופת is used. See Malbim's commentary to Ex. 7:3 for a different explanation.

4. אות and מופת often appear together. In the singular, they appear together three times, and in the plural twelve times.
5. There is a statement in *Sifrei* Num. 23 that the two words have the same meaning. On the other hand, *Sifrei* Deut. 83 (on Deut. 13:2) makes the distinction that an אות is *ba-shamayim* (citing Gen. 1:14), while a מופת is *ba-aretz*. (But this is inconsistent with Joel 3:3 which refers to *moftim ba-shamayim u-va-aretz*.)
6. *Midrash Lekaḥ Tov* suggests that an אות is a sign about something in the distant future, but a מופת is a sign for something that is imminent.
7. I doubt that any explanation for מופת is going to work for all the instances. But the proponent of the explanation can always argue that his explanation was its original meaning and then the meaning of the word expanded. (This is why I prefer an explanation for the original meaning that at least connects it to a known root.)
8. My intuition tells me that the word started out as referring to a supernatural event/wonder. When a sign/prediction is made that comes true that too is a "wonder" on some level. Perhaps a sign/prediction then came to be called a מופת even at the time it was made.
9. Finally, a leading modern scholarly lexicon is the one authored by Ludwig Koehler and Walter Baumgartner: *The Hebrew & Aramaic Lexicon of the Old Testament*. It is generally filled with hypothetical suggestions. But it is not willing to make **any** suggestion about the origin of our word, merely writing: "? etym." [=uncertain etymology].[165]

* * *

I would like to acknowledge the post of Rabbi Reuven Chaim Klein of Jan. 8 2019, "The Sign is Coming," at his site "What's in a Word?," which provided many of the above sources.

* * *

It is somewhat of a wonder that I am able to continually write weekly columns without going to the library. (As stated in the introduction

---

165. Similar is the essay in *TDOT*, vol. 8, p. 174. It states that the word's etymology is "still completely uncertain" and makes no suggestion.

to this book, I would like to thank Rabbi Moshe Schapiro, Rachel Berliner, and Rebekah Shoemake of the Yeshiva University library who continue to scan me what I need.)

13. מות: The Meaning of Death

We all know the verb מות and its meaning "to die." But what about the word מתי? At the *seder*, we all recite the following phrase from Deuteronomy 26:5: *va-yagar sham bi-metei me'at*. See also Genesis 34:30 where Jacob complains to Simon and Levi about their endangering him. He states: *va-ani metei mispar*. This word מתי appears 22 times in *Tanakh* in various forms, always in the plural.[166] It always has a meaning like "men" or "people."[167]

Isn't this surprising, a word with root letters מת refers to individuals who are alive, despite the fact that מות means "to die"?

Of course, I am tricking you, because this is a common phenomenon in the Indo-European languages. For example in English, we have the word "mortal." This English word is derived from Latin, where *mori* means "die," *mors* means "death," and *mortalis* means "mortal."[168] The underlying idea is that man has always been viewed as a frail creature that will die eventually. (This is in contrast to the ancient gods, who were believed to live forever.) Another Indo-European language reflecting this same relationship is Greek. Here, *thanatos* is the word for death, and *thnitos* is the word for mortal.

At Deuteronomy 33:6, in Moses' blessing to Reuben, we have both of our מת words in the same sentence: *yeḥi Reuven ve-al yamot, vi-yehi* **metav** *mispar*.

But the use of both words here may just be wordplay, with the two roots not being related. There is much wordplay in *Tanakh*.[169]

---

166. *Metei* is the construct form for the plural *metim*. Scholars have to guess what the singular would have been. Usually they guess *mat*.
167. Or perhaps "warrior." See Isa. 3:25. This is one of its meanings in Akkadian as well. See Tawil, p. 229.
168. I thank Avi-Gil Chaitovsky who pointed this out to me.
169. A well-known wordplay in *Tanakh* involves the letters *ayin*, *resh*, and *mem* at Gen. 2:25 and 3:1. The two similar looking words are not related, as the first

Even though the connection between live individuals and death is clear in the Indo-European languages, it may just be a coincidence in Hebrew that both use the root letters מת.¹⁷⁰ On the other hand, perhaps there is a connection here and one day it will be understood. The idea that מת originally meant "mortal," as in the Indo-European languages, has been suggested.¹⁷¹

* * *

Now let us address the word מות with its meaning "die." Scholars typically search for concrete meanings of words to try to figure out what they originally meant. Here "die" seems pretty concrete.¹⁷² Nevertheless, some suggestions I have seen for an origin are: 1) a relation to מוש: depart; and 2) a relation to מוט: totter, and 3) a relation to an Arabic word with a root similar to מת that means "spread out."¹⁷³ Regarding the third, the *Tanakh* has a root מתח which means "spread out." It appears only once, at Isaiah 40:22.¹⁷⁴

* * *

Now let us return to Deuteronomy 33:6: *yeḥi Reuven ve-al yamot*,

---

comes from a different root, ערה, with its meaning "bare." I have discussed wordplay in *Tanakh* in *Roots and Rituals* (2018), pp. 180–83.

170. There is a tradition that Ibn Ezra made an interesting pun about our two roots. Supposedly, he wrote that the difference between the חיים and the מתים is that the חיים are עומדים, while the מתים are שוכבים. He is referring to the vocalization! The vocalization under the *mem* of live individuals (*metim*) is a *shewa*, in which the dots are vertical. This is in contrast to the vocalization under the *mem* in the word for deceased individuals (*meitim*), in which the dots are horizontal!

I do not believe that this statement is found in any of Ibn Ezra's known writings. But there are sources that attribute this statement to him. (I thank Dovid Wasserlauf for telling me about this.)

171. See *TDOT*, vol. 9, p. 98.
172. The essay on מות in *TDOT* (vol. 8) has only a miniscule discussion (at p. 190) of the word's etymology. It offers no specific suggestions (unlike Mandelkern). But it does point out that the root occurs in the other Semitic languages and in Egyptian.
173. See, e.g., the concordance of Mandelkern for all three suggestions.
174. But the root perhaps also underlies the word אמתחת (= sack), which only appears in Genesis chaps. 42–44. See Klein, p. 37. Tawil, p. 25, disagrees and gives it a different etymology relating to Akkadian.

vi-yehi metav mispar. The expression *metei mispar* appears five times in *Tanakh*. It is evident in each case that the meaning is "few."[175] Literally, this blessing seems to mean: "Let Reuben live and not die, and let him be few in number." What kind of blessing is this?

One approach is that of Ibn Ezra. He suggests that the negative אל applies to both parts of the sentence. The import of the second phrase is *al yehi metav mispar* = let him not be few in number.[176] The 1917 translation of the Jewish Publication Society of America interpreted similarly: "Let Reuven live, and not die, In that his men become few."[177] Rabbi Hertz's own comment below this translation is interesting as well: "Living in Transjordania, he was exposed to constant attacks from numerous enemies."

* * *

As this essay comes to its demise, here are some final thoughts:

1. It is widely agreed that the *metu* in the Biblical names Metushael and Metushelach comes from *mat* with the meaning: "man."
2. The "mate" in the word "checkmate" may be related to our word. It depends on whether "checkmate" derives from Arabic (a Semitic language) or from Persian.
3. The modern Hebrew word for "chess" is שחמט. This spelling was at the suggestion of Hayyim Nahman Bialik (early twentieth century). He wanted to avoid the use of מת in the name of the game!
4. Finally, the "mort" in the word "mortgage" is also related to a death meaning.[178] I have seen different interpretations of precisely why. ("Gage" means "pledge.")

* * *

While still alive, Mitchell First can be reached at MFirstAtty@aol.com. After that, he hopes his address will be something like MFirst@shamayim.com and not: MFirst@sheol.com.

---

175. When the *Tanakh* wants to refer to something as "numerous," it refers to them as "not being able to be counted." See, e.g., Gen. 16:10.
176. Ibn Ezra suggests something similar many other times. See, e.g., his comm. to Prov. 30:3.
177. Seforno takes the same approach.
178. I thank my son Daniel for pointing this out to me.

14. מטה: מטה and Other Words for "Stick" in *Tanakh*

The *Tanakh* has several words for sticks: **mateh, shevet, mishenet,** and **makel**. What is the difference between them?

Let us analyze the easiest one first, משענת. The root here is שען. This verb means "lean, support." A *mishenet* must originally have been a stick used for assistance in walking or when one needs a temporary rest from walking, i.e., a cane. This word appears several times in *Tanakh*. One of them is in the well-known verse at Psalms 23:4: *shivtekha u-mishantekha heimah yenaḥamuni*.

What about מטה? The root here is נטה. This word needs to be analyzed as if it were written מנטה. The initial *nun* root letter dropped. This is a common phenomenon in Hebrew.[179]

The root נטה has several meanings in *Tanakh*: "stretch out/extend," "incline," and "bend down." (Surely these are related but that is another discussion.) Perhaps a מטה was originally a stick that was used to extend one's reach.

(By the way, what is the root of the word *mitah*, a "bed" or "couch" in *Tanakh*? That would also be נטה. Perhaps the original meaning of *mitah* was a place of reclining.[180] Another related word is *le-matah*, downwards, from the "bend down" meaning.)

What about מקל? This is a difficult one. Postulating an initial *nun* that dropped does not help us, as there is no Hebrew root נקל. The essay in *Theological Dictionary of the Old Testament* writes that the etymology is uncertain, but notes a relation to an Egyptian word for such an object: *maqira*.[181] (Switches of the L and R sound between different languages and even within the same languages are common.[182]) This source concludes that the Egyptians borrowed the

---

179. I wrote about this in *Roots and Rituals*, pp. 176–180. Here is another common word with a dropping of its initial *nun*: matanah (= gift). This should be read as if it were מנתנה, from the root נתן = give.
180. *BDB*, p. 641.
181. Vol. 10, p. 549.
182. One example is the Greek word *margarites* (= pearl) which is *margalit* in post-Biblical Hebrew.
  In 1953, T. Lambdin wrote an article where he attempted to collect all words in *Tanakh* that were likely of Egyptian origin or that had a significant

word from Western Semitic. (Hebrew is one of the Western Semitic languages). This source also opines that the word is a primary noun, i.e., it did not derive from a verb.

We could try postulating that the root was קלל. We are used to this root as meaning "curse." But it originated with a meaning like "light." (Just like כבד originally meant "heavy" before it meant "respect.") קלל as "curse" started with a meaning "make light of."

So it is possible that the root of our word was originally מקלל from the root קלל. Then perhaps the reference was to a stick that was lightweight, or to some other meaning related to this root (e.g., swift?). The final ל dropped. This happens often with doubled letters. S. Mandelkern is one source that mentions a possible connection with the root קלל. Also, M. Clark, in his etymological work, puts מקל in the קלל entries, but he does not explain how he connects them. (But note that the *dagesh* in the ק of מקל suggests that the missing root letter, in the mind of the post-Talmudic Masoretes, was not the *lamed* at the end but a letter between the first and second letters.)

Some scholars note the word קלקל with the meaning "shake" as Ezek. 21:26.[183] This might be another angle to help understand our word's origin.

Now let us get to the ubiquitous word שבט. There is no verb שבט in Hebrew. In Akkadian, there is a verb like this which means "to strike, beat." So it is possible that our noun came from this verb! This seems to be the view of E. Klein. But it is also possible that this verb in Akkadian came after the noun.

The noun *shevet* appears 191 times in *Tanakh* (in its various forms). It has two main meanings: "stick" and "tribe." This same phenomenon occurs with the word *matteh*. I have seen an explanation that after being used to refer to the *matteh* and *shevet* of the tribal leader, the word expanded to mean the tribe itself, i.e., to everyone under the command of the one who holds the *matteh* or *shevet*.[184]

---

possibility of being of Egyptian origin. He did not include this one. See *Roots and Rituals*, pp. 188–192, where I discussed the ones he did include.
183. See, e.g., *BDB*, p. 596.
184. For some other explanations, see the post of May 24, 2020 (*shevet* and *matteh*) at balashon.com.

Did the noun *shevet* have a particular connotation originally? Many suggest this. But it is hard to maintain, given that the noun appears in many different contexts. It may simply have meant a wooden stick that could be used for a number of purposes.

One context where *shevet* was often used is that of shepherds. It was an important weapon in holding off wild animals and thieves from the flock. It was also an aide in guiding the flock. It was also used for counting the flock or for separating out certain animals from it, e.g., for tithing purposes (see Lev. 27:32).

Tanakh also uses the word *shevet* outside the context of shepherds. It is an instrument of education, punishment and discipline, both for individuals and for nations. See, e.g., Isa. 14:29 (the *shevet* that struck the Philistines).

Eventually it developed into a symbol of leadership, power and dominion. See, e.g., Gen. 49:10: *lo yasur shevet mi-Yehudah*. I.e., from its basic meaning, it expanded to mean the one who holds the *shevet*.

Finally, there is one more word in *Tanakh* for a "stick." The word is שרביט. It appears only in the book of Esther (four times). A widespread view is that it is an Aramaism of the word *shevet*. There are other occasions when the Aramaic form of a word adds an "R" sound. See, e.g., the word כרסא (= throne) at Dan. 5:20, which is an Aramaic form of the Hebrew כסא.[185]

* * *

It has been observed that despite the over one hundred references to *matteh* in the book of Numbers and twenty-seven in the book of Exodus, the word nowhere appears in the book of Deuteronomy. A suggestion to explain this is that *matteh* is generally used where the focus is on the tribes as separate entities. In Deuteronomy, in contrast, the focus of the book is a much more national one. Hence *matteh* is omitted and *shevet* is the term used.[186]

* * *

Now let us try to provide some insight into the phrase at Ps. 23:4:

---

185. This Hebrew word is borrowed from Akkadian but had its origin in Sumerian. See Klein, p. 281 and Tawil, p. 168–69.
186. I thank Rafi Ganz for this observation and explanation.

shivtekha u-mishantekha heimah yenaḥamuni. This chapter begins with a statement by David that God is my shepherd (23:1). Then at verse 4, the statement is made that God's *shevet* and *mishenet* will comfort him.

Rav S.R. Hirsch suggests: "I take comfort in the knowledge that whatever I receive from Thee, be it chastisement or support, is indeed Thine and comes solely from Thee." Rashi too views the *shevet* here in a similar manner, as inflicting *yissurim*.

But *Daat Mikra* interprets the verse as follows: The speaker, who is speaking as a sheep, is saying: I can relax and feel secure knowing that the shepherd has a *shevet* to strike the wild animals and help lead the way for me, and that he has a *mishenet* to lean on when he navigates the hills and rocks. If we follow the *Daat Mikra*'s interpretation of the verse, its import is that we all should be comforted due to the protection that God provides us.

To close with a few more interpretations: Radak interprets *shivtekha* as *yissurin*, and *mishantekha* as the Torah (since we lean/rely on it). Malbim views *shivtekha* as the adversity that David encountered in his life. It comforted him because he knew its purpose was to steer him in the path of righteousness. Finally, in the view of *Metzudat David*: *shivtekha* refers to being hit with the *shevet* of *yissurin*, but immediately God brings us back/provides us support (= *mishantekha*). This way we know right away that God does not abandon us.

* * *

As a personal injury attorney, Mitchell First needs to carry around a stick to help protect himself from difficult clients.

15. ממזר: The Etymology of the Word *Mamzer*

The word ממזר appears only two times in *Tanakh*: at Deut. 23:3 and Zech. 9:6. According to our Sages, it refers to a child who is the result of certain forbidden relations. (There are different views about precisely which such forbidden relations. See, e.g., *Sifrei* Deut. 248 and *Yevamot* 49a.) The question for this essay is what is the root of the word ממזר and whether we can see evidence of the Sages' interpretation in the root.

As further background, the verse that follows 23:3 is one that prohibits marriage with males of Ammon and Moab. There is a view that ממזר is the name of a nation or ethnic group. (One can support this from the use of the word at Zech. 9:6, see below.) But there is no known nation or ethnic group by the name ממזר. Moreover, the prohibition at Deut. 23:4 refers to עמוני and מואבי. If ממזר was the name of a nation or ethnic group, we would expect ממזרי at 23:3.

On the simplest level, we would expect the root of ממזר to be מזר, with the initial *mem* serving to turn the verb into a noun. There are only two times that a root מזר perhaps appears in *Tanakh*: at Job 38:32 and 37:9. In the first, the context supports a meaning related to the constellations (similar to מזל, see 2 Kings 23:5). As to the second, it may have a constellation-related meaning here. Or perhaps the root at 37:9 is a different root such as זרה, with its meaning "scatter." So we do not have a Biblical root מזר that is helpful to the understanding of our word.

There is a root מזר in Arabic and in some dialects of Aramaic. It has meanings like "rotten, foul." It is used in Arabic in the context of eggs. It has been suggested that our word ממזר can be explained if there was once such a root in ancient Hebrew.[187]

Perhaps this meaning is found in the Hebrew of the Mishnah. At *Ḥullin* 12:3, we have a reference to eggs that are מוזרות. In such a case, one does not have to send away the mother bird. From the context, the meaning seems to be destroyed and unable to produce a young bird. One could read the "rotten, foul" meaning into this word. Similarly, R. Judah Ibn Balaam (eleventh cent.) understands this word as meaning מקולקל (= damaged, defective) and cites this Mishnah as evidence that a *mamzer* is one whose *yiḥus* is מקולקל.[188] But admittedly there are many ways to understand this word in the Mishnah.[189]

---

187. See *BDB* and *KB*.
188. The view of Ibn Balaam is included on AlHatorah.org (citing the translation from the Arabic by M. Peretz).

R. Yonah Ibn Janaḥ is another who believes that the root is מזר and connects it to this Mishnah.

In his commentary on Zech. 9:6, Ibn Ezra cites Ibn Balaam for the view that ממזר is the name of a nation. This is a misattribution by Ibn Ezra. Rabbi Ezra Frazer has advised me that this was the view of a Karaite. (In his comm. on Deuteronomy, Ibn Ezra mentioned this view and attributed it to *aḥerim*.)
189. See the discussion of the early nineteenth-century Mishnah commentator *Tiferet Yisrael*.

Many see the word ממזר as being based on the word זר, with its meanings "strange, foreign."

At Joel 1:17, there is a word ממגרות which means some type of storehouse. Almost everyone agrees that the root of this word is גור, with its "dwell" meaning. This would be an example of a verb that had two *mems* added to its root to generate the noun. Radak (*Sefer Ha-Shorashim*) and Ibn Ezra are among those who explain ממזר in this way: זר plus the addition of two initial *mems*. But the addition of two initial *mems* (as opposed to one) is rare. I doubt there are other examples of this in *Tanakh*.[190]

Could ממזר be an abbreviation of מעם זר or מאום זר? Both would mean "from a foreign nation." These explanations have been suggested by some scholars.

Naḥmanides connects ממזר to the word מוזר and writes that this individual, the product of forbidden relations, will be *muzar me-aḥiv*, i.e., a stranger to his neighbors. They won't know where he came from. The male who sired him will distance himself from him, and even his mother will abandon him as a baby. Therefore, even in the city of his birth, his origin will be unknown.

Bekhor Shor interprets ממזר to mean "born *mi-mi she-zar* to his mother." By זר, he presumably means "foreign, not permitted to." ממי is probably his attempt to explain the double *mem*.

Malbim suggests that the meaning may be that this מום is זר to *Bnei Yisrael*. It is uncommon for *Bnei Yisrael* to produce children through prohibited relations.

Both Talmuds (BT *Yev.* 76b and JT *Kidd.* 3:14) include a statement deriving *mamzer* from *mum zar*. This derivation is found earlier at *Sifrei* Deut. 248.

Now I will mention some approaches that are not based on the word זר with its "strange, foreign" meaning.

Malbim suggests that perhaps a *mamzer* is called this because the מום is from *zera ha-nizra* (a seed that was planted).

Another suggestion is that there may have been a Biblical root זור with a meaning like "loathsome, abhorrent." See Num. 11:20 (זרא) and Job 19:17 (זרה).[191] Many of the forbidden relations that produce a

---

190. No one that I have seen cites any other example.
191. There is a similar root in Arabic with this meaning. See Soncino to Job

mamzer are considered a תועבה, similar to this "loathsome, abhorrent" meaning.[192]

With regard to the meaning at Zech. 9:6, the context is God describing the future defeat of certain Philistine cities: "A *mamzer* will dwell in Ashdod and I will cut off the pride of the Philistines." Perhaps the reference is to a community of *mamzerim*. But a widespread view is that the word *mamzer* is used loosely here and refers to something like "half-breeds."[193]

Perhaps this is a clue to the original meaning of the word. If the meaning here is "half-breeds," this would suggest that there was once a root מזר in Hebrew that meant "mixed." A scholar who suggests this is Ephraim Neufeld. He thinks that originally a *mamzer* meant an offspring of persons of two different nations and then it expanded to include children who were the offspring of incestuous and adulterous unions.[194]

There is a long discussion of the etymology of our word at *Daat Mikra* to Zech. 9:6. Many different views are mentioned.

My own opinion is that a Hebrew root מזר is the most likely basis for our word. The Mishnah in Ḥullin is strong evidence that such a root once existed in Hebrew. Perhaps the interpretation of the word by R. Judah Ibn Balaam comes closest to the truth.

* * *

Mitchell First had been meaning to write about this topic for years. He does not recall what negative interaction with a specific individual may have finally motivated him!

16. עבר הנהר: The Meanings of *Ever Ha-Nahar* and *Ever Ha-Yarden*

A well-known speech is given by Joshua in Shechem: "*Be-ever ha-Nahar yashvu avoteikhem mei-olam...*" (Josh. 24:2). נהר here

---

19:17. But perhaps there is no independent Hebrew root זור with this meaning. This meaning may just be an expanded meaning of the "strange" meaning.
192. This suggestion was made by *Ha-Ketav Ve-Ha-Kabbalah*.
193. See, e.g., Soncino.
194. See his *Ancient Hebrew Marriage Laws* (1944), pp. 224–227. Neufeld also points to an Akkadian word *mazu* that means "to mix."

(and in many other verses) is a reference to the Euphrates river in Babylonia. עבר means "across, at the other side of, beyond." Here, from Joshua's perspective, he is referring to the area beyond the **east** side of the river.

We also have the phrase at 2 Samuel 10:16 from the time of David: "Haddadezer sent and brought forth the Arameans who were *mei-ever ha-Nahar*." Assuming the river is the Euphrates, here too it would seem that the reference is to its east side.

Several decades later, at 1 Kings 14:15, the prophet Achiah warns that the people of Israel will eventually be scattered *mei-ever la-Nahar*. Here too the reference (a prediction) is probably to the east side of the Euphrates.

But in the books of Ezra and Nehemiah the reference is consistently to the **west** side of the River, to an area that includes *Eretz Yisrael*. We have the phrase in Hebrew one time in the book of Ezra and three times in the book of Nehemiah. We also have the phrase in Aramaic, *avar Nahara*, many times in the book of Ezra.

What is going on here? Why did the meaning change? Yoel Elitzur, in his fascinating book *Places in the Parasha* (2020), p. 8, explains: "The earlier occurrences of the expression 'beyond the River' were based naturally on the perspective of the Land of Israel: We are 'here' and they – Assyria, Babylonia, and Haran – are 'beyond the Euphrates.' Only much later do we find sources that unintentionally take the opposite approach, identifying ourselves as the 'other': Assyria, Babylonia, and Susa represent the epicenter of the world, while we in the Land of Israel are resigned to the region 'beyond the Euphrates.'...[195] The watershed moment at which 'beyond the Euphrates' reversed its meaning was, in all likelihood, the rise of the Assyrian empire."

He explains that we have an inscription from the Assyrian king Esarhaddon (early seventh century BCE) which uses the term *eber nari* to refer to the region of *Eretz Yisrael* and some of its surrounding

---

195. Elitzur points out a contemporary analogy. The terms "Middle East" and "Near East" are commonly used to refer to Israel and its neighbors, and "Far East" is commonly used to include China and Japan. All these terms are Eurocentric terms. Nevertheless they are widely used by non-Europeans.

areas like Ammon.[196] From the Assyrians, this use of the term passed to the Babylonians and then to the Persians.

But what about 1 Kings 5:4 relating to Solomon? He preceded the rise of the Assyrians. Here we read that Solomon controlled "*be-khol ever ha-Nahar* from Tifsaḥ to Azah, over all the kings of *ever ha-Nahar*...." Here *ever ha-Nahar* includes *Eretz Yisrael*.

The solution is easily seen. According to *Bava Batra* 15a, the book of Kings was authored by Jeremiah, a prophet associated with the destruction of the Temple in the sixth century BCE. Modern scholars also date the book of Kings to this century since it continues through the destruction of the Temple. Accordingly, Elitzur explains that 1 Kings 5:4 "reflects the mindset of the author of the book of Kings and not that of Solomon or the people of his time."

* * *

Now we will discuss *ever ha-Yarden*.

A famous claim is that the first verse in Deuteronomy must have been written after the time of Moses. Moses is giving a speech on the east side of the Jordan River and the verse refers to the location as *be-ever ha-Yarden*. The claim is that this verse must have been composed **west** of the river, i.e., after the time of Moses.

Both S.D. Luzzatto and the commentary of Rabbi J.H. Hertz reject such a claim. Both explain that the term *be-ever ha-Yarden* does not have to mean "across the river." Rather, it can simply mean "on the side of the river," and apply to both the eastern and western sides.

In his study of the term, the scholar B. Gemser agreed.[197] He found twenty-four cases where the *Tanakh* added specifications after the expression, such as מזרחה (east), or ימה (west). That these specifications were necessary indicates that one cannot merely look at the term and conclude that it always meant "the **other** side." He writes that there are at least sixteen passages where the neutral translation "side" makes sense.

We already discussed Deuteronomy 1:1. Here is another case that Elitzur and Gemser cite. Where is the location *Goren Ha-Atad* in

---

196. See Elitzur, p. 8.
197. *Vetus Testamentum* 2 (1952), pp. 349–355.

connection with the travel to Jacob's burial? The site is described as being *be-ever Ha-Yarden* (Gen. 50:10). Yet it was also supposed to be on the way to Ḥevron where Jacob was to be buried, in a procession that started in Egypt. There was no reason for the delegation to take a circuitous route to the east side of the Jordan river. Translating the term here to refer to a region on the west side of the river solves the problem.

Gemser is willing to apply his approach to *ever ha-Nahar* as well. For example, at 2 Samuel 10:16, he suggests that we do not have to assume that Haddadezer brought those Arameans all the way from the east side of the river.

Gemser concludes his article, published in 1952, with an observation about the country Jordan.

I will give a little background. When this entity was first set up in 1921, it was named "Transjordan." This name was appropriate because it was set up in Eastern Palestine where it was finally decided at this time that the Balfour Declaration of 1917 would no longer apply east of the Jordan river. The precise borders of "Palestine" had not been defined in the declaration itself.[198] In 1946, Transjordan became an independent state. But then came the war of 1947–1949. Jordan ended up with the area that is commonly referred to today as "the West Bank," which had been planned as an Arab state in the 1947 plan for the partition of Western Palestine. (Jordan's annexation was recognized by no countries except the U.K. and Pakistan.) In 1949, Transjordan renamed itself "Jordan" since it was now on both sides of the river.

Gemser mentions this as a loose modern analogy. The new name of the country was broad enough so it could indicate areas on both sides of the river.

Mitchell First lives in Teaneck, New Jersey, "on the other side of Route 4."

---

198. If they had tried to do that, it could never have been issued! It was hard enough for the British War Cabinet to agree to issue that brief statement itself! But there is much documentation of an original intent to apply the Declaration to a large area east of the Jordan river, up to the Hejaz railway (a railway that ran north-south from Damascus to Medina). See, e.g., Balfour's memorandums of June 26 and Aug. 11, 1919, cited in J. Peters, *From Time Immemorial* (1984), p. 518. (In the June 26 memorandum as quoted in the book, I suspect the word "left" was a mistake by either Balfour or Peters and should read "east.")

17. ערב: The Meaning of *Erev Rav* at Exodus 12:38

When the Israelites left Egypt, Exodus 12:38 tells us that an *erev rav* also went with them. One of the meanings of the root ערב is "mix," so a common translation here (following the King James Bible) is "mixed multitude."

Can we say anything more about them? Let us review some interpretations:

- Targum Onkelos: *nukhrain sagiin* = many strangers.
- Rashi: *taarovet umot shel gerim.*
- Ibn Ezra: people from Egypt who mixed themselves in with them.
- R. Aryeh Kaplan: "a great mixture [of nationalities]."

Now let us review some of the commentators who write more expansively:

1. S.D. Luzzatto ("intermarriage" interpretation): He cites to Nehemiah 13:3: "They separated all the *erev* from Israel." From Nehemiah 9:2, it seems likely that *erev* at 13:3 is referring to intermingling by way of intermarriage.[199] Luzzatto concludes: "Therefore, it seems to me that this *erev rav* had previously mixed with the Israelites, and that they were Egyptian men who had married Israelite women and Egyptian women who had married Israelite men..."[200]

    While *erev* with this meaning fits the context in Nehemiah, there is no contextual evidence which would point to this meaning at Exodus 12:38.[201]

2. Rabbi Dr. J.H. Hertz ("riffraff-opportunist" interpretation): "The mass of non-Israelite strangers, including slaves and prisoners of war, who took advantage of the panic to escape from Egypt." (This is also the first interpretation given in *Daat Mikra*.)

3. *Daat Mikra* (second interpretation): Non-Israelites who came to join the Israelites and to mix with them.[202]

---

199. See also Ezra 9:2.
200. Translation from the edition of D. Klein.
201. There is evidence of such intermarriage at Lev. 24:10.
202. See also the first sentence of Luzzatto quoted below.

Daat Mikra cites *Exodus Rabbah* 18:10.[203] Here we are told that the *kesherim* of Egypt, the ones who loved the Israelites, participated in the *pesaḥ* sacrifice and left with them.

Daat Mikra also cites Philo (first cent.). Here are Philo's words at *Life of Moses* I, sec. 147: "Moreover, there also went forth with them a mixed multitude of promiscuous persons collected from all quarters, and servants, like an illegitimate crowd with a body of genuine citizens. Among these were those who had been born to Hebrew fathers by Egyptian women, and who were enrolled as members of their father's race. And, also, **all those who had admired the decent piety of the men, and therefore joined them; and some, also, who had come over to them, having learnt the right way, by reason of the magnitude and multitude of the incessant punishments** which had been inflicted on their own countrymen."

* * *

Luzzatto also writes at 12:38: "It has been said that these were Egyptians who mixed with the Israelites in order to become proselytes, upon seeing the prodigious wonders that God had done for them... It seems to me, however, that even if some people were stirred to become proselytes, there would have been no reason for them to leave with the Israelites, for the Israelites had never said they were going away permanently, but were supposed to return immediately."[204]

Luzzatto has raised an interesting issue. From Moses' statements to the Israelites at 12:17 and 25–26, it seems that they knew they were not coming back, but Moses did not share this with Pharaoh. Pharaoh seemed to assume that they would return after the holiday he granted. See, e.g., 12:31 (*ke-daberkhem*). What the non-Israelites would have thought is a difficult question. If they were living among the Israelites, presumably they would have known what the Israelites' plan was. But if they had not been living among the Israelites, probably they would not have known. Nevertheless, they might have attempted to leave with the Israelites anyway. Once out, they could have continued on their own.

* * *

---

203. *Exodus Rabbah* is a late midrash. Rashi, for example, never cites it.
204. Translation from the edition of D. Klein.

A scholar Shaul Bar suggested a novel interpretation of the phrase *erev rav*.²⁰⁵ There are three verses in *Tanakh* where the word *erev* is used and it could mean "mercenaries," i.e., people that are paid to fight on your side. This would come from a different meaning of the root ערב, the "take on a pledge" meaning, or the "exchange" meaning. The three verses are Jer. 25:20 and 50:37, and Ezek. 30:5. For example, Jer. 25:19-20 reads: "Pharaoh king of Egypt, and his servants, and his princes, and all his people, and all the *erev*...." The word that Targum Yonatan uses in all three verses for *erev* comes from the root סמך, which means "support." See also Rashi on all three verses and especially on Jer. 25:20: *u-mishanto aleihem le-ezrah* (= he relies on them for help). See also Soncino to Jer. 50:37: "foreign traders or mercenaries." So perhaps *erev* meant "mercenary" at Exodus 12:38. Bar also argues that if it does, we can better understand how the Israelites can be described as *ḥamushim* when they left, assuming that this word means "armed."²⁰⁶ Bar concludes that "it is most probable that the term ערב רב in Exod 12:38 refers to mercenaries who intermarried with the Israelites and left armed with them at the time of the Exodus."

While I appreciate the creativity of this attempt at a solution, there is nothing in any surrounding verses that suggests that we have a reference to mercenaries in the phrase *erev rav*. (Moreover, as Bar admits, the vocalization under the *ayin* in the word with the "mercenary" meaning is a *segol*, while here it is a *tzere*.)

* * *

Two final points:

- There are no passages in either Talmud that give an interpretation of *erev rav* except for the passage at *Betzah* 32b where an *amora* who was not treated with kindness criticized those who treated

---

205. See his "Who Were the 'Mixed Multitude'?" *Hebrew Studies* 49 (2008), pp. 27-39.
206. There are many possible interpretations of this word. I discussed them in an essay in *Links to Our Legacy*, pp. 26-30. I argued for the interpretation: "arrayed in military formation." This interpretation is based on the idea that ancient armies marched in a format of five sections: front, rear, two wings, and center.

him and said that they must be descendants of the *erev rav*. He observed that, in contrast, the seed of Abraham are *meraḥem al ha-briyot*. But perhaps these statements were only made with homiletical intent.²⁰⁷

- Another issue is whether the *erev rav* are to be identified with the *asafsuf* of Num. 11:4. The identification is more compelling if we can view *erev rav* as one word. The Samaritan Torah has this reading. In this reading, the fourth and fifth letters are just reduplicative, like *yerakrak*. The reduplicative term may also be a form of disparagement. Many sources, ancient and modern, make the identification. The fact that "mix" and "gather" are words with a similar meaning supports the identification. On the other hand, if the groups were the same, we would expect the same word to have been used and it was not.²⁰⁸

* * *

Mitchell First is an attorney and Jewish history scholar. Unlike *erev rav* and *asafsuf*, these terms in no way mean the same thing.

18. פלא: Insights into This Wondrous and Marvelous Root

1. Our topic is the word פלא and its derivatives such as נפלא. As one scholar has written, this root usually describes "extraordinary phenomena, transcending the power of human knowledge and imagination... [T]he usual translation of the niphal as 'be marvelous' comes close to the basic meaning."²⁰⁹

    The common English translation of פלא is "wonder" so I will generally use that, but I agree with the above analysis.

    Our root occurs many times in *Tanakh*. One example is in *Oz Yashir* (Ex. 15:11). God is here described as *oseh feleh* = doing wondrous things.

---

207. But see Rambam, *Matanot Aniyyim* 10:2 ("whoever is cruel and not merciful, his lineage is suspect...").
208. For further reading on this topic, see D. Zucker, thetorah.com, Jan. 30, 2020, "Erev Rav: A Mixed Multitude of Meanings."
209. *TDOT*, vol. 12, p. 534.

Another example is Ex. 3:20. God says that He is going to strike Egypt *be-khol nifli'otai* (= with all My wonders). *Niflaot* in general, when referring to acts of God, refers to actions that are unfathomable to human beings and at variance with human understanding.

Finally, another example of our root is at Psalms 118:23 (Hallel): "This was God's doing; *hiy nifleit be-eineinu* (= it is wondrous in our eyes)."

2. There is another root in Hebrew, פלה, that means "separate." A main issue in analyzing our root is whether פלא is related to this other root. After all, wonderful things are separate from normal things. Many scholars believe the two roots are related. But I am going to follow the approach that the roots are distinct. This is the approach taken in the essay in *Theological Dictionary of the Old Testament* (vol. 12, p. 536).

3. Sometimes we have a word where the third root letter has dropped and the word could be from either פלא or פלה. One example is Ex. 33:16: ונפלינו. But from the context, it is evident that this word is from פלה: *ve-niflinu ani ve-amekha mi-kol ha-am*....

4. At Ex. 9:4, although the plain sense of והפלה here is "separate," both Targum Yonatan and Naḥmanides give interpretations related to פלא = wonder.

5. What about the meaning at Deut. 17:8? Here we have: *ki yippale mimkha davar la-mishpat*... The translation in the *Pentateuch* of Rabbi Dr. Hertz at the top (the 1917 Jewish Publication Society of America translation) is: "If there arise a matter too hard for thee in judgment..." But the commentary of Rabbi Dr. Hertz correctly suggests "extraordinary," instead of "hard." Another interesting use of the root is at 2 Sam. 13:2 in the context of Amnon being in love with Tamar but being unable to do anything about it (*va-yippale be-einei Amnon la'asot lah meumah*). It can be concluded from both of these examples that the root פלא is used when individuals are confronted with tasks and obstacles that are beyond their imagination and ability.

6. A main issue in the root פלא are those five occasions in the Torah where it is used in connection with vows. For example, the first

is Lev. 22:21: *le-falle neder*. The phrase does not fit the "marvel, wonder" meanings. Also, making a *neder* is not something beyond human imagination and ability.

Rashi here writes: *le-hafrish be-dibburo*, giving it a meaning relating to "separate," i.e., to set aside through his statement. Similarly, Rashi on Deut. 17:8 writes that the root פלא is always one of *havdalah u-ferishah*. Similarly, Ibn Ezra on Lev. 22:21 suggests the meaning *le-faresh*.[210] (Here is a sample of other commentators: R. Saadiah translates our word as: *la-tet be-lev shalem*.[211] *The Living Torah* uses the word "presents." Rav S.R. Hirsch makes a very speculative attempt to relate this פלא to our other meaning of פלא.)

One solution is to treat these words in the vowing context with the root פלא as deriving from פלה and its meaning "separate." Radak suggests this in his *Sefer Ha-Shorashim*, entry פלא. But perhaps it is simplest to view the use of the root in the vowing context as fitting within the root פלא and indicating an "extraordinary" type of speech.[212]

7. At Judges 13:18, an angel tells Manoah and his wife (the future parents of Samson) not to ask what his name is and instructs that it is פלאי. Many Rishonim understand the meaning here as "covered." But most likely, the meaning is something like "high and beyond human comprehension." One can see this meaning at Psalms 139:6 where our root appears and is parallel to נשגבה (= high). See also Radak, *Sefer Ha-Shorashim*, פלא. His translation of our phrase: "My name is *nifla ve-nisgav mei-lehodia lekha*." See also *Judges*, Anchor Bible, p. 222: "beyond comprehension." See also *Daat Mikra* to Psalms 139:6, which cites Deut. 17:8.

8. I previously discussed the possible roots of the word מופת and came to no definite conclusion. One suggestion I mentioned was that of Nahmanides that it is a shortened form of מופלאת, from our root פלא. (See his comm. to Deut. 13:2.) He wrote that מופת is used when something is done that involves a change of the

---

210. But compare his commentary to Num. 6:2 when the verb is used in the case of a *nazir*.
211. This is the translation in the *Torat Hayyim* from the original Arabic.
212. See *Daat Mikra* on Num. 6:2 which explains the meaning as: *nivdal ve-yotzei min ha-kelal*.

natural forces of the world. As I learned more about the root פלא, his suggestion sounds more attractive. (Without discussing the root of the word מופת, Malbim writes something similar. A מופת is something that involves a change of nature and is מפליא for all to see. See his comm. to Ex. 7:3.)

9. פלא is the first name of the child with a long name mentioned at Isa. 9:5: *pele yoetz kel gibbor avi ad sar shalom* (= wonderful in counsel is God the mighty, the everlasting father, the ruler of peace).

10. Of course, it is interesting that our word is used in the *Asher Yotzar* prayer: *u-mafli la'asot*. *The Complete ArtScroll Siddur* translates the entire phrase as "Who heals all flesh and acts wondrously."

The phrase *u-mafli la'asot* is taken from Judges 13:19 and the above story about the angel who informed the parents of Samson about his forthcoming birth. The phrase *u-mafli la'asot* is used in conjunction with the angel's ascent to heaven on fire that came from an altar. There is a widespread view that to better understand the phrases in our prayers one has to see how they are used in their original context. One wonders what message is being conveyed by the borrowing of this phrase from this story!

In a different context, the phrase in our Rosh Hashanah liturgy *harat olam* (= birth of the world) is taken from Jer. 20:17. There it means "eternally pregnant"! So it seems that Biblical phrases are sometimes creatively borrowed into our prayers without the borrowing indicating an underlying message. I think this is what occurred with *u-mafli la'asot*.

11. I always wondered about the phrase פלני אלמני. (I wonder why I keep using the term "wonder"!) This phrase appears three times: at 1 Sam. 21:3, 2 Kings 6:8, and Ruth 4:1. Also, at Dan. 8:13, we have פלמני, which is probably a contraction of the two words.

The root פלה = "separate" is likely the root of the first word. The second word likely derives from אלם with its meaning "silent." Therefore, the phrase means something like "the separate (= certain, distinct) person who is not mentioned."[213]

* * *

---

213. See, e.g., *BDB*, p. 811 and *Daat Mikra* to Ruth 4:1. At 1 Sam. 21:3 the reference is to a place that is not mentioned.

Mitchell First had always thought *ploni almoni* was essentially jibberish like "Joe Shmoe"! It is wonderful that he continues to learn new insights!

19. פסים: What is the Meaning of כתנת פסים?

כתנת is an easy word. It appears many times in *Tanakh* and is a type of garment. But what is the meaning of that word פסים?

Aside from the Joseph story at Gen. 37:3, the phrase *ketonet passim* only appears in one other story in *Tanakh*, the story of Tamar at 2 Samuel 13. (The phrase appears three times in the Joseph story and two times in the Tamar story.) In the Tamar story, we are told that it was a type of מעיל (= upper garment, coat) that *benot ha-melekh ha-betulot* wore.

Where do we get the well-known translation "coat of many colors"? The Septuagint (third century BCE, Egypt) used the word *poikilos* to translate the word פסים in the Joseph story. (It used a different word in 2 Samuel.) *Poikilos* is usually understood to mean "various colors." This translation was followed in the King James Bible of 1611. The 1917 translation of the Jewish Publication Society often followed the King James Bible and they did so here as well.[214]

Targum Onkelos had used the word פסי which is subject to different interpretations. But Targum Yonatan used the word מצויר. I have seen this translated as "many colors." But I have also seen this translated as "with pictures," "with designs," or "embroidered." If it did mean "many colors," then we would have another early source for the "many colors" translation.

There are those who view פס or פסים as a kind of material. For example, Rashi calls it *kli milat*. From other statements in Rashi we see that he means "fine wool."[215] R. Saadiah Gaon had written that פס or פסים was "silk."

But there are many other approaches to the word. As an introduction, I have to explain that פס has several meanings in Aramaic/Rabbinic Hebrew:

---

214. See the translation at the top in the *Pentateuch* of Rabbi Dr. Hertz.
215. See the ArtScroll edition of Rashi.

One meaning is "strip," stripe."²¹⁶ This meaning is not found elsewhere in *Tanakh*.

The other meanings are "hand" and "ankle/foot."²¹⁷ Most likely, פס has these meanings because it means "end." The hand and the ankle/foot are the ends of the arms and legs. This meaning of פס is related to the word אפס. In *Tanakh*, we have *afsei aretz* many times with the meaning the "ends of the earth."

We have the "hand" meaning in the Aramaic section of *Tanakh* at Dan. 5:5: *pas yeda*.²¹⁸ We have the "ankle" meaning at Ezek. 47:3: אפסים. (I am not concerned with the initial א, since the meaning of פס as "end" probably derives from אפס.)

Let us now look at the various interpretations of פסים that have been proposed. Based on the "hand" and "ankle, foot" meanings, our phrase can mean a coat that goes all the way down to the hand, or all the way to down the ankle/foot, or all the way down to all of these. *Genesis Rabbah* 84:8 and others suggest the first of these approaches. A late midrash edited by S. Buber takes the second of these approaches,²¹⁹ as do others. S.D. Luzzatto and R. David Zvi Hoffmann are among those who follow the third approach.²²⁰

It is widely viewed that such a coat would symbolize that the wearer was one who was exempt from manual labor.²²¹

There are Rishonim who view *ketonet passim* as a garment with various colors. The earliest with this view are Ibn Balaam, Ibn Janaḥ, Radak (in his Genesis commentary, and in his *Sefer Ha-Shorashim*) and Ralbag (on 2 Sam.). But how do they come to this conclusion?

---

216. See Jastrow, p. 1191.
217. See, e.g., Mishnah *Meg.* 4:8, Mishnah *Ohalot* 1:8 and Jastrow, p. 1191.
218. *Pas* probably means that part of the יד from the wrist to the tip of the finger. See Jastrow, p. 1191. A similar expression is at Dan. 5:24.
219. It is included in AlHatorah.org on Gen. 37:3.
220. See also Josephus who writes in the context of Tamar: "long-sleeved tunics reaching to the ankle." See *Antiquities*, VII, 8, 1. The Septuagint in the context of Tamar had used a Greek word that meant "long-sleeved" relating to the arm. (Josephus had omitted mention of the *ketonet passim* in his discussion of Joseph.)
221. In contrast, Rav S.R. Hirsch views the "end" meaning as not indicating the length of the coat, but as indicating that the coat had special trimming on its edges.

When partial quotes from these sources are brought, it sometimes seems that they are getting it from the "stripe" meaning of פס. (A striped garment can imply that the stripes are of different colors.) But when I read all the above sources carefully, I realized they are all deriving their interpretation from the "hand" meaning. They are understanding פסים as implying a garment made of separate patches that are the size of a hand, and viewing the implication of separate patches as the patches being of different colors. (Of course, a garment can be composed of patches and not be multi-colored. But it is surely the luxurious implication of the *ketonet* that leads them to suggest that we are dealing with patches of different colors.)

It is not clear to me what motivates this unusual interpretation. The interpretation of פסים as describing the length of the coat is a much simpler one.

A creative approach is found in Bekhor Shor and Hizzekuni: a beautiful coat לפייסו (to pacify him). But this meaning of פיס is not a Biblical meaning. It is found in Rabbinic Hebrew, borrowed from Greek (and related to our word "appease.")

Among modern translations, the Koren has "coat with long sleeves" and R. Aryeh Kaplan has "long colorful coat."

The phrase *l-b-sh p-s-m* is referred to in a clothing list from Ugarit (Syria) dated not later than the thirteenth century BCE, but the precise meaning is unclear.[222]

There are Babylonian temple texts from around 600 BCE that refer to *kitu pishannu* or *kutinnu pishannu*. This was a ceremonial robe that had various gold ornaments sewed onto it.[223] *Pisshanu* is an Akkadian term for stitched-on ornaments. But even if we assume a linguistic connection, these texts are much later than the Joseph story.[224]

---

222. Tawil, p. 300.
223. See E.A. Speiser, *Genesis* (Anchor Bible), and Tawil, p. 300.
224. *Daat Mikra* on 2 Sam. 13:18 includes a photo with the caption reading: "women dressed in *ketonet passim*; wall fresco in ancient Egypt" (my translation from the Hebrew). After investigation, I found that this is a photo from a famous Egyptian tomb painting from 1900 BCE from the tomb of Khnumhotep II at Beni-hasan which depicts women and men (all described as foreigners) wearing multicolored tunics. But there is nothing here to indicate any connection to the term *ketonet passim*!

After all of that, what do I think? The simplest approach is that *ketonet passim* means a coat that goes all the way down to the hand, or all the way to down the ankle/foot, or all the way down to all of these, based on the פס = end meaning. As stated earlier, such a coat would symbolize that the wearer was one who was exempt from manual labor.

I would like to acknowledge the article by Rabbi Dr. Ari Zivotofsky in *Jewish Action* 2018, which provided many of the above sources.

Finally, as to כתנת, it is a word that appears (sometimes with slight modification) in many ancient languages, Semitic and non-Semitic. In Greek, their related word is *chiton*. It has been suggested that the Latin word *tunica* (the basis for our English word "tunic") was probably originally *ktunica*.[225]

* * *

Mitchell First thinks that the most creative explanation is the one first found at *Genesis Rabbah* 84:8: פסים symbolizes Joseph's troubles: *Potiphar, Soharim, Yishmaelim* and *Midianim*!

20. פתה: *Pen Yifteh Levavkhem* (Deuteronomy 11:16)

We all recite this phrase regularly in the second paragraph of *Shema*. But what does it mean? The word that needs a proper translation is יפתה.

ArtScroll, in the various works it publishes, consistently translates this phrase as "lest your heart be seduced." Similarly, the 1917 Jewish Publication Society of America translation (at the top in the *Pentateuch* of Rabbi Dr. Hertz) has "lest your heart be deceived." An early rabbinic source, *Sifrei* Deut. 43, names the *yetzer ha-ra* as the party doing the seduction/deception.[226]

But there is a problem with the above translations. *Yifteh* is in the *kal* construct. It is not in the *nifal*. The *nifal* would be *yipateh*. "Be deceived" and "be seduced" are translations that correspond to the

---

225. *TDOT*, vol. 7, p. 384.
226. "*She-lo yit'eh etkhem yetzer ha-ra.*"

nifal, where some other party is causing the deception/seduction. That is not the import of the *kal*.[227]

I have seen the alternative translation "be tempted."[228] This is better as one could interpret this as meaning being tempted by oneself.

Rav S.R. Hirsch translates: "that your heart does not open itself to being led astray."[229] Let us evaluate this suggestion.

The verb פתה occurs 28 times in *Tanakh* in various constructs. In the *nifal*, it means that you were led by another to do a foolish thing. In the *piel*, you are persuading or misleading someone else. But what does the verb mean in the *kal*? The verses in the *kal* that are most analogous to ours are Proverbs 20:19 and Job 31:27.

As further background, in Aramaic the *kal* has the meanings "open" and "expand." We see the "expand" meaning once in *Tanakh* at Gen. 9:27: "God will cause to expand the (borders of) *Yafet*." But here our verb is in the *hifil*.

Is the "open" meaning of the verb פתה found in *Tanakh*? Most likely, "open" is the meaning of פתה in the *kal* at Proverbs 20:19. Here the verb is parallel to גולה and its meaning "reveal." Since the "open" meaning is found for the *kal* here, we can accept the suggestion of Rav Hirsch regarding Deut. 11:16.

One scholar has made a similar suggestion. He translates the phrase: "lest your mind become so open that you turn aside…"[230] He explains further that "open" here has the meaning "open-minded." He writes: "that was exactly the complaint of the prophets and of Deuteronomy against the people – they were too tolerant of alien gods."

---

227. See, e.g., the commentary of S.D. Luzzatto, who points out that the meaning here is יפתה מאליו.
228. See, e.g., *The Living Torah*. Rabbi Jonathan Sacks also uses this translation, as does *The Koren Siddur*, American edition (2009). *Siddur Avodat Halev* (2018) in its translation has "be deceived." But in its commentary it cites the passage as if "be tempted" was its translation.
229. See also the Siddur of R. Hirsch: "lest your heart open itself to temptation."
230. T.J. Meek, "Old Testament Notes," *Journal of Biblical Literature* 67 (1948), pp. 235–36. Note that our verse referred to the *lev*, but Meek loosely translates it as the "mind." In an essay in the "Liturgy" section of the present book, I explain that in *Tanakh* it is the heart and the kidneys that control man's decisions. The brain and the mind are not mentioned in *Tanakh*. The brain's importance was not discovered until the fifth century BCE.

Now I will offer another approach to our word *yifteh*. Let us look at the other very analogous verse, Job 31:27. This verse has the phrase *va-yift ba-seter libbi*. This is not only another instance of our root in the *kal* but also a verse using it with the word לב. The previous verse referred to the sun and moon shining as it is normal for them to do. Then comes verse 27 where Job refers to the possibility (which he denies) that he might have had foolish thoughts regarding paying homage to the sun and the moon.[231] But if he would have, he would not have been misled by the sun and the moon. He would have been thinking these foolish thoughts on his own. That is why the verb is in the *kal*. The *Daat Mikra* commentary on Job 31:27 suggests that the same explanation applies to Deut. 11:16. The meaning is: thinking foolish thoughts on one's own.[232] This is also essentially the translation of our phrase offered in *Theological Dictionary of the Old Testament*: "simple and foolish."[233]

To sum up, I have provided alternative approaches to the "be seduced/be deceived" approach which was grammatically problematic. My suggestions are an approach to פתה based on an "open" meaning and an approach based on a "be foolish" meaning.

* * *

A remaining issue is whether the "open" meaning and the "foolish" meaning are related. Aside from the verb with a meaning related to "foolish," the noun פתי for a foolish person appears many times in *Tanakh*.

A simple explanation of the relationship is that the "open" meaning came first and that the "foolish" meanings are expansions. A foolish person is one who is open to different ideas (whether wisdom or folly). But he finds it hard to discern the truth. See, e.g., *Brown-Driver-Briggs*, p. 834 and Prov. 14:15 (*peti ya'amin le-khol davar*). See also Rav S.R. Hirsch on Gen. 9:27. Probably, the noun "foolish person" developed first (from the "open" meaning), and the verb "to be foolish" developed later.

* * *

---

231. See the commentary in the Soncino.
232. This is essentially what *Daat Mikra* on 11:16 has: *yihiyeh le-feti ve-kal daat*. Earlier, Hizzekuni had taken this approach.
233. Vol. 12, p. 169. *KB* suggests: "be simple, gullible."

Now I want to mention a different problem that I can now probably explain. Seven times in *Tanakh* we have a word פתע that means "sudden." Twenty-five times we have another word פתאם that means "sudden." But why is one with *ayin* and one with *aleph*? We even have the words together several times with their contradictory spellings. *Peta pitom* is at Num. 6:9 and Isa. 29:5. *Pitom le-peta* is at Isa. 30:13.

The most likely explanation is that the original word for "sudden" is פתע. But when there is a *mem* after these letters, this makes it hard to pronounce the *ayin* properly, so an *aleph* became the letter instead. But why that synonym פתאם had to arise at all I cannot (yet) explain.

I included this topic here because I have seen the suggestion that פתע is related to פתה = "be foolish" and that the latter originally meant "to act suddenly, without consideration." This is mentioned as a possibility in E. Klein.[234] But I think the connection of פתה = "be foolish" with the meaning "open" is more likely.

* * *

The father of the prophet Joel was named פתואל. This is the only time this name is in *Tanakh*. *Daat Mikra* suggests that it comes from the "expand" meaning of the root פתה, and that the name is analogous to the Biblical name רחביה.[235] Interestingly, in the Greek translation of the Torah, the name of the father of Joel begins with the Greek letter for "B." This translation gave him the same name as the father of Rebekah!

* * *

Mitchell First is a scholar and an attorney. As a scholar, he has an open mind. In the field of law, both sides are trying to mislead the jury.

21. רגע: The Multiple Meanings of the Root רגע

It is easily seen that the root רגע has three different meanings in *Tanakh*. For example, it has the meaning "rest" a few times. An example is Deut. 28:65: *u-va goyim ha-hem lo targia* (= among those

---

234. Klein, p. 536. See also Rav S.R. Hirsch to Gen. 9:27.
235. Introduction, p. 6.

nations you will have no rest). It also seems to have the meaning "**move, stir up**" a few times. One example is Isa. 51:15 which describes God as *roga ha-yam*. That phrase is followed by *va-yehemu galav* (= its waves roar). This implies that the *roga* preceding it has a "move, stir up" meaning. Finally, *rega* has the meaning "**brief period of time**" many times in *Tanakh*. See, e.g., Num. 16:21: *va-akhalleh otam ke-raga* (= I will consume them in a moment).

Do all three meanings have a common origin? The widespread view is that the "brief period of time" meaning and the "move" meaning are related. This has an analogy in English. It is widely accepted that the English word "moment" derives from the word "movement."[236] (Think of the hands of a clock!)

The harder question is whether the seemingly opposite meanings of "rest" and "move" have a common origin. There is a cognate in Arabic that means something like "returned to rest after wanderings." Based on this, it has been theorized that one meaning of רגע focused on the "rest" aspect of this idea, and the other meaning focused on the "movement" aspect. But this is farfetched. More likely, "rest" and "move" are separate רגע roots which coincidentally have a common spelling.[237] (It has been suggested that the "move, stir up" meaning is related to the root רגז.)

The root רגע also appears at Job 7:5. This perhaps reflects a different רגע root altogether. (I will discuss this verse shortly.)

Three times in *Tanakh* we have the word ארגיעה or ארגעה: Proverbs 12:19, Jer. 49:19 and Jer. 50:44. The contexts in each indicate suddenness. A widespread understanding among scholars is that this word refers to a person moving his eye: "I twinkle [my eye]." See, e.g., Soncino to Prov. 12:19. In none of these three verses is the word for "eye" in the verse. It has been further suggested that the original meaning

---

236. But Mandelkern suggests the opposite approach is possible as well. Each *rega* is a brief period of rest during the continuum of time. One who adopts this view is Rav S.R. Hirsch (comm. to Deut. 28:65).
237. See Klein, p. 606. In contrast, the essay in *TDOT* (vol. 13, pp. 326–27) argues for one underlying root and claims that most scholars today agree. It states further that "most OT occurrences can be derived from the concrete notion of a 'blink of an eye'..." But I fail to see how this approach can explain the several "rest" meanings.

of רגע as "moment" was the twinkling movement of the eye.[238] (I will discuss this further below.)

Daat Mikra takes a different approach to the three ארגעה / ארגיעה verses. It suggests the meaning of ארגיעה is: "I will do this in one *rega*." See their comm. to Jer. 49:19.

At Job 7:5, we have Job stating that his skin was *raga*. This is a very difficult verse. In the first part of the verse, Job stated that his flesh was clothed with worms and clods of dust. After רגע, the next word is וימאס. This last word may mean "became repulsive" but many translate it as if the root was מסס and the meaning: "melted, flowed." So what could *raga* mean here? Targum Yonatan has רטט, which means "shake." Some of the Rishonim have בקע, which means "break open." (They see this meaning in the רגע verses in connection with the sea, so they have this meaning available to be used here.) Malbim sees the "rest" meaning here: rest from the worms. *Brown-Driver-Briggs* suggests "harden," and suggests that this is possibly a special development of the "rest" meaning. *Daat Mikra* suggests, based on the sea-wave verses, that the meaning is that his skin has folds and valleys like waves. But perhaps this word in Job 7:5 comes from a different רגע root altogether.

Since the verb רגע can mean either "movement" or "rest," sometimes a verse is ambiguous as to which meaning is intended. For example, at Job. 21:13 we have: *u-ve-rega* they go down to *She'ol*. The subject is wicked individuals. Does this mean they suddenly go down to *She'ol* or they peacefully go down? (Job 34:20 supports the former. But the טוב in the verse perhaps supports the latter.) Another example of such an ambiguity is at Isa. 51:4.

Rav S.R. Hirsch is one who believes that רגע never has the "move" meaning. (Many scholars take this approach as well.) In his commentary to Deut. 28:65, he understands each *rega* as a brief period of stopping or suspending a motion, and he interprets the three sea verses as referring to "calming" the sea. But this is very difficult since the expression in two of these three sea verses is followed by "its waves roar."

I mentioned earlier that it has been suggested that the original

---

238. See, e.g., *BDB*.

meaning of רגע as "moment" was the twinkling movement of the eye. One of the reasons this is suggested is that this is the literal meaning of "moment" in Egyptian. "Moment" is written in Egyptian with the hieroglyph for "eye."

Finally, there is a humorous question in the Talmud at *Berakhot* 7a: How long is a רגע? One answer: כמימריה = as long as it takes to say the word![239]

* * *

Now let us talk about another time-related word, שעה. In *Tanakh*, we only have this time-related word in an Aramaic section of *Tanakh*: chapters 3, 4, and 5 of the book of Daniel. We have שעה, שעתה, and שעתא, a total of 5 times. But the meaning is not one-twelfth of the time from sunrise to sunset. Rather, the meaning is a brief period of time. (It is only later, in the Mishnaic period, that we begin to have this root with the "one-twelfth" meaning sometimes.)

There is a version of the *asher yatzar* blessing from the time of the Talmud that has the added phrase *afilu sha'ah eḥat* (= we would not be able to stand before you even one *sha'ah*). See, e.g., *Berakhot* 60b, glosses of the Gra.[240] R. Barukh Epstein had this text. In his *Barukh She-Amar*, pp. 17–19, he discusses the word שעה extensively and explains that it obviously does not mean "one twelfth of the time from sunrise to sunset" here. Rather, it means a brief moment, the equivalent of רגע.

There is a root שעה in the Hebrew section of *Tanakh*, appearing 15 times. Fundamentally, it means "look at intensely, pay attention to." See, e.g., Gen 4:4 (regarding God's attitude to the offering of Abel). Some have suggested that the Hebrew and Aramaic meanings of שעה are related.[241] But the widespread view is that they are not.

In the modern period, a word was needed for "clock." Already in the Mishnah (*Kelim* 12:4) we had a term for the sundial: *even sha'ot*. In the period before modern Hebrew, a word used for clock was

---

239. There is much more about the word *rega* here.
240. On this reading, see also I. Baer, *Siddur Avodat Yisrael* (1868), p. 37.
241. See, e.g., *BDB*, p. 1116 (Aramaic section) and Mandelkern, p. 1347 (Aramaic section).

moreh sha'ot. But in 1885, Yeḥiel Michael Pines coined the term שעון, following the trend of coining shorter terms.[242]

* * *

As an attorney, Mitchell First makes much effort to move his litigations quickly. But as a scholar, he often finds it better to contemplate and go slow.

22. רפא and רפה: The Two Meanings of *Refaim* in *Tanakh*

The word רפאים (*Refaim*) appears many times in *Tanakh*. But it has two different meanings. Sometimes it refers to an ancient race of giants. Other times it refers to dead people in the underworld. Can we make any sense of this? Also, what about that word רפא which means "heal"? Does it have any connection with the word רפה which means "weak"? This essay is going to address these topics.

Let us start with the easiest question, the possible relationship between רפא and רפה. With regard to the verb רפא, even though we are used to thinking of it as meaning "heal" (as this is its widespread meaning in *Tanakh* and in our prayers), most likely it started out with a more concrete meaning. Most likely it originally meant: "restoring a wrong, sick, broken, or deficient condition to its original and proper state."[243] For example, at 1 Kings 18:30 it refers to repairing a destroyed altar, and at 2 Kings 2:21 it refers to purifying a spring of water.

With regard to the verb רפה, even though we think of it as meaning "become weak," most likely, it started out with the concrete meaning of "sink down."[244] For example, at Ezekiel 1:24 it refers to the dropping down of angels' wings, and it is often used in *Tanakh* in connection with hands dropping down.[245]

While a relationship between "heal" and "weak" might have been

---

242. I wish to acknowledge the post at balashon.com of Feb. 22, 2016, from where I obtained some of the above material on the root שעה.
243. *TDOT*, vol. 13, p. 597.
244. *TDOT*, vol. 13, p. 614.
245. For a similar but slightly different approach, see Rav S.R. Hirsch to Deut. 4:31.

something that could be explained, the original meanings of the words רפא and רפה do not sound like they have any relationship.

* * *

The ancient רפאים who were giants are mentioned eleven times in the books of Genesis, Deuteronomy, Joshua and Chronicles. For example, at Deut. 3:11, we are told: "Only Og king of Bashan remained from the remnant of the *Refaim*..." and the verse continues with a description of the size of his bed. At Deut. 2:10-11, the *Refaim* are mentioned in a context with the tall *Anakim*.

The impression one gets from this verse and from Deut. 2:20 is that the *Refaim* were a race that had died out by the time of Moses. Also, at Genesis 15:19-21, they are listed with the several other commonly listed pre-Israelite inhabitants of the land: e.g., *Ḥiti*, *Prizi*, and *Emori*.

In contrast, in the books of Isaiah, Psalms, Proverbs and Job, eight times we have the word רפאים with the meaning "dead people" (or spirits of these dead people). For example, they are mentioned parallel to *meitim* at Isaiah 26:14 and Psalms 88:11, and they dwell in the depths of *She'ol* at Proverbs 9:18.[246]

With regard to the "dead people" meaning, the simplest explanation is that this meaning derives from רפה, with its meanings of "sink down" (to the underworld) or "powerless." See, e.g., the *Brown-Driver-Briggs* lexicon which mentions both of these suggestions.[247] The ה dropped in the plural and it became רפאים.[248]

Is there a way to connect the two different meanings of רפאים: "giants" and "dead people"?[249] I will mention some approaches that have been suggested:

---

246. Also, many scholars interpret the Biblical word תרפים (a type of household idol) as derived from *refaim* with this meaning.
247. At Deut. 2:11, Rav S.R. Hirsch adopts the "powerless" approach. So does Mandelkern, p. 1106.
248. This happened as well with the word טלה = lamb. Its plural is טלאים. See Isa. 40:11. I am sure there are many other examples.
249. It is of interest that in the Greek translation of *Tanakh*, most of the time a Greek word for "giants" is used for both.

- The word was originally used in a legend about a giant who was banished to the underworld. The name was subsequently applied to all the dead in the underworld.
- Taking the "dead people" meaning as primary, the name was applied to that race of people because their race was dying out or had died out at the time of Moses.[250]
- Those giants caused fear to others, as much fear as seeing a dead person.[251]

Since we can explain the "dead people" meaning with simple explanations derived from רפה, we should reject that first suggestion. The other two suggestions are creative but farfetched.

We should also note that רפאים, in its "giants" meaning, seems to be used as an ethnic term to describe a people who were giants, and not as a descriptive term for "giants."[252]

(This has ramifications in the concordance of Mandelkern. His concordance has a separate section for proper nouns, i.e., names whose first letters would be capitalized in English. He places the entries with the "giants" meaning in this separate later section.)

Of course, many scholars believe that the term *Refaim* with its "giants" meaning was originally a descriptive one.

There is another interesting twist in our analysis. At 2 Samuel, chapter 21, we have the singular of *Refaim* four times and the implication is that it is referring to giants. What is the singular form used? It is רפה each time.[253] Moreover, this רפה word is part of the phrase *yelidei ha-Rafah* and similar phrases each time. This gives the impression that the tradition in ancient Israel was that the *Refaim* who were giants were descended from an individual named רפה.[254]

* * *

---

250. Many scholars take this approach. So do Rav S.R. Hirsch (comm. to Deut. 2:11) and Mandelkern.
251. See, e.g., S.D. Luzzatto to Deut. 2:11.
252. But when the reference is to the people who were giants, both Targum Onkelos and Targum Yonatan translate the word with a word from the root גבר, treating the word as descriptive.
253. But in the later parallel passage at 1 Chron. 20, the רפה spelling is changed to רפא.
254. But it is possible to interpret the individual רפה as being a collective noun and referring to a group. The Soncino commentary suggests this as a possibility.

A few more thoughts:

1. There are findings from ancient Ugarit that may be relevant to our analysis, but the *Encyclopaedia Judaica* describes the Ugaritic material as "fragmentary and difficult to interpret." Nevertheless, it does attempt a summary.[255]
2. At Deut. 2:20, we are told that the Ammonites called the *Refaim* by a different name: *Zamzumim*. Here are the comments in the *Etz Hayim* Torah commentary: "[This] name...seems to be an imitation of their speech. It means, roughly, 'the Buzz-buzzers,' i.e., the people whose speech sounds like buzzing." See the similar comments in the *Pentateuch* of Rabbi Dr. Hertz: "people whose speech sounded uncouth." Gen. 14:5 perhaps refers to this same group, using the name *Zuzim*.
3. *Emek Refaim* is referred to 7 times in *Tanakh* (but nowhere in the Torah). It could be translated "Valley of the Dead" or "Valley of the Giants." Targum Yonatan uses the word גבריא, implying a preference for the latter.[256] Most of the scholarly sources I have seen also prefer the latter and *Daat Mikra* adopts this interpretation as well.[257]

* * *

I am reminded of the following story: At the time of the drafting of Israel's Declaration of Independence, there was a dispute between the Orthodox and the secular. The Orthodox wanted a mention of God's name in the declaration. The secular objected. Then someone suggested the phrase *Tzur Yisrael*. The secular could agree to this phrase and the Orthodox could interpret it as a reference to God.

---

255. *EJ* 14:79-80. For another summary of the Ugaritic material, see *TDOT*, vol. 13, p. 604.
256. See, e.g., Targum Yonatan to Josh. 15:8.
257. Comm. to Josh 15:8. The only difficulty might be its location. It is a valley near Jerusalem, west of the Jordan River. But *Daat Mikra* points out that the ancient *Refaim* also lived on the west side of the Jordan River and not just on its east side. See also *Daat Mikra* to 2 Sam. 21:16.

The Septuagint gives *Emek Refaim* a meaning related to death. See *TDOT*, vol. 13, p. 614.

A weakness with the "death" meaning is that the underworld was not tied to a specific geographic location in *Eretz Yisrael* or on earth.

What allowed this compromise to work? The fact that Hebrew has no capital letters! A capital letter or a lower-case letter would have allowed for no ambiguity and offended one of the groups![258]

23. שכל: *Sikkel et Yadav* (Genesis 48:14)

At Genesis 48, we are told that Joseph brings his two children to Jacob to be blessed. Verse 13 tells us that he put Efraim to the left of Jacob and put Menashe to the right. Verse 14 provides Jacob's response: Jacob put his right hand on Efraim, the younger, and his left hand on Menashe. The verse continues: שכל *et yadav ki Menashe ha-bekhor*.

After Jacob gives the blessing, Joseph responds: "Not so, my father, for this one (=Menashe) is the first born, put your right hand on his head." But Jacob refuses. He has seen the future and the younger will be greater.

Our question is what does שכל mean and what is the meaning of the phrase: שכל *et yadav ki Menashe ha-bekhor*?

First, let me provide some background. As to the word כי, although it usually means "because," there are a few times where it seems to mean "even though." The Even-Shoshan concordance counts over 4000 instances of the word כי in *Tanakh*! (With such a large number of occurrences, it has a few other meanings as well.) A famous dispute is the meaning of כי at Ex. 13:17: *ki karov hu*. Does it mean "because the way of the land of the Pelishtim was near," or "although the land of the Pelishtim was near"?[259]

As to the root שכל, it appears many times in *Tanakh*. It always has a meaning related to doing something wisely. But there is also a root סכל that appears many times in *Tanakh* and means "doing something foolishly."

Now let us return to our phrase at Gen. 38:14. On the simplest level, the phrase means something like: Jacob "put his hands [in this manner] with wisdom because Menashe was the firstborn." This

---

258. I would like to thank Jeff Neugroschl for getting me interested in the roots רפא and רפה.
259. Or perhaps some other meaning of כי fits best here.

translation makes no sense in the context. But if we translate כי in its less frequent use as "even though," we have a sensible (but awkward) reading of the phrase: Jacob put his hands in this manner with wisdom, even though Menashe was the first born. This is essentially the translation of Rashi.

Let us see some other possibilities:

- Rabbi Dr. Hertz: Jacob purposely, against Joseph's wish, did what he did. (Presumably Rabbi Dr. Hertz is translating כי in the next phrase as "even though.")
- Hizzekuni: Jacob directed his hands with wisdom, and for this reason merely switched his hands. Because Menashe was the first born, Jacob did not want to slight Menashe by physically moving him.
- Rabbeinu Ḥananel (quoted in Rabbeinu Baḥya): Jacob was הרכיב his hands, one on top of the other. Rabbeinu Ḥananel seems to be understanding שכל to mean something like "crossed his hands." R. Ḥananel, in his commentary on *Bava Metzia* 25a, had cited *Targum Eretz Yisrael* for this interpretation.[260]

Many scholars adopt this interpretation and find support for it in Arabic. For example E. Klein writes that, in Arabic, a *shikal* is a rope for tying together an animal's legs.[261]

But it is obviously weak to rely on Arabic to translate a Biblical word. Although Arabic is a Semitic language, most of its words are

---

260. The standard *Mikraot Gedolot* has this interpretation in the name of Yonatan b. Uzziel. Here שכל is translated with the word פרג and one of the meanings of this word is "exchange." See Jastrow, p. 1213. In contrast, Targum Onkelos translates the word with a word from the root חכם.

261. Klein, p. 657. *BDB* writes something similar, also citing Arabic.
Interesting is *The Living Torah*. R Kaplan uses the phrase "deliberately crossed." Is he translating שכל as "deliberately" or as "crossed"? The ArtScroll Stone edition is also interesting. In its translation, it translates our word as "maneuvered." But in its commentary the only explanation that it includes is that the hands were "crossed." Probably, they chose the word "maneuver" for the translation because it fits with the "wisdom" meaning. Then the commentary explains the type of maneuver. (Probably, R. Kaplan took the same approach. He is translating שכל as "deliberately" and then "crossed" is just what Jacob did but it is not stated explicitly in the text.)

only known to us from the time of the Quran (seventh century). Moreover, I do not think the subsequent phrase flows properly in this translation of שכל, whether the subsequent phrase means "because Menashe was the firstborn" or "although Menashe was the firstborn."

Nowhere else do we have the Hebrew root שכל with a meaning like "cross." In my view, there is insufficient basis to invent this new meaning for our Biblical root, even though there is an early Aramaic translation that takes this approach, and even though Jacob did cross his hands.

- Rabbeinu Baḥya understands the phrase to mean that Jacob physically switched the two brothers.[262]

But the most interesting explanation is that of S.D. Luzzatto. Based on the meaning of the different root סכל, he believes the meaning of the phrase is: Jacob put his hands in a way that looked foolish, since Menashe was the first born, and was entitled to the blessing with the right hand.[263]

The view of Luzzatto reads well into the entire verse. It fits the verse even better than the view of Rashi. But can we adopt it? We would have to postulate that שכל could be interpreted as if it were spelled סכל. It turns out that there are other ש letters in *Tanakh* that are interpreted as ס:

- At Ecc. 1:17, we have the spelling שכלות for "foolishness." The normal spelling of the word is סכלות (six times).

- At 2 Sam. 1:22 the word נשוג is consistently understood as if the root was סוג (move away). See similarly ישיגו at Job 24:2.[264]

- At Isa. 19:10, the word שכר is widely understood as if the root was סכר.[265]

---

262. But how he is translating שכל is unclear.
263. Ralbag had earlier interpreted שכל as if it were written סכל, but he defined סכל with a meaning like "crooked" and the implication that the hands were crossed. See similarly the earlier view of Rashbam (written too succinctly).
264. On both, see Mandelkern, p. 792.
265. See *Daat Mikra*. Also, at Ex. 33:22, we have the word ושכתי ("and I will

While I was initially hesitant to give some credence to Luzzatto's interpretation, now that I have the above examples,²⁶⁶ I am more willing to do so.

שׂכל with its wisdom-related meaning is rare in the Torah. It is only found at Gen. 3:6, and Deut. 29:8 and 32:29. (But admittedly סכל with its foolishness-related meaning is only found one time in the Torah, at Gen. 31:28.)

Finally, in favor of Luzzatto's interpretation, as opposed to Rashi's, is that the use of כי with the meaning "even though" is rare. Even-Shoshan lists only thirteen such instances out of the over 4000, and even some of these can be questioned.

* * *

A few final thoughts:

- There are of course many more interpretations of our phrase at Gen. 48:14. See AlHatorah.org on our phrase and M. Kasher, *Torah Shelemah, Va-yeḥi*, sec. 88.
- The Biblical שׂ often evolved into ס in Mishnaic/Rabbinic Hebrew (e.g., the Mishnaic ארוסין). We even have such an evolution in a late book of *Tanakh*, the book of Ezra. See Ezra 4:5: סכרים (hired).
- In a widespread Christian view, Gen. 48:14 alludes to Jacob having made the sign of the Cross, and the subsequent verse 19 indicates that the younger religion (Christianity) will be greater than the older religion (Judaism).²⁶⁷

* * *

Both as an attorney and a scholar, Mitchell First knows the difference between statements made with "wisdom" and statements made with "folly."

---

cover"). This is consistently understood as having the same meaning as if the initial root letter here was a ס. But admittedly here the original root may have had a שׂ. See also שׂעירם at Deut. 32:2. Rashi and many others understand this word as if that *sin* was a *samekh*. But here too שׂ may have been the letter in the original Hebrew word for "storm."

266. I thank Sam Borodach for providing some of them.
267. I thank Daniel Chazin for sharing this with me (based on a presentation he heard from R. Meir Soloveichik).

24. שער: Is There a Connection in *Tanakh* Between Hair Standing Up and Fear?

There is an interesting Rashi at Deuteronomy 32:17. This verse describes the Israelites as sacrificing to gods that לא שערום אבותכם. What does that middle word mean? The first opinion that Rashi offers is that their ancestors' hair did not stand up out of fear. Rashi explains that hair stands up when people are in fear. Rashi's source for this interpretation is *Sifrei* Deut. 318. (Rashi offers a second interpretation as well: their ancestors did not deify them, relying on the possible "demon" meaning of שער.)

I wondered for decades about that first interpretation in Rashi. Is there really a connection between hair standing up and fear? The first step in my analysis was to survey the root שער in *Tanakh*.

Of course, a main meaning of the root שער is hair. Also, a goat is called a שעיר because of its unusual amount of hair. (The name of the animal literally means: "the hairy one.")

Then there is the word שערה for "barley." Most likely it is called this due to its hairy appearance as it grows in the fields.[268] (Whoever would have imagined this! Of course to Biblical scholars who are farmers this etymology would probably be obvious!)

Also, four times in *Tanakh* we have שעיר in the singular or plural where the context supports, or perhaps supports, a "demon" meaning. See particularly Lev. 17:7. The other three verses are Isa. 13:21, 34:14 and 2 Chr. 11:15. A widespread (but not unanimous) view is that if a "demon" is intended in these verses, it is a demon in the shape of a goat.[269]

The root שער also has a meaning like "be whirled away."[270] This

---

268. One can see photos of this online or see the sketch at *Daat Mikra* to Ex. 9:31.

269. See, e.g., *BDB*, p. 972, *KB*, p. 1341, Klein, p. 672, and Radak, *Sefer Ha-Shorashim*. According to Rabbi Dr. Hertz, p. 486, "worship of the goat, accompanied by the foulest rites" was widespread in Lower Egypt (= northern Egypt).

At Isa. 34:14, שעיר with the possible "demon" meaning is in the same verse as לילית. This is the only reference to Lilith in *Tanakh*. For more on this demon in extra-Biblical sources and later midrashic sources, see *EJ* 11:245.

270. See, e.g., Ps. 50:3 and 58:10, and Job 27:21. See also Dan. 11:40.

meaning is usually viewed as related to the root סער, with its "storm" meaning. Also, at Isa. 28:2 and Nah 1:3, we have שער with a meaning like "storm."[271]

Going back to our original question, the root שער also has a meaning related to "fear" in a few verses. Let us analyze these verses.

At both Ezek. 27:35 and 32:10, there is a double use of שער. The first verse has שער שערו שערם ומלכיהם. The second verse has ומלכיהם ישערו עליך שער. The context in both verses is that the kings are or will be terrified.[272] The Jewish Publication Society translation of 1917 translates the phrase in both verses as "horribly afraid."[273] Probably, the translation uses the word "horribly" because of the double use of שער. Most of the rabbinic commentaries on both verses and the *Daat Mikra* translate the expression as if the meaning is related to סער (storm, tempest). But several standard scholarly works translate both phrases as if the meaning is something like "hair bristled with terror."[274] According to my trusty Random House Dictionary, "bristle" means "to stand or rise stiffly like bristles."

At Job 18:20, we have *aḥazu sa'ar* (= stricken with panic). See also Jer. 2:12 for another fear-related meaning of שער.[275]

The *Brown-Driver-Briggs* and Koehler-Baumgartner lexicons do not postulate a separate "fear" meaning for שער. They subsume this meaning within the "hair" meaning.[276] Fundamentally they view the root as meaning "hair" and that this expanded to "hair bristling, fear."

Most significantly, in a different verse, Job 4:15, where the root means "hair," and the context is fear (see Job 4:14), we have *tesammer*

---

271. See also perhaps Job 9:17. Most likely, *sin* was the original first letter in this meaning of the root. See *TDOT*, vol. 10, pp. 291–92. Based on this, some want to connect this "storm" meaning with the "fear, shudder" meaning. See, Klein, p. 673, and *TDOT*, ibid.
272. עליך in the second verse probably means "because of you."
273. The King James Bible had "sore afraid" in the first verse and "horribly afraide" in the second.
274. E.g., *BDB*, p. 972, and *KB*, pp. 1343–44.
275. In all four of the verses where שער has a meaning related to fear, it is parallel to a verb from the root שמם.
276. *BDB*, p. 972, and *KB*, pp. 1343–44.

sa'arat besari. The root סמר means "stand up."²⁷⁷ The entire phrase means: "The hair of my flesh stood up."

So going back to our verse at Deuteronomy 32:17, Rashi's first understanding is a plain sense understanding. "Rising hair" and "fear" are connected in *Tanakh*.

But is "rising hair" the best understanding of שערום in this particular verse? It turns out that most scholars today take a different approach to our verse than Rashi did. שערום in our verse is parallel to ידעום. In the language of South Arabic, a language that can be documented to have existed in the late Biblical period, there is a root that is the equivalent of the Hebrew *shin-ayin-resh* that has the meaning "to know." This root passed on to classical Arabic with this meaning.²⁷⁸ This root with its initial *shin* letter is not that different from our *sin-ayin-resh* root. Because of the parallel to ידעום, modern scholars prefer this approach based on South Arabic to our word, and give שערום the "know" meaning here.²⁷⁹ The "know" meaning is also a better fit grammatically in our sentence. "They did not hair them" is too awkward a reading.

On our verse 32:17, Rav S.R. Hirsch and Rabbi Dr. Hertz agree with Rashi's first interpretation, while Rashbam prefers Rashi's second interpretation.

* * *

There is one unusual use of the root שער in *Tanakh*. At Deut. 32:2, we have *sei'rim* with a rain-related meaning, falling on *desheh*. The phrase is parallel to *revivim* in the same verse, falling on *eisev*. *Revivim* appears a few times in *Tanakh* and can be translated as "copious showers," from the root רבב, abundant. So perhaps *se'irim* should be translated as parallel to *revivim* and with a meaning like "heavy rains" (related to the root סער). Or perhaps it means something like light rain. See, e.g., Ibn Ezra (and the explanation in n. 14 in the *Torat Ḥayyim*: thin, like hair). Or perhaps it is related to *sei'rim* with a demon/deity

---

277. As to this meaning for סמר, see also Ps. 119:120, and see *Daat Mikra* to both verses. A מסמר in *Tanakh* is a nail.

278. Our sources for classical Arabic begin in the seventh century. We do not have too many words from South Arabic.

279. See, e.g., *BDB*, p. 973, *KB*, p. 1344, Klein, p. 673 and Kaddari, p. 1130. This is also how the word is translated in the Septuagint.

meaning and refers to the heavy rain supposedly produced by those demons/deities. See, e.g., S.D. Luzzatto (citing I.S. Reggio). Finally, E. Klein suggests a very strange idea: the rain clouds look like goats.[280]

* * *

Mitchell First's father was involved in naming the SAR Academy school (in Riverdale, N.Y.) in the late 1960's. It was an abbreviation of Salanter-Akiba-Riverdale (the three schools that merged). No connection to "demons," "goats," or "storms" was intended. His father wanted to name the school RASHI: Riverdale-Akiba-Salanter Hebrew Institute. But for reasons related to school politics this suggestion was rejected.

25. Interesting Words in *Hallel*

Hallel comprises chapters 113–118 of the book of Psalms. I will discuss these words in the order they appear.

עקרת: Here the meaning is "barren, without children." Most of the time in *Tanakh*, the meaning is similar, as the root עקר means "to uproot," and the adjective means "uprooted."

But we know in Hebrew today that the עקר (*ikar*) is "the main thing." This is the case already in Mishnaic Hebrew. See, e.g., Avot 1:17. How could this root have these two almost opposite meanings?

The explanation is that in the Hebrew part of *Tanakh* (= most of *Tanakh*, its older part), the verb עקר means "to uproot." But there are also Aramaic parts of *Tanakh* (parts of Daniel and Ezra, and Jer. 10:11). Here, in the fourth chapter of Daniel, three times we have the root with a meaning like "the root of a tree." The root of a tree is the basis of a tree.[281] Very likely, from the "uproot" meaning the word developed a meaning of "root, basis."[282]

---

280. In my view, the סער = heavy rain approach is the simplest and most likely explanation, as it provides a good parallel to *revivim*. (I am here assuming that *desheh* and *eisev* do not require a different type of rain, which may not be the case!)
281. See *Daat Mikra* to Dan. 4:12.
282. Klein, p. 483. Daniel 7:8, a verse in the Aramaic section, has the "uproot"

People today sometimes refer to an important woman as an *akeret ha-bayit*, borrowing the expression from our verse in Psalms. They intend the later meaning "basis." But in the verse they are citing, *akeret* means "barren/uprooted." I had always thought this was an error from modern times. But I learned recently that *Midrash Tanḥuma* adopts such an interpretation on a similar verse, Gen. 29:31. This verse has the phrase *ve-Rachel akarah* and this midrash comments: *ve-hi hayta ikar ha-bayit*.[283] This comment is surely only a homiletical one as it does not fit the context. Nevertheless, it is found in this ancient source and later sources repeat it.[284]

לועז: The root of this word is לעז. This is the only time this root appears in *Tanakh*. Fortunately, the root appears in the Mishnah and Tosefta. For example, Mishnah *Megillah* 2:1 tells us: *korin otah le-loazot be-laaz* = we may read [the Megillah] for those who speak a foreign language in a foreign language. Probably, the verb originally meant "speak unintelligibly"[285] and this later expanded to include "speak a foreign language."

חלמיש: This word appears five times in *Tanakh*. From all these verses, it is easy to determine that it has a meaning like "hard rock." But the word always bothered me because it has what seems like four root letters. Scholars are very good at finding parallels in Akkadian and Arabic to our word, but the sources I have seen typically avoid suggesting what the original three-letter Semitic root was.

Fortunately, I found a good suggestion in the commentary of Rav S.R. Hirsch,[286] the concordance of S. Mandelkern,[287] and the book *How the Hebrew Language Grew*.[288] There is a root in Hebrew חלם that means "strong." There is evidence for it only two times in *Tanakh*, at

---

meaning. So we cannot simply say that Hebrew had the "uproot" meaning and Aramaic had the "root" meaning. Rather, an expansion from "uproot" to "root, basis" is likely what happened.

283. See H. Zelcer, *Thoughts on our Daily Prayers* (2020), p. 89.
284. As Zelcer points out, the interpretation is repeated in *Ruth Rabbah*, Zohar and Malbim. Also, Rashi on *Gittin* 52a writes something similar.
285. *BDB*.
286. Gen. 25:6.
287. P. 398.
288. Horowitz, p. 189.

Job 39:4, and Isa. 38:16.[289] That is likely the root of חלמיש. The *shin* added at the end is merely a suffix, as in the words חרמש, רטפש (from רטב), and עכביש.

עצביהם: The root here is עצב. This root has two different meanings: 1) pain/grieve (many times) and 2) form/shape (see Job 10:8 and Jer. 44:19). From the context, עצביהם at Psalms 115:4 means "their idols." This obviously comes from the "form/shape" meaning.

It is hard to believe that the two Hebrew עצב meanings, "pain/grieve" and "form/shape," have a common origin. Arabic has two different *ayin* letters, written and pronounced differently. (Most likely, Arabic has preserved what was in the original, hypothesized Semitic language.) The "pain/grieve" meaning has one such *ayin* letter and the "form/shape" meaning has the other such *ayin* letter. This strongly suggests that the two Hebrew עצב roots do not have a common origin but only look similar due to the merger of the two different *ayin* letters.

Now I would like to mention some very creative (but very unlikely) approaches that have been suggested to connect the "idols" meaning of the root עצב to its "pain/grieve" meaning:

- S. Mandelkern theorizes that the root עצב could fundamentally mean *avodah*, i.e., hard work that makes you tired. The word was then transferred to idols because they too have *avodah* done for them.
- Rav S.R. Hirsch suggests that the "idol" meaning originated as "powers and forces who maliciously made life hard and took pleasure in the toil and worry of men."[290]

שאול (= netherworld): Most likely, the root is שאה = desolation, and the *lamed* is just a suffix, and not part of the root. (Another example of a *lamed* which is merely a suffix is the *lamed* in the word כרמל, with its "garden-land" meaning.) I discussed this root at length in *Roots and Rituals*.

חלצת (*ḥillatzta nafshi mi-mavet*): The root here is חלץ which means

---

289. In the liturgy, it appears in the prayer that asks for healing of the sick: להחלימו.
290. Gen. 3:16. Similarly, he interprets אלילם as "refusers, who always say No!"

"release." The root has this meaning often in *Tanakh*. I discussed this root at length in *Roots and Rituals*.²⁹¹

אתהלך: The root here is הלך = walk. But what is the role of the *hitpael* here? We are all taught that the *hitpael* typically means to do something to yourself. So is the meaning here: "I will walk myself"? The explanation is that the *hitpael* has other functions as well.²⁹² One of them is to do something continually. Throughout *Tanakh*, when הלך is in the *hitpael*, it means to "walk continually."

שער: The noun *shaar* with the meaning "gate" appears many times in *Tanakh*. But two times we have the word *shaar* with the meaning "measure": at Gen. 26:12 (*meah she'arim*), and at Prov. 23:7. (We all know the medieval version of this word: שיעור = a set measure of learning.) Are the "gate" and "measure" meanings related? After all, the price of merchandise may have typically been determined at the town gate. See, e.g., 2 Kings 7:1.

The idea that the original Semitic language had an alphabet of more than twenty-two letters helps us understand what happened here. Our present letter *shin* is the result of a merger of two older letters. One of the original letters was pronounced "sh" like our *shin*. But another was pronounced with a "th" sound. Just like Hebrew has a twenty-two letter alphabet, Aramaic also has a twenty-two letter alphabet. The original Semitic letter that was pronounced "th" usually became a *shin* in Hebrew, but it usually became a *tav* in Aramaic. Since some dialects of Aramaic have the word תרעא for gate, this suggests that this word had an original "th" letter, unlike the original word for "measure."²⁹³

That our Hebrew *shin* is the result of a merger of two different root letters explains why we do not have to stretch to find a relationship between other words such as: *shemen* and *shemonah*, *ḥeresh* (= deaf) and *ḥarash* (= cut, plow), *shelaḥ* (send) and *shulḥan*, and *she'ar*

---

291. An interesting question is what the root means in the phrase *ḥillutz atzamot* in *Birkat Ha-Ḥodesh* (based on a similar phrase at Isa. 58:11). Can this phrase mean "release of bones"? I also discussed this at length.
292. I discussed the *hitpael* stem extensively in *Roots*, pp. 240–47 (in my article on the meaning of התפלל).
293. See Horowitz, p. 107. There is also evidence from Ugaritic that the words do not derive from a common root. See the essay in *TDOT*.

(remainder) and *she'eir* (kin). In all of these pairs, the latter most likely had an original "th."[294]

* * *

Mitchell First feels a great release in finally getting to the root of the word *ḥalamish*. It had been grieving him over the years and he had erroneously suspected that it was a לועז word.

26. Hendiadys: Two Separate Words Understood as One Idea

A few years ago I wrote a column about the meaning of the phrase *yad va-shem* (Isa. 56:5). *Yad* here means "monument" and *shem* here probably means something like "memorial." On a literal level, the verse refers to the establishment of two different things. But many interpret these two words as one idea, ignoring that middle *vav*. They believe the meaning is "a *yad* that serves as a *shem*" (= a monument that serves as a memorial).

After I wrote the column, someone sent me an email explaining that there was a term for this style of writing and that it occurs throughout *Tanakh*.[295] It is called "hendiadys."[296] I have since learned much about this style and would now like to explain it.

Hendiadys has been defined as "the expression of one single but complex concept by two separate words.... The important aspect of hendiadys is that its components are no longer considered separately but as a single unit in combination."[297]

The typical hendiadys has two nouns with a *vav* between them. But hendiadys occurs with other forms of words as well. (It also sometimes occurs even without that middle *vav*.)

This style is found in ancient Semitic languages like Ugaritic and Akkadian. It is also found in Greek, Latin, and English.[298]

---

294. See Horowitz, pp. 106–07.
295. The one who sent me the email was Rabbi Menahem Meier, founding principal of Yeshivat Frisch.
296. The word "hendiadys" derives from a Greek phrase that means "one through two." I.e., something that is one idea is represented by two words.
297. Watson (see below), pp. 324–25.
298. The Wikipedia entry "Hendiadys" even cites an example from Shakespeare.

A main purpose of hendiadys when it involves two nouns is the extra emphasis that results when two nouns are used, instead of a noun with a modifying adjective.

Hendiadys has other functions as well, e.g., to produce assonance or rhyme, or preserve rhythm.[299]

Some scholars believe that there are only a small number of hendiadyses in *Tanakh*. But a widespread view is that there are many.

Already at Genesis 1:2 we have: *tohu va-vohu*. This is believed by many to be a hendiadys with the meaning: "formless void."

There is a dissertation online that discusses hendiadys extensively and itemizes many possible hendiadyses throughout *Tanakh*, going through all the Biblical books. It is by Rosmari Lillas and titled: *Hendiadys in the Hebrew Bible* (Univ. of Gothenburg, 2012).[300]

* * *

When first proposed by Christian Hebraists in the late sixteenth and early seventeenth centuries, here are some of the hendiadyses that were suggested:[301]

> Gen. 19:24: *gafrit va-esh*, literally "sulfur and fire." The suggestion is that it is one concept that meant either "burning sulfur" or "sulfurous fire."
>
> Gen. 23:4: *ger ve-toshav*, literally "foreigner and resident." This is to be understood as *ger toshav*, i.e., a *ger* who is a *toshav*.[302]
>
> Jer. 22:3: *mishpat u-tzedakah*, literally "judgment and righteousness." The suggestion is that it meant "righteous judgment."
>
> Jer. 29:11: *aharit ve-tikvah*, literally "an end and a hope." The suggestion is that it meant "a hoped for end."

---

299. Watson, ibid.
300. Gothenberg is in Sweden, in case, like me, you did not know.
301. I am not claiming that Rishonim and early Aharonim did not interpret the individual verses below in a manner that achieves the same result. But I do not think they discussed something like this as a general principle.
302. There are a few others verses with *ger ve-toshav*. Interestingly, at Lev. 25:47, we have *ger ve-toshav* and *ger toshav* in the same verse.

Job 4:16: *demamah ve-kol*, literally "silence and voice." The suggestion is that it meant "low voice."[303]

* * *

Let us now look at some others that have been suggested over the past few centuries:

Gen. 1:14: *le-otot u-le-moadim*: as signs to mark seasons
Gen. 1:22: *peru u-revu*: be abundantly fruitful
Gen. 2:15: *le-avdah u-leshamrah*: for the task of tending it
Gen. 3:16: *itzvoneikh ve-heironeikh*: your pain in childbearing
Gen. 4:12: *na va-nad*: restless wanderer
Gen. 11:4: *ir u-migdal*: a towering city
Gen. 12:1: *mei-artzekha u-mi-moladetekha*: from your native land
Gen. 13:13: *ra'im ve-ḥataim*: wicked sinners
Gen. 18:19: *tzedakah u-mishpat*: correct judgment
Gen. 22:2: *et binkha et yiḥidekha*: your only son
Ex. 15:5: *markevot Paroh ve-ḥeilo*: his chariot army
Ex. 15:6: *eimatah va-faḥad*: dreadful terror
Ex. 15:25: *ḥok u-mishpat*: binding ordinance
Deut. 7:12: *et ha-brit ve-et ha-ḥesed*: the brit of ḥesed
Jer. 3:2: *bi-zenutayikh u-ve-raatekh*: your evil harlotry
Job 10:12: *ḥayyim va-ḥesed*: life of ḥesed

Also, here are a few that occur several times: *ot u-mofet, ḥesed ve-emet, ḥelek ve-naḥalah, toshav ve-sakhir,* and *yayin ve-shekhar*. (The last means "wine that makes one inebriated.")

Regarding *ḥesed ve-emet*, this precise phrase appears twenty-three times in *Tanakh*. An important one is at Ex. 34:6 in the first of the two verses where the thirteen Divine attributes are specified. The complete phrase here is *ve-rav ḥesed ve-emet*. The commentary of S.D. Luzzatto on this section lists twelve different ways that have been proposed to count the thirteen attributes. In all but one, *ḥesed* and *emet* are listed as separate attributes. But if *ḥesed ve-emet* is a hendiadys here, these

---

303. We have *kol demamah* elsewhere, at 1 Kings 19:12.

three words amount to only one attribute. *Daat Mikra* understands the phrase as a hendiadys and only counts it as one attribute. *Daat Mikra* offers a few different ways to understand the phrase, but in all their approaches it is a hendiadys and counts as only one attribute. See similarly the Conservative movement's flagship Torah commentary *Etz Hayim* (2001) on this verse.[304]

Note also that in the last blessing of the *Amidah*, Ashkenazim recite: *torat ḥayyim ve-ahavat ḥesed*. Sephardim recite: *torah ve-ḥayyim ahavah ve-ḥesed*. Are there different meanings here? No, the two phrases are hendiadyses and the Ashkenazic text has merely made their meaning explicit.

* * *

It is of course ironic that a style often meant for purposes of emphasis is little known today, resulting in the passage being misunderstood. It is important to be on the look-out for this style when reading Biblical passages.

As to the Hebrew word for this style, E.Z. Melamed uses *Shenayim She-Hem Eḥad* in the title of his article (see below).[305] But in the text he often uses הד״ר (= hendiadys)! R. Gordis (see below) uses: *eḥad derekh shenayim*.[306]

For further reading, see E.Z. Melamed, *Shenayim She-Hem Eḥad (EN ΔIA ΔYOIN) Ba-Mikra, Tarbitz* 16 (1945), pp. 173–189, R. Gordis, *The Word and the Book* (1976), pp. 40–43 and W. Watson, *Classical Hebrew Poetry* (1986, second ed.), pp. 324–328.

* * *

Mitchell First came across one overly creative hendiadys suggestion: *etz ha-daat tov va-ra* should be interpreted as "the tree that enables evil enjoyment"!

---

304. "The Hebrew words *ḥesed v'emet* appear frequently together to express a single concept.... When used together, the two words express God's absolute and eternal dependability in dispensing His benefactions." See similarly *Daat Mikra* to Gen. 24:27 (on *ḥasdo va-amitto*).
305. This is also the term that *Daat Mikra* uses for this style.
306. In a different context I know that often a scribal error occurs when a scribe returns to the correct word, but on a later line. This will result in an omission. In English this is called a homeoteleuton error, but in Hebrew, this is called more simply a דומות error.

27. Miscellaneous Words of Interest

אשנב: This is a word for window. It appears only at Judges 5:28 and Prov. 7:6. But what is its root? There is no root שנב in *Tanakh*. One interesting suggestion is that the root is נשב and we have an example of a metathesis. נשב means "blow,"[307] and opening a window enables the wind to blow. Note that our English word "window" derives from the word "wind."

גשם: In the Hebrew portion of *Tanakh*, this root means "rain." In the Aramaic portion of *Tanakh*, in the book of Daniel, this root means "body." Most likely, there is no connection between the two root meanings. (The latter root later expanded into meanings like: substance, matter, carry out, and concretize.)

דשן: The book of Leviticus, at 6:3, in the context of the daily burnt offering, tells us that every morning it was the duty of the priest to go to the altar and "take up the דשן which the fire has consumed" and place it next to the altar. *Deshen* is usually translated here (and in the few other verses in the sacrificial context) as "ashes."

Now let us look at some of the other occurrences of the root דשן in *Tanakh*. It usually has a positive meaning. For example, at Psalms 92:15, referring to the righteous who flourish, we are told that, in their old age, *desheinim ve-raananim yihyu*. רענן means "fresh." דשנים must mean something similar and positive. At Proverbs 28:25, we are told that "one who puts his trust in God ידשן."

How do we explain these different meanings? The answer is that *deshen* in *Tanakh* means "fat," in a positive way. When *deshen* is used in the context of offerings, it really means what is produced when the fat is burned. The regular term for ashes in *Tanakh* is אפר. The translation "ashes" in the offering context is a poor one. It should have been translated as "remnants of the fat." Unlike אפר, *deshen* is not at all a symbol of grief. (In the well-known verse at Psalms 23:5, it means "to put a lot of something on," related to the word "fat." "Fattened my head with oil" would be a rough translation.)

---

307. נשב is the root of *mashiv* in our well-known phrase *mashiv ha-ruaḥ*. The first word should be understood as if it is spelled מנשיב = causes the wind to blow. In the Rosh Hashanah liturgy, we have *ruaḥ noshavet*.

הורים: The root הרה in *Tanakh* meant: become pregnant, obviously referring only to a female. The word הרה referring to the father, and the root הורים referring to both parents, arose only in post-Biblical times.

One can disagree with this approach based on Gen. 49:26. Here we have the word הורי, and Rashi and many others interpret this word as "parents." But Rashbam, S.D. Luzzatto and modern scholars believe that this word means "mountains," parallel to גבעת later in the verse. These terms are parallel more than thirty other times in *Tanakh*![308]

חשמל: This word appears only at Ezek. 1:4, 1:27, and 8:2. From the contexts, it seems to mean something radiant. Tawil notes an Akkadian word *elmeshu*, and claims that this is the Akkadian cognate to חשמל. According to Tawil, *elmeshu* refers to a "precious stone with the characteristic sparkle and brilliancy of fire."[309]

The Talmud discusses the meaning of חשמל at *Hag.* 13b. Two interpretations are given. In both, חשמל is an abbreviated form of other words.

When the book of Ezekiel was translated into Greek, the word *elektron* was used for חשמל. *Elektron* in Greek referred to an alloy of gold and silver. In modern Hebrew, in part due to this Greek translation, it was decided to use חשמל as the word for electricity.[310] There were many who opposed this secular use of the word חשמל.

Tawil also equates the word חלמיש with *elmeshu*. (I have given a different explanation for this word in the essay "Interesting Words in *Hallel*" in this book.)

---

308. On this issue, see the post at balashon.com of July 18, 2008. Jastrow, p. 340, takes a different approach. He connects the "father" meaning with the root ירה and its meaning "instruct."

309. P. 108.

310. An interesting analogy is the case of the modern word משרד for office. Where did this common word come from? In *Tanakh*, שרד appears only a few times, always in the book of Exodus, always in the phrase *bigdei serad* or *bigdei ha-serad*. The phrase refers to clothing made for priests but the meaning of שרד itself is unclear. In the Greek translation of the Torah, *bigdei serad* was translated as "service garments" (probably due to a confusion with the word שרת). The Greek translation gave Eliezer Ben-Yehuda the idea to use משרד for office: a place of service. See Klein, pp. 395 and 681.

כרך: This is a word for a walled city. We all know the word from Mishnah *Megillah* 1:1 (*kerakhin ha-mukafin ḥomah*…). It is also found in the Haggadah: Hillel used to *korekh* the various Passover items and eat them together. Fundamentally, the word means something like "encircle" or "wrap." I always thought that a walled city was called a כרך because there was a wall encircling the city. But it turns out that there is another approach. There is a Greek word *charax* that meant "fortification." This word originally meant the pointed stakes used to make the fortification walls, but later came to mean the fortification itself. So it is possible that this Greek etymology is the correct etymology of the word כרך as "walled city."[311]

In *Tanakh*, the root כרך only appears one time. It is the root of the word *takhrikh* (= robe), at Esther 8:15. A robe encircles a person.

לוה: This word means both "borrow" and "join." At first glance, these meanings do not seem to be related. After all, the borrower is taking something away from the lender.

But when one borrows something, one is connecting himself on some level with the lender. So the scholarly world is split on the issue of whether these meanings might have had a common origin. *Brown-Driver-Briggs* and many others list "borrow" and "join" as two separate roots and do not even mention the possibility of a common origin. On the other hand, *Theological Dictionary of the Old Testament* does raise the possibility.[312]

Some others who advocate for a common origin are S. Mandelkern and Rav S.R. Hirsch (comm. to Ex. 22:24). Mandelkern points out that in Latin, a debt is called an "obligation." This word comes from a Latin word *leig* that means "to bind."[313]

Proverbs 22:7 has: "The borrower is the servant to the lender." This supports the idea that there is a connection between the two.

מונית: The word "taxi" is short for "taximeter," a car with a meter that calculates the cost of the ride. Initially the word "taxi" was used in modern Hebrew. But in 1948, the word מונית was introduced, named

---

311. See the post at balashon.com of March 2, 2017.
312. See vol. 7, pp. 475 and 477.
313. So does the word "ligament," the connective tissue in one's body.

for the מונה (meter) inside the car. At that time the public was asked to start using this word and stop using the foreign word "taxi."

מין. This word, in Rabbinic Hebrew, means both "species" and "heretic."[314] I am not going to discuss the topic of the relationship between them.[315] But at Sukkot time, circulating around the internet is a poster with a picture of seven heretics with the caption *Shivat Ha-Minim!* The seven heretics are: Elishah ben Avuyah, Baruch Spinoza, Shabbetai Tzvi, Jacob Frank, Benjamin Disraeli and two female heretics.

The female heretics are Sarah-Theodora and Leila Murad. The former was the second wife of Tsar Ivan Alexander, who ruled Bulgaria from 1331–1371. Sarah converted to Eastern Orthodox Christianity and accepted the name Theodora. She was known for her fierce support of her new religion and was one of the instigators of a church council against the Jews. She restored many churches and built many monasteries. Murad achieved fame as an Egyptian singer. She converted to Islam. Her father had been a *chazzan*. She died in 1995.

מלאך: Based on its four-letter structure with an initial *mem*, we could suspect that the root of this word is לאך. But there was no such verb in *Tanakh*, so we did not know what the verb meant. But when Ugaritic was discovered, scholars learned that this language had a verb that was the equivalent of the Hebrew לאך, with the meaning "send."[316] We can all understand that a מלאך is one who is "sent."

But what about that word מלאכה? In *Tanakh*, מלאכה often refers to work involving skills of the hands. It is often used in connection with the work of the Tabernacle, the Temple and sacred objects. There is a phrase *mislaḥ yadekha* (= activity of your hands, from the root שלח) which appears six times in *Tanakh*.

Probably the שלח aspect of this idiom refers to your hands being sent out (= extended) from your body when you do this work. See *Daat Mikra* to Deut. 12:7. So we see that the work of one's hands is

---

314. The word מינים is found in many of the versions of the twelfth blessing of the *Amidah* (= *la-malshinim*), See B.S. Jacobson, *The Weekday Siddur* (1978), pp. 194–95. It is not in the version in *The Complete ArtScroll Siddur*.
315. But see Klein, p. 342 for some insights.
316. See *EJ* 2:957. The similarity to the Hebrew verb הלך (= go) is probably not coincidental.

connected to a meaning related to "send" in this expression. Probably this is the "send" aspect in the term *melakhah* as well and perhaps just like *mislah yad*, there was once a phrase *melekhet yad*, which was then shortened to *melakhah*.[317]

מעגל: This word means "path" in *Tanakh*. The root of this word is עגל, which means "round." But at Proverbs 4:11, we have *ma'aglei yosher*, implying a מעגל that is straight. How can a path be both round and straight? The explanation is that מעגל refers to a straight path, made by the wheels of a wagon![318]

סהר: *Beit Ha-Sohar*, a term for prison, appears eight times in *Tanakh*, but only in Genesis chapters 39–40. (In *Nakh*, the term for prison is "*Beit* כלא.") *Beit Ha-Sohar* may have originated based on a round shape of original prisons.[319] Or perhaps the term originated because prisons are typically surrounded by walls. (The word "surrounded" obviously derives from the word "round.")

The word סהר is found at Song of Songs 7:3 (*agan ha-sahar*, describing a navel). It either means "round" or "moon" there. The "round" meaning of the word may have originally meant "to be round like the moon."

In Rabbinic Hebrew and in Aramaic, we have words like סהר (*sahar*) as an enclosure for cattle, and סהרא and סהרה as "moonlight."[320].

At Judges 8:21 and 8:26 and Isa. 3:18, we have שהרנים (*saharonim*) which probably refers to ornaments in the shape of the moon or a crescent.

---

317. See *TDOT*, vol. 8, p. 326. See also the post of balashon.com of Sept. 22, 2020. Klein (p. 348) seems to imply that the original meaning of מלאכה was "mission," but I do not find this convincing. (But we do now better understand the use of the word at Jonah 1:8.)
318. See, e.g., *BDB* and the Soncino comm. to Prov. 2:9. But I have seen some who take the unlikely position that מעגל refers to a "circular path." See similarly Rav S.R. Hirsch's creative explanation of our word at Ps. 23:3. I would like to thank Mollie Fisch for getting me interested in this word.
319. See, e.g., Radak, *Sefer Ha-Shorashim*.
320. See Jastrow, p. 960.

Finally, in modern Hebrew, a סהרורי is a word for a lunatic and for a sleepwalker.

עטש: This root appears only one time in *Tanakh*, at Job 41:10. It means "sneeze." It is surely an onomatopoeia, as it sounds like our "achoo"! There is another word for "sneeze" that appears only one time in *Tanakh*, at 2 Kings 4:35: ויזרר.[321]

עכשו: This word looks like a real challenge, as עכש is not a root. The likely explanation is that עכשו is just a contraction, probably from *atah kemo-shehu* (= now the way it is).[322] I also learned recently (in a post by Rabbi R.C. Klein) that עכשו pre-dates the Mishnah and is found in a Dead Sea Scroll: 4Q225.

פקוח נפש: This phrase does not literally mean "saving a life." It means "opening [to save] a life." The meaning expanded to this idiomatic meaning because an important case in rabbinic times was the issue of opening up a heap of debris on Shabbat to attempt to save a life.[323]

צדקה: This word has two different meanings in *Tanakh*. Once, in an Aramaic section at Dan. 4:24, we have this word with the meaning "charity," and "charity" is a common meaning of the word in Rabbinic Hebrew. But elsewhere in *Tanakh*, the meaning of the word *tzedakah* is always "righteousness" or "justice" or something similar.[324] The issue then arises what *tzedakah* means in the famous line in *U-Netanneh Tokef*. If the meaning is its original meaning, then it is "righteousness" or "righteous acts in general" that affect the decree, not the specific monetary righteous act of "charity."[325]

---

321. I would like to thank Alan Schwartz for pointing out this word to me. Klein suggests that this word is perhaps an onomatopoeia.
322. See Jastrow, p. 1080. Klein suggests something similar: *ad ke-shehu*.
323. See, e.g., *Ketubot* 15b.
324. See, e.g., *Daat Mikra* to Prov. 10:2 and Dan. 4:24, and F. Rosenthal, "Sedaka, Charity," *Hebrew Union College Annual* 23 (1950–51), pp. 411–430.
325. I wrote about this in a column in 2021. If we look at *U-Netanneh Tokef* itself, we cannot determine the meaning of *tzedakah* there. But we can analyze the passage in the Jerusalem Talmud (*Taanit*, second chapter) on which our line in *U-Netanneh Tokef* is based and suggest the proper interpretation of *tzedakah* in this passage. I concluded tentatively that the meaning was the

רווק (*ravak*): This is a word for a single man in the Mishnah and thereafter. Many believe it derives from the root רוק with its meaning "empty." The reason suggested is that a single man is one whose home is empty of wife and children.

תו: "again, furthermore." For this insight, I have to credit my daughter Rachel. When she was in her teens, she came across this word and I told her what it meant. Then she said: "It does not have enough root letters." So I looked in Jastrow and saw that she was correct! It is a shortened form of תוב. I.e., it is the Aramaic equivalent of the Hebrew: שוב ("return," "come again").

* * *

Adonis: This is a name of a Greek god (of beauty and desire) and is based on that word familiar to all of us, אדון, the name of a Canaanite God. *Adon* was the Canaanite name for the Sumerian-Babylonian god *Tammuz*. *Tammuz* was a god of fertility, and there was a ritual of crying and mourning every summer to commemorate its departure due to the heat.[326] The Canaanites passed this mourning ritual on to the Greeks.[327]

For grammatical reasons (related to Greek having a nominative case), the Greek language has to add endings like "es," "is," "as," and "on" to foreign nouns. The name משה for example, became "Moses" in the Greek translation of the Torah.[328] This is the explanation for the "is" at the end of "Adonis."

Naples (city in Italy), **Nablus**, and **Carthage**: Naples is a form of "Neapolis." This name means "new city," from *neo* + *polis*. There were

---

monetary one. I intend to research this issue further. (I would like to thank Barry Lichtenberg for first mentioning this issue to me.)
326. This ritual is alluded to at Ezek. 8:14. It is of course ironic that we cry in *Tammuz* as well!
327. See *EJ* 15:788.
328. Another example is the individual on whose name the Christian religion is based. His name in Greek: Iesous, likely from ישוע. Another example: Yirmiyahu becomes Ieremias in Greek. Finally, this is also the reason for the "es" at the end of the name "Xerxes," the botched Greek name for Ahashverosh. (Please always remember that the Greek language did not have a letter for the "sh" sound. שרש was never going to transliterate well.)

many cities with the name "Neapolis" in the ancient world. I have seen the observation that, in the ancient world, "creating colonies was all the fad but coming up with snazzy new names apparently wasn't." (In the U.S. today, there are many towns named "Newton," from new + town.)

In Israel, the city of Shechem is called "Nablus" by the Arabs. Nablus also comes from *neo* + *polis*, but Arabic lacks a letter for "p." (Their letter that is cognate to פ is pronounced "F.")

The new area of Shechem was founded in the year 72 by Vespasian, just west of the original Shechem. The new area was originally called Flavia Neapolis = "Vespasian's New City." (Vespasian's full name was Titus Flavius Vespasianus.)

In this context, I also have to mention the ancient city of Carthage (in modern Tunisia), founded by colonists from Tyre (= Phoenicians) in the late ninth century BCE. The name in English "Carthage" derives from the Latin "Carthago," which ultimately derives from the Canaanite *kart* + *ḥadash* = city + new.[329]

Quarantine: This word originally referred to a period of forty days that a ship suspected of carrying contagious diseases was isolated in port in fourteenth-century Italy.

Thomas: This name is derived from the Aramaic name תאומא meaning "twin." (Of course, the Hebrew form is at Gen. 38:27 and other places in *Tanakh*.) The English "Thomas" is a transliteration of the Greek. Greek added an "as" ending to the Aramaic form.

Utopia: The word "utopia" means "an imaginary place." In Greek, "*topos*" means "place," and the prefix "*ou*" means "not." So the combination of *ou* plus *topos* means: it is not a place.

* * *

Regarding the last word, Mitchell First wonders what a person who knows Greek thinks when he sees "OU Kosher"!

---

329. I thank Leonard Berkowitz for this insight.
We all know the Aramaic word *karta* for "city" from *Kah Ribbon*. At the end of this *zemer*, Jerusalem is called *karta de-shufraya* (= city of beauty).

Abbreviations of Frequently Cited Sources

Menaḥem Zevi Kaddari, *Millon Ha-Ivrit Ha-Mikrait* (2006). Cited as "Kaddari."
Ernest Klein, *A Comprehensive Etymological Dictionary of the Hebrew Language for Readers of English* (1987). Cited as "Klein."
Ludwig Koehler and Walter Baumgartner, *The Hebrew & Aramaic Lexicon of the Old Testament* (1995, revised edition). Cited as "KB."
Marcus Jastrow, *A Dictionary of the Targumim, the Talmud Babli and Yerushalmi, and the Midrashic Literature* (1903). Cited as "Jastrow."
Hayim ben Yosef Tawil, *An Akkadian Lexical Companion For Biblical Hebrew* (2009). Cited as "Tawil."
Solomon Mandelkern, *Heikhal Ha-Kodesh* (1896). Cited as "Mandelkern."
Francis Brown, S.R. Driver, and Charles A. Briggs, *A Hebrew and English Lexicon of the Old Testament* (1906). Cited as "BDB."

I also frequently cited to *Theological Dictionary of the Old Testament*. This is a 15 volume work which spanned the years 1974–2006. Each article is by a separate author. Cited as *"TDOT."*

* * *

All citations to *The Complete ArtScroll Siddur* are to the third edition (1990).
All citations to the *Encylopaedia Judaica* are to the 1972 edition. This work is cited as *"EJ."*
All translations from Josephus are from the Loeb Classical Library edition.

I also frequently cited to balashon.com, an excellent site on the etymology of Hebrew words, ancient and modern, by David Curwin of Efrat.

Corrections Page

Page 13, first line: four (instead of "three").

Page 48, note 39: I wrote that "I am not aware of their source..." I retract that sentence. I now know that there is a *Seder Tikkunei Shabbat* from 1612 or 1613 and that it has the *Shalom Aleikhem* prayer. It also has the typical reading of one *ha-sharet* followed by three *ha-shalom*. It also has the readings that I mentioned in the first full paragraph on p. 50. I thank Michoel Chalk for pointing all this out to me.

Page 65: I wrote that the prayer was found in the *siddur* of R. Eliezer b. Nathan of Mainz (c. 1090–1170). I wrote this because the prayer is found at pp. 518–19 in *Siddur Ha-RAB"N*, a work published in 1991. But I did not read the introduction to this work carefully. In the introduction, the authors explain that the purpose of this work was only to publish the *siddur* comments of *RAB"N* and that the text that they published as their *siddur* text was not connected to him. There is no evidence whatsoever that *RAB"N* knew of our prayer.

Similarly, at p. 70, when I refer to the *siddur* of R. Eliezer b. Nathan, it is not our earliest text of *Maoz Tzur Yeshuati*. But the text printed in this 1991 *siddur* does have the interesting variant that I mentioned. (That variant is not unique to this text.)

I thank Yonatan Brander for informing me of my misreading of the *Siddur Ha-RAB"N* work.

I still believe that the sixth stanza was part of the original prayer. I cited a reason on p. 65 ("Also, it would have..."). Also, both A. Frankel and Y. Melamed take the position that the sixth stanza was part of the original prayer and explain their reasoning.

The earliest manuscript that we have of the prayer (Hebrew Union

College Acc. 962) dates from the late fourteenth or early fifteenth century. But it is a fragmentary one. The several pages that have survived continue only to the middle of the fourth stanza.

Page 75, note 152. I refer to a future article of mine in *Ḥakirah* that was supposed to appear in volume 32. It did not appear there. I expect it will appear in volume 33.

Page 99: Regarding the recently discovered Rashbam commentary on Psalms, there is much information on this commentary at AlHatorah. org. Please click on the "i" icon next to this commentary on any particular Psalms verse.

Page 141, item 6: I wrote that paragraph before I read Clark Clifford, *Counsel to the President* (1991). Clifford explains there, in a very dramatic first chapter, that Secretary of State George Marshall was vehemently against any form of recognition of the new Jewish State. The idea of limiting the initial recognition to de facto only was a very last minute compromise worked out between Clifford and Marshall's representative, Undersecretary of State Robert Lovett. Marshall went along, very reluctantly. I highly recommend this chapter.

Page 236, שער paragraph, fourth line: modern (instead of "medieval")

Page 242, note 310. Add: A similar translation is found in Targum Onkelos: *levushei shimusha*. See Targum Onkelos to Ex. 31:10, 35:19, 39:1 and 39:41. (Probably this influenced Ben-Yehuda as well.) I thank Jonathan Tavin for pointing this out to me.

Mitchell First, Jan. 2023

www.ingramcontent.com/pod-product-compliance
Lightning Source LLC
Chambersburg PA
CBHW030112240426
43673CB00002B/56